D0236845

Please renew/return this item by the last date shown.

From Area codes 01923 or 020:	From Area codes of Herts:
Renewals: 01923 471373	01438 737373
Enquiries: 01923 471333	01438 737333
Textphone: 01923 471599	01438 737599

www.hertsdirect.org/librarycatalogue

GETTING OUR WAY

Also by Christopher Meyer

DC Confidential

GETTING OUR WAY

500 Years of Adventure and Intrigue:
the Inside Story of British Diplomacy

CHRISTOPHER MEYER

Weidenfeld & Nicolson

LONDON

First published in Great Britain in 2009
by Weidenfeld & Nicolson

3 5 7 9 10 8 6 4

This book is published to accompany the three-part television series
Getting Our Way, presented by Sir Christopher Meyer
and produced by Wingspan Production for the BBC.
Executive Producer: Archie Baron. Produced and Directed by Helena Braun.

A CIP catalogue record for this book
is available from the British Library.

ISBN- 97 8 02978 85875 1

Typeset by Input Data Services Ltd, Bridgwater, Somerset

Printed in Great Britain by CPI Mackays, Chatham, Kent

Weidenfeld & Nicolson

The Orion Publishing Group Ltd
Orion House
5 Upper Saint Martin's Lane
London, WC2H 9EA

The Orion Publishing Group's policy is to use papers that are natural,
renewable and recyclable products and made from wood grown in sustainable
forests. The logging and manufacturing processes are expected to
conform to the environmental regulations of the country of origin.

www.orionbooks.co.uk

To Catherine, as always.

CONTENTS

ACKNOWLEDGEMENTS

The origins of *Getting Our Way* are to be found in the fertile genius of Archie Baron, Creative Director of Wingspan Productions. I had previously worked with Archie on a television documentary for the BBC called *Mortgaged to the Yanks*. Afterwards we thought of doing something more ambitious about Britain and America, in advance of the US presidential elections in 2008. But after a while our conversations – and this was Archie's idea – turned to making a documentary series about British diplomacy and how Britain had played its hand in the world over the last five hundred years. The BBC liked the idea; and, lo and behold, it commissioned a three-part series for television. *Getting Our Way* was born.

I was very keen. From my earliest years at school I had loved history. As a diplomat, I was time and again reminded of how much is to be learnt from the past; and how ignorance of history can lead modern politicians into error and misjudgement. It was, I thought, worth making the series just to remind viewers of Britain's diplomatic past. But it would also offer a platform for a set of arguments, dear to my heart, about the abiding importance of diplomacy and the national interest. *Getting Our Way* is, therefore, both a documentary series and a book with an opinion.

The idea of a book flowed naturally from the television series. But, once again, it was something inspired by Archie Baron's energy and creative imagination. He fired me up to put pen to paper. Sometimes, in this whole endeavour of television series and book, I see myself a little like the Chinese Emperor Qianlong from Chapter 4 within, borne aloft on my lonely author's palanquin by the strength of others. Archie was among the strongest: always encouraging, inspiring, enthusing, sometimes cajoling.

There were many others who bore me aloft and kept me going. There was huge cross-pollination between the book and the television series. I am not sure whether the *Getting Our Way* production team appreciate how much they motivated my writing. They were extraordinarily talented and always the best of company. I owe a great debt of gratitude to Helena Braun, the producer/director, who contributed so much. She had the steadiest of hands on the tiller, while having to put up with my quibbling over the script and tantrums when I got tired at the end of a day's shooting. I also want to thank the jovial Will Jacob, cameraman and sound recordist extraordinaire, as well as the King of Puns; assistant producer Kim Lomax (more of her below); and Nick Boy, quartermaster and logistics wizard. We had a few laughs.

My warm thanks also to Julian Alexander of LAW and Jayne Rowe of Wingspan, whose quick efficiency sorted out contractual and other matters for both television and book with a minimum of fuss.

All kinds of people, too numerous to list, helped us on location around the world. But a special mention is owed to Sir David Tang, not only for the wisdom he brought to the Chinese episodes of the documentary and book, but for his generous hospitality and help in Hong Kong and Beijing.

Of course, none of this would have happened without the BBC's confidence in the project. Five names in particular are on the *Getting Our Way* roll of honour: BBC Commissioning Editors Mark Bell and Martin Davidson; and successive BBC Four Controllers Janice Hadlow, George Entwistle and Richard Klein.

This book benefited from a great deal of research done for the television series. It was intimidating in its thoroughness. In the time available I would never have been able to get on top of it on my own. I am indebted to Kim Lomax and to Jo Foster for their high-quality contributions, under great pressure, to the historical chapters. Without these as a foundation, the book would never have seen the light of day in 2009. Any mistakes are, of course, my own.

My thanks, as ever, to my agent, Jonathan Lloyd, at Curtis Brown; to Alan Samson, my publisher at Weidenfeld and Nicolson; and to my editor, Lucinda McNeile. No writer could be in better hands. I am grateful also to Jeremy Lee of JLA for his help on the television side.

Throughout the writing of this book, my grumpiness and self-absorption have tested the patience and good humour of my wife, Catherine, to the outer limits. She not only showed the forbearance of a saint, but did everything possible to ensure that, over the months, I could write undisturbed by the distractions of daily life. *Getting Our Way* could be dedicated only to her.

London, August 2009

INTRODUCTION

You can and should be prouder of who you are, what you have done and what you represent. Stop apologising for who you are, and focus instead on what you do.[1]

This is a book which uses history to make the case for the revival of British diplomacy. It is an argument for a coherent foreign policy under a re-energised Foreign Office, driven by a clear-eyed vision of the national interest.

Getting Our Way recounts nine stories from Britain's diplomatic annals over the last five hundred years. Diplomats are at the centre of each narrative. It is an inside account of their extraordinary experiences, sometimes in the face of physical danger, often at history's hinge. The book covers a period in which Britain's power has waxed and waned: from the puny island nation of the sixteenth century, to the global superpower of the nineteenth century, to the more modest post-imperial status today of a major European power. In these radically differing circumstances, we see how Britain has viewed its interests in the world and sought to advance them; how allies have become enemies and enemies allies. Time and again, we see the enduring wisdom of Lord Palmerston's[2] observation in 1848 that 'we have no eternal allies and we have no perpetual enemies. Our interests are eternal and perpetual, and those interests it is our duty to follow.'

For all that has changed in international affairs since his time, Palmerston's insight is as valid today as it was 161 years ago. Foreign policy – what is to be done – and diplomacy – how it is to be done –

begin and end with the national interest. Without that, all is drift and muddle. Nowadays, to our damage as a nation, we have allowed the necessary rigour of foreign policy to become diluted by fashionable but fraudulent notions of the post-modern state, which elevate the daft utopianism of 'global values' at the expense of the national interest.[3] Meanwhile, diplomacy shrivels within the confines of an undernourished Foreign Office.

Getting Our Way records diplomatic successes and failures over the centuries in all four corners of the earth. But the companion of success has invariably been an unsentimental foreign policy, executed by robust, proficient and well-resourced diplomacy.

Diplomacy rivals prostitution as the oldest profession. Like street-walking, it has never enjoyed a wholly favourable reputation. Often confused with its clandestine cousin, espionage, it has for centuries been associated with deviousness and duplicity. Only the other day, when I was giving a talk on foreign policy, a woman came up to me afterwards and expressed astonishment that I had actually given straight answers to questions. 'I expected', she said, 'the usual wishy-washy "on the one hand, on the other" that you get from diplomats.' In modern times diplomacy has also become associated with appeasement of one kind or another, of kowtowing to foreign governments. The venerable Conservative politician, Lord Tebbit, was once reputed to have said that just as the Ministry of Agriculture protected the interests of farmers, so the Foreign Office provided the same service to foreigners.

These criticisms have acquired the rancid flavour of class warfare, a deeply ingrained British pastime. For centuries diplomacy recruited from the aristocracy and upper classes. When I joined the Foreign Office in 1966, recruitment had become more widely meritocratic; but it was overwhelmingly a male meritocracy drawn from Oxbridge and a few other universities. Today, the recruitment pool is vastly bigger in every way. But, the old myths persist. The image of a diplomat, clad in pinstripes, quaffing champagne, leading the good life in a magnificent embassy, dies hard. The press, with its Pavlovian attachment to cliché, perpetuates the myth with relish.

In 1984, Britain's then Foreign Secretary, Sir Geoffrey – now Lord – Howe,[4] pulled me out of our embassy in Moscow and made me his press secretary and Foreign Office spokesman. He told me that one of my main tasks was to improve the FO's public image. So, to show that British diplomacy was tough, I recommended a campaign against foreign diplomats who failed to pay their parking fines in London. This resulted for a while in a draconian regime, which led to the naming and shaming of diplomatic miscreants and much yelping from London's Diplomatic Corps. But, it pleased the *Evening Standard*, which had a low opinion of the Foreign Office ('we are as a matter of editorial policy hostile to diplomats,' said its formidable political editor, Charles Reiss, at our first somewhat tense encounter); and, as far as I was concerned, that was all that mattered.

Then, to show that the Foreign Office was not stuffy, I persuaded its chieftains to agree to a BBC proposal to put Geoffrey Howe on *Jim'll Fix It*, a television show that went out every Saturday at teatime. My earlier attempt at image-management had ended in the disaster of a documentary called *Caviar and Cornflakes*, which confirmed every FO stereotype, and then some. *Jim'll Fix It* had a huge audience and was presented by Jimmy Savile, one of the top television personalities of the 1980s. Every week it brought to life someone's wish or ambition, usually a child's. In our case, it was a girl who wanted to be an ambassador. So, we fixed it for her and sent her to Moscow for a week. She acquitted herself brilliantly; and even the Soviet foreign ministry played ball. No one would bat an eyelid nowadays. But, twenty years ago, it caused some con-sternation in the Foreign Office to see Her Majesty's Secretary of State for Foreign and Commonwealth Affairs sitting alongside the flamboyant Savile, a demure schoolgirl, and a chart-topping black brother-and-sister group called Five Star.

The programme was considered a success; and I suppose that several million viewers got a better understanding of what an ambassador is for. But the attempt to strike a populist note went beyond currying favour with the press and public. It reflected a long-standing malaise in King Charles Street, which, though it has mutated over the decades, persists to this day.

I joined the Foreign Office on a warm autumn's day in 1966. I was astonished at the lack of formal preparation for the job. I had found the Civil and Diplomatic Service entrance exams rigorous, exhausting and often quite fun. In those days they took place in three stages, by the end of which hundreds of unsuccessful candidates had been knocked out. The whole process took weeks. I remember being so drained that I was left with barely enough energy or motivation to do the revision for my university finals, which followed soon after. At each stage, you waited tensely for the Civil Service Commission letter that would tell you, in strangely small typescript, whether or not you had been successful. Only a score or so survived the final stage to be admitted to the upper reaches of the Civil and Diplomatic Services.

My induction course lasted about a month. It was led by an engaging, rugby-playing giant of a man, Ewen Fergusson.[5] I do not remember much about it. I was given a handbook on diplomatic etiquette, sent to some lectures and made to spend a fortnight in a registry, learning how to file papers. Then, one morning, I was taken to the West and Central Africa Department, told that I would be responsible for French-speaking African countries plus Liberia, and shown my chair and desk. 'You will be sitting next to Mr Renwick.[6] He will show you what to do,' I was informed. I sat down and the first thing I saw was an enormous in-tray, filled with files held together with red tape and what were known as Treasury tags: pieces of red string with little metal bars at each end that were threaded like cuff-links through holes punched in the files. As I stared at the pile, paralysed like a rabbit in headlights, Robin Renwick leaned over to me and said, 'I think you will want to give priority to Upper Volta.[7] They haven't paid the rent on their embassy and they have done a bunk to Paris.'

And that was that. I was now, at the tender age of twenty-two, a wet-behind-the-ears but fully functioning British diplomat, expected to advise my seniors, including George Brown, the Secretary of State, on all aspects of relations with some fifteen African states. I was put unsparingly to the test in my very first month. As I wrestled with the Upper Voltans, I was summoned to the office of the Minister of State, a genial Scottish politician called George Thomson. He was about to receive an official visit from a member of the government of the Central African Republic. I was there to interpret between English and French. The usual pleasantries of a courtesy call were easy enough to translate. But, just as I was beginning to relax and enjoy myself, the African told Thomson that one of the main exports from his country was *roselle*. What on earth was *roselle*? With panic rising in my gorge, and unwilling to admit to ignorance, something made me blurt out 'jute' in translation. To my horror, instead of moving on to another subject, Thomson eagerly pressed the African minister to describe the precise properties of *roselle*. Thomson hailed from Dundee, where jute mills had once been the backbone of the economy. He knew a lot about jute. There ensued a lively conversation in which Thomson said 'jute' and the African minister said *roselle*. Thomson promised to look into the possibility of importing *roselle* into Dundee. After the meeting, he asked me to follow matters up vigorously. This could be a way of helping Dundee and a poor African country. I raced back to my office and looked in my dictionary. *Roselle* was not there. I tried out the mystery word on a friend in the French Embassy; but he had not heard of it either. He promised to ask around. The next day, Jean-Pierre called back. What was a British minister doing, he asked, talking to a politician from the Central African Republic about importing a plant that was variously used as a diuretic, laxative and food-colouring agent? My heart sank. I saw my career slipping beneath the waves before it had hardly begun. 'Oh, and by the way,' added Jean-Pierre, 'it's also used sometimes as a substitute for jute fibre – if that's of any interest to you.' Of any interest to me!? I kissed my French-English dictionary. History does not relate, I believe, whether *roselle* proved to be of any use to the moribund jute mills of Dundee.

That was the British way of doing things: to learn on the job. It still is to some extent. The British diplomatic tradition is not to be overly abstract or intellectual. It is in some contrast to Continental Europe, where diplomacy is often taught at specialist academies. The annals of diplomacy record, perhaps apocryphally, a long and arduous negotiation with the French over some initiative, at the end of which the leader of the French delegation throws up his hands and exclaims: 'I agree this will work in practice. What concerns me is whether it will work in theory.' In Germany, after years of studying things like international law, virgin diplomats are not let loose until they are sniffing the approach of middle age. In Britain we do not have academies. We do not teach diplomacy, we teach foreign languages. We leave international law to the lawyers. As for the rest, we learn by example, just as in nature animals show their young how to hunt. I gathered a vast amount from having my desk in what is known as the Third Room. Besides Robin Renwick, there were two other older diplomats working in the same room as me. It was noisy and sometimes distracting. But, as I was meant to, I observed and listened to what was going on around me and learnt in a week more than I could be taught by an instructor over a term.

There was something else too which made this an exhilarating experience for someone just out of university. Despite the Italianate magnificence of Gilbert Scott's building, and the stuffy reputation of the Foreign Office, everything was surprisingly informal. Long before Tony Blair insisted that he be addressed as 'Tony', the use of first names was the norm in King Charles Street. I discovered that I was expected to address everyone this way, with the exception of the Secretary of State, other ministers, and the Permanent Under-Secretary, who was the head of the Diplomatic Service. There was a formal hierarchy of ranks as there is in the armed services. But more often than not it was by-passed. Quite often, lowly creatures like myself would be summoned to the office of the Secretary of State or of some great mandarin, so that I could brief them, say, on Liberian politics or tensions between Rwanda and Burundi. For a while the Foreign Office experimented with what it called the 'team system', which removed two layers of bureaucracy. It worked brilliantly, pushing down responsibility to the lowest level possible. It was heady stuff for a young diplomat. You got to know personally almost everyone who mattered very quickly. It inculcated a terrific *esprit de corps* and high morale. Needless to say, bureaucracy reasserted its deadening hand and in due course the two layers were restored.

From this pragmatic system emerged a Diplomatic Service that was widely respected by its peers. I remember being told by a Japanese diplomat how Tokyo had studied several of the European diplomatic services and had concluded that the British was best. It was admired in particular for its professionalism, negotiating skills, and profound knowledge of abroad. The Foreign Office was organised around great clans of specialists: Arabists, Kremlinologists, sinologists and the like. A huge effort was put into language training. I spent a year learning Russian full-time. It was two years for the Chinese- and Japanese-speakers. You were meant to acquire a thorough understanding of the country for which you were the specialist; and if you were actually posted there, you were expected to do this without falling into the dreaded trap of 'going native' – of representing Ruritanian interests in Britain, not the other way round. It is all too easy to do. You make a vast effort to understand a country – to speak the language, make friends, burrow deep into its *mores* and culture, travel its length and breadth – and before you know where you are, you are more familiar with it than with Britain. Unless you are vigilant, your sympathies can be pulled along in the wake of your understanding and knowledge. Before going to Washington as Britain's Ambassador in 1997, I was given the crisp instruction 'to get up the arse of the White House and stay there'. Once comfortably ensconced in this part of the American anatomy, where, as a distinguished US general recently told the White House, 'the sun don't shine',[8] I had always to remind myself that the purpose of the contacts made in this intimate position was to advance the British interest.

It did not take me long to realise that I was joining an organisation as troubled as it was talented. There was a spectre stalking the august corridors of the Foreign Office. It took the form of an American Secretary of State, Dean Acheson, who had served President Harry Truman between 1949 and 1953. Only four years before I became a diplomat, in a lecture to officer cadets at West Point, he had made the sharply perceptive observation that 'Great Britain has lost an empire and has not yet found a role'. His words, which have passed into the realm of historical cliché, caused outrage in a Britain already highly sensitive to its diminished post-war status. It did not help that they had come from America, our intimate wartime ally.[9] It is a useful antidote to the careless rapture of today's Special Relationship rhetoric (alive and well during President Obama's visit to London in April 2009) to realise that in the early post-war decades it was above all the United States that confronted Britain with its decline. This was a period marked by strained and difficult passages between London and Washington. Immediately after the end of the war in 1945, the newly elected, and nearly bankrupt, Labour

government sought a substantial loan from the Truman administration. The negotiations were so hard-fought and acrimonious
that they aroused an intense mutual hostility; and the strain killed
John Maynard Keynes, the ailing British delegation leader. In 1956,
President Eisenhower's administration humiliated Britain by
exploiting the weakness of sterling to force a halt to the Anglo-
French expedition to seize the Suez Canal from Egyptian President
Nasser. The swelling national crisis of confidence and identity, felt
with especial keenness inside the Foreign Office, was aggravated still
further by General de Gaulle's veto in 1963 of our application to join
what was then the European Economic Community.

In 1968 I was posted to Moscow and then, two years later, to our
embassy in Madrid. It was an awful time to represent Britain abroad.
We seemed in a state of terminal economic decline and national
demoralisation. British diplomats abroad are paid and taxed in
sterling. As the pound kept on sinking in value, the relentless fall in
our purchasing power measured almost exactly Britain's rate of
decline. Even the Communist East Germans, in a characteristic
piece of Goebbels-style hyperbole, claimed to have overtaken our
GDP. In late 1973 I returned home from Madrid to a litany of
horrors: the miners' strike; the three-day week; the energy crisis;
working in the Foreign Office by the light of a small Camping Gaz
lamp; double-digit pay rises, devoured by inflation worthy of a
banana republic; and to a surly Customs officer, who searched my
car from top to bottom. Could it get worse?

The Foreign Office, meanwhile, suffered a prolonged agony of
introspection, reflected in inquiry after inquiry into the purpose and
nature of British diplomacy: the 1964 Plowden review; the 1969
Duncan Committee report; the creation in 1971 of the House of
Commons Defence and External Affairs Sub-Committee, which
published a series of reports on overseas representation; and, most
far-reaching of all, the 1977 report of the Central Policy Review Staff
(CPRS), which in essence recommended the abolition of the Diplomatic Service and its integration into the home Civil Service. As the
government's response in 1978 to the CPRS report pointed out,

The frequency of all these reviews has been a clear reflection of Britain's
need ... to adjust ... to the post-war world ... to the dismantling of the

Empire, to the withdrawal from East of Suez ... More than any other single factor [entry into the European Community][10] has altered the international framework within which British foreign policy operates.[11]

At the time of the CPRS report I was in London, working as a member of the Planning Staff of the Foreign Office. This was supposed to be a collection of egghead diplomats whose task was to look at long-term strategic issues. We wrote worthy papers on things like the interdependence of nations, a newly fashionable concept born of the realisation that the oil-producing countries had their hands on our windpipe; or Eurocommunism, a hot-button issue of the Cold War era (what do you do if a NATO member-country like Italy votes for a communist government? Answer: not much). The good and the great of the Foreign Office would read the papers, congratulate us on the perspicacity or otherwise of their content, and then consign them to the dusty archives of eternity.

When not boring ourselves rigid writing these papers, the Planners served as the Foreign Secretary's special forces, taking on *ad hoc* tasks at his personal request. In 1977–78 the key task for the Planning Staff was to destroy the CPRS report, which represented an existential threat to the Foreign Office; I was entrusted with drafting the counter-blast. The Foreign Secretary of the time was David, now Lord, Owen, who at thirty-eight was the youngest holder of the job since Anthony Eden in 1935. The tough, talented and ambitious Owen, who had just become Foreign Secretary on the unexpected death of Anthony Crosland, was having none of a report that would have shot his job from under him. In due course, the CPRS boarders were repelled. Better than that, the government's response endorsed the primacy of the Foreign Office in the conduct of foreign policy, even while acknowledging the 'meshing of foreign and domestic affairs' as a result of our membership of the European Community. The key conclusion, which had Foreign Office mandarins purring from one end of King Charles Street to the other, was that:

Responsibility for the overall conduct of overseas relations in the broadest sense of the term will continue to be vested in a single Cabinet Minister, namely the Secretary of State for Foreign and Commonwealth Affairs ...

Note that this conclusion was reached despite the separate existence of a Ministry of Overseas Development, created by the then Labour government.

So, game, set and match to the Foreign Office. For a while it regained its footing and self-confidence. But, thirty years later, the FO has, according to numerous witnesses, fallen again on hard times, surrendering swathes of responsibility for foreign policy to other players in the Whitehall community and continuing to live a crisis of confidence and identity. The notion, for example, that the Foreign Secretary is responsible 'for the overall conduct of overseas relations' has been undermined by the activism abroad of the Prime Minister's office and the autonomy and funding given to the Department for International Development, which, with a budget at least three times that of the Foreign Office, pursues its own agenda abroad. A bright, middle-ranking woman diplomat, who can expect to be a contender in due course for the top jobs, told me recently that she was a member of a group of dissident Young Turks inside the Foreign Office. 'If', she said, 'we go on the way we are, we will just end up a Ministry for Consular Affairs, rescuing distressed travellers and tourists.'[12]

How was this allowed to happen? After all, following the bleak under-achievement of the 1970s and the earlier wrenching readjustment to the loss of empire, Britain enjoyed more than a generation of economic renaissance, which enabled us to play a confident and assertive role in the world. How is it possible that the wise and careful Lord Hurd, a former Foreign Secretary and professional diplomat, could get up in the House of Lords earlier this year and speak of 'a malaise becoming increasingly apparent' in the working of the Foreign Office; of an organisation that has been 'hollowed out', because it is no longer 'a storehouse of knowledge providing valued advice to ministers and is increasingly an office of management ... of a steadily shrinking overseas service'? Hurd's conclusion was that the Foreign Office should be 'the coordinator, the guide and the shepherd' in foreign affairs and that it should 'repair and restore its tradition of excellence'.

What lies beneath accusations made in 2008 by the human resources consultancy, Couraud, hired by the Foreign Office itself, of 'institutional timidity', 'a cultural fear of failure', 'people getting to the very top of the Office by never making any mistakes'? Couraud tells us that 'mediocrity flourishes because mediocrity is seen to be safe ... We have never come across an organisation so stuffed full of talent. How can it continue to get so many obvious "common sense" issues wrong?' Or take another consultants' report, this time by Collinson Grant in 2005 and again commissioned by the Foreign Office. It delivered the verdict that: 'The entire organisation needs to be challenged and reformed, but the leadership lacks the skills needed and the will to upset the status quo.' The then Permanent Under-Secretary, Sir Michael Jay, was excoriated by the House of Commons Foreign Affairs Select Committee as 'part of the problem'. It is all quite mystifying to people like myself, who regularly meet young diplomats. They are as bright and talented as they have ever been.

The use of outside consultants is itself part of the problem: the symptom of weak leadership that cannot see what needs to be done; or, if it does, dares not make changes without some sort of validation from the private sector. This is not a phenomenon peculiar to the Foreign Office. New Labour's obsessive reliance on the alchemy of consultants has infected much of Whitehall. But as Britain re-covered its strength under Margaret Thatcher, Foreign Office self-confidence failed to keep pace. It did not help that one of the Great Beasts of the Conservative government, the Foreign Secretary, Lord Carrington, fell on his sword over the Argentine invasion of the Falkland Islands in 1982. It did not help to have an overbearing, even intimidating, Prime Minister, who seized the reins of the most important foreign policy areas of the day – the US, the Soviet Union, the EU, South Africa – a model that Tony Blair was to emulate several years later, albeit without Thatcher's rigour and grasp of detail. In her twelve years as Prime Minister Margaret Thatcher went through five foreign secretaries. She regarded the Foreign Office with suspicion. A *Sun* leader-writer of my acquaintance at the time used regularly to characterise the FO as a bunch of 'pin-striped appeasers'. It was an authentic Thatcherian echo. It was not surprising that, under Thatcher's tough monetarism, the Foreign Office budget came under sustained pressure. When I applied to take time out in 1988 to study American politics at Harvard, a fearful Foreign Office told me never to utter the word 'sabbatical' in Thatcher's presence. She thought them a waste of money. Instead I was to say 'career-development attachment'. I did. She asked me what it was. I replied with some trepidation that it was a sort of . . . sabbatical. She did not seem to mind.

It was around this time that the Foreign Office got it into its head that, to deflect charges of being fuddy-duddy and out of touch, it should organise itself on business lines borrowed from the private sector. There would be modernisation based on the latest information technology. This was when the rot set in – when corporate management seemed to become as important as the conduct of foreign policy. It has been a sorry tale: generations of failed computerisation projects, some in-house, some sold to King Charles Street by consultants; a privatised global telecommunications system, which in my time passed through the hands of German and American companies in a series of buy-outs to end up under the control of a Hong Kong Chinese corporation; departmental reorganisations recommended by consultants, which in due course had to be dismantled when they proved unworkable.

It got worse under New Labour, as deference to the world of business and consultancy reached a climax. The culture of targets, set by the Treasury, acquired the madness and mendacity of Soviet statistics. In Washington as Ambassador, I had to engage in an annual objectives-setting exercise. In principle, it is absolutely right to set clear goals for your embassy. But, the Foreign Office, throttled by the Treasury's grip on its budget, insisted on a bureaucratic exercise of elephantine proportions. The Office had its own objectives. Each department within the Office had theirs. Each embassy and high commission had theirs, as did individual officials. The idea was that there should be a 'cascade' of objectives from the top to the bottom. Getting all these objectives to fit together took ages. Finally, like the annual promulgation of the theses of the Communist Party of the Soviet Union, the objectives would be published, often months into the year to which they were meant to apply. They were, for all practical purposes, dead on arrival. Meantime, we just got on with the job for which there was only one authentic objective: advancing the national interest, using our judgement, common sense and professional skills to work out how to get from A to B.

In any case, the methodology of objectives-setting was almost entirely fraudulent. Quantitative targets are fine for road building or hospital cleaning. But much of diplomacy is not susceptible to this kind of measurement. I was instructed by London to put into my personal objectives a set number of public speeches for the year. There was no interest in their subject or audience: never mind the quality, feel the width. I plucked the number thirty-five out of the air. Fine, was the response. At the end of the year I duly reported that I had met my quota. Well done, was the response. But, this kind of target-setting measures nothing. Your embassy, each of your staff, you yourself can report a 100 per cent success rate; and it will tell you very little about the quality of your diplomacy.

In 2006, Sir Ivor Roberts, retiring from the Diplomatic Service as British Ambassador to Italy, sent a valedictory despatch of unusual candour to the Foreign Secretary. For over a century it had been the custom that retiring ambassadors should write a despatch, making observations on, and drawing conclusions from, their final posting and diplomatic career as a whole. Like all despatches they were addressed to the Foreign Secretary and circulated to all posts. Many of these despatches have been of very great value, with more frankness than is usual in diplomatic communications. Ivor Roberts' was one such, with his trenchant and well-aimed criticism of the culture of managerialism and permanent revolution in the Foreign Office:

The culture of change has reached Cultural Revolution proportions ... Can it be that in wading through the plethora of business plans, capability reviews, skills audits, zero-based reviews ... we have forgotten what diplomacy is all about? ... Why have we failed so signally to explain to the likes of the Cabinet Secretary that well-conducted diplomacy cannot properly be measured ...? We manage or contain disputes; very rarely do we deliver a quantifiable solution.

The content was sufficiently newsworthy to leak in due course to the press. As such it followed in the footsteps of the similarly well-crafted and timely farewell despatch sent by Sir Nicholas Henderson from Paris in 1979. He addressed Britain's decline and what we should do about it. His despatch duly found its way into the pages of the *Economist*.

Unlike Henderson, who was hauled out of retirement by an

approving Thatcher and rewarded with the embassy in Washington, Ivor Roberts' despatch fell on deaf ears; and, for the first time since their inception, valedictory despatches were as a result severely curtailed in their distribution. Meanwhile, the Foreign Office website continues to be riddled with the jargon of management consultancy. There is much talk of corporate leadership, audit and risk, business strategies, 'change owners' and what appears to be the terrible sin of 'change-bunching'. Innovation has become a virtue in its own right, as if permanent revolution were necessary for the effectiveness of British foreign policy.

Reform and modernisation are periodically necessary. Today's Foreign Office is a better place for the true meritocracy of its recruitment. It is a better place too for its light, airy canteen. For lunch in the 1970s I had to descend into a subterranean chamber, where sweating cooks of gargantuan girth would emerge from the steam to ladle you Cornish pasties the size and consistency of hand grenades.

But, the price paid for necessary improvements has been high. I still have ringing in my ears something said to me on my first day in the Foreign Office in 1966. 'Always remember this is a service, not a business.' That has seemed to me ever since a pretty good principle for all Whitehall. But, over a generation or more, it has become progressively diluted. Consultants, special advisers, and sundry outsiders – many with civil service status on short-term, high-paying contracts – have been increasingly entrusted with tasks once reserved for the mainstream civil service. Many top civil servants are themselves paid huge salaries – the £130,000 a year, plus expenses, that I received in my last year in Washington in 2002–03, is relatively modest when set against the pay today of public service jobs with comparable responsibility. The weary argument that these sums are necessary to recruit and retain quality just does not wash. You are not supposed to be in public service for the money. The implicit deal when I joined was clear: we will pay you modestly (£60 a month after tax in 1966), in return for which you will get job security, a final-salary pension and a decoration if you do well – and, by the way, you will go wherever we choose to post you. That admirable ethos looks to me in pieces, perhaps beyond repair. Like much of Whitehall, the Foreign Office today cannot make up its mind whether it is a service or a business.

This has not been great for British diplomacy – and that at a time when conflicts in Iraq and Afghanistan have yet again validated Clausewitz' dictum that war is the extension of politics by other means. The poor, bloody infantry can win a thousand firefights in Helmand province, and earnest officials from DFID[13] can make their plans for a bridge here, a dam there; but until these efforts are linked to a political process, underpinned by diplomacy, they are so much waste of blood and treasure.

Getting Our Way examines, through its cast of diplomatic characters, the three pillars of the national interest: Security, Prosperity and Values. Sometimes these pillars are, as they should be, mutually reinforcing. Sometimes one – especially Values – will be in conflict with the others. Either way, there are sharp lessons to be drawn from the past to guide us through the turbulence of a world where, far from ending, history has resumed with a vengeance. The sharpest of them all is that, despite the profound changes in international affairs over the last five hundred years – geopolitical, demographic, economic, environmental, technological – a nation that loses sight of its interests, and neglects its diplomacy, is a nation lost. Britain risks such a fate.

PART I
SECURITY

The first duty of government is to ensure the security of the nation. For most of our history this has meant protection from invasion, armed attack and subversion. It still does. But, nowadays, we have to take a broader view of our security and to add a new order of threats – economic, environmental, criminal, cyber, health and so forth. It makes foreign policy a much more complicated business than in most of the period covered by this book. Yet, at bottom, it remains a matter of confounding our enemies and strengthening our alliances.

The following three chapters show how Britain's diplomats have sought to buttress the nation's security at very different stages of our history. Sir Henry Killigrew sets out in the later sixteenth century on a dangerous mission to Scotland, when Britain's very survival as an independent, Protestant nation is under threat from foreign invasion and domestic conspiracy. Two hundred and fifty years later, with Britain assuming the mantle of superpower after victory in the Napoleonic Wars, Viscount Castlereagh reorders the map of Europe at the Congress of Vienna to avoid further entanglement in the Continent's disputes. A century and a half later, with British power now in decline, Sir David Ormsby-Gore, one of my predecessors as Ambassador to the United States, manoeuvres artfully to acquire nuclear weapons from the United States, so guaranteeing not only Britain's security in the Cold War, but also its place at the top table of nations. Britain lives still with Sir David's legacy.

I

ALL SECRECY AND CIRCUMSPECTION:
Killigrew in Edinburgh

Henry Killigrew might not have looked much like a hero as he rode towards Woodstock Palace in Oxfordshire in September 1572. A serious and professional Cornish gentleman, he would never seize the limelight in the same way as a Sir Francis Drake or a Sir Walter Raleigh. But Queen Elizabeth had summoned him to attend a confidential meeting with her two closest advisers – William Cecil, Lord Burghley, and Robert Dudley, Earl of Leicester – because she needed an able and experienced diplomat, and Killigrew had, over the course of several missions in Europe, earned himself a reputation for a discreet and skilful touch. With England standing on the verge of international conflict, it fell to Henry Killigrew to save the day. After bidding farewell to his monarch, he would saddle his horse and ride with all haste to a city in the grip of civil war, where he would enter negotiations with the foreign power judged to pose the most immediate threat to England's security – Scotland.

Elizabeth I's grip on the throne had been shaky from the start. Legally, she was a bastard. Her father, Henry VIII, had left her with a murderous legacy of religious conflict and dynastic instability. Her predecessor, Mary I, had bequeathed a poison pill of her own by marrying the heir to the Spanish throne, soon to be King Philip II. This gave the most powerful Catholic monarch in Europe a personal, religious and political stake in England's future. And to make matters worse, Elizabeth was an unmarried woman. As long as she refused to pick a husband and produce an heir, preferably male, the country would be plagued by plots, and rumours of plots, over the succession.

Ironically, the root of Elizabeth's problems lay in Henry's determination to shore up the Tudor dynasty. After the divisive civil war of the previous century – the Wars of the Roses – from which they had emerged victorious, the Tudors were congenitally insecure about their grasp on power. When his Spanish wife, Catherine of Aragon, failed to produce male heir, Henry VIII applied to the Pope for a divorce so that he could marry Anne Boleyn. The Pope's refusal led Henry – a religious conservative, who saw no particular attraction in the Protestant rite – to break with the Catholic Church and open the door to the Reformation with the creation of the Church of England. This was hugely divisive since many English Catholics, while loyal to their sovereign, refused to abandon their allegiance to Rome. Worse, it had all been to no avail: Anne Boleyn bore him a daughter – Elizabeth – whom Henry subsequently declared illegitimate, at the same time ordering her mother's execution. Though a subsequent Act of Succession restored Elizabeth's place in the line of succession, she remained a bastard in the eyes of the Catholic Church.

After Henry's death in 1547, the brief reign of his sickly son, Edward VI – the only male progeny given him by his six wives – saw the consolidation of Protentantism as the state religion, but accompanied by unrest and rebellion. When the fifteen-year-old king died in 1553, he was succeeded by his half-sister, Mary I, daughter of the discarded Catherine of Aragon. The equally brief reign of 'Bloody Mary' pushed tensions sky-high, as she set about returning England to Catholicism by burning hundreds of Protestants at the stake as heretics.

Elizabeth herself never showed any of the doctrinal intolerance that had marked her half-sister, but there was never any doubt that Elizabeth would be true to her father's legacy and keep Britain free of the Papacy. Her legitimacy and security as sovereign were entwined with the fate of the Church of England. Within a year of ascending the throne, an Act of Parliament made her its Supreme Governor.

Meanwhile, Europe in the sixteenth century was, as ever, a treacherous snake pit of constantly shifting alliances, played out in wars, dynastic marriages and betrayals. But the terrain was changing. Nation states and city states were emerging from a medieval world, in which the Pope and Holy Roman Emperor had once struggled for European primacy. Now the Papacy was fighting for its spiritual authority against the Protestant Reformation, while its secular authority began a terminal decline. The Holy Roman Empire had split between the Austrian and Spanish branches of the Habsburg dynasty, and the so-called Italian Wars, which had raged from the end of the fifteenth to the middle of the sixteenth century, dragged in most of Western Europe, including, for a while, England. By the middle of the sixteenth century, Spain had the clear edge in the struggle for supremacy with France, as the latter descended into a half-century of religious wars between Protestants and Catholics. (It was not until the French king, Henri IV, put an end to these in 1598 that France was able to begin the long climb to great-power status under Louis XIV a century later. That in turn would trigger a century-long struggle between France and Britain for world supremacy, from which the latter would emerge victorious on the battlefield of Waterloo in 1815.)

As a small country on the outskirts of Europe, sixteenth-century England lacked both wealth and military muscle. Its various armed interventions on the Continent were, for the most part, marked by incompetence. Elizabeth frequently complained about her generals, once remarking of the Earl of Essex, who was somewhere in France, that 'where he is, or what he doth, or what he is to do, we are ignorant'. Fortunately, England showed greater skill at tacking between France and Spain, playing one off against the other.

The advent of the Reformation, and the division of Europe between Protestants and Catholics, had made the balancing act a more perilous, high-stakes game, since it had become infused with religious fanaticism. Elizabeth, a conservative like her father, started out reasonably tolerant of Catholics, but this proved no protection against the full force of the Catholic Counter-Reformation: the perennial threat of either Catholic conspiracy at home or Catholic invasion from abroad – or some combination of the two. The crisis that hit Elizabeth within two years of her ascending the throne in 1558 had three distinct, but linked, features: religious – the threat of schism; dynastic – stemming from rivalries rooted deep in the Middle Ages; and national – the jostling for position between embryos of the modern nation-state. It was a sign of much graver things to come. And it originated in Scotland.

The Scots had been England's enemy for hundreds of years. Since the thirteenth century they had been in intermittent alliance with France against England. The famous 'Auld Alliance' reached a climax in the middle of the sixteenth century when James V of Scotland married a French wife, Mary of Guise, a member of one of the great French Catholic noble houses. James died in 1542, a few days after the birth of his daughter, also called Mary and later to become known as Queen of Scots. The child Mary was sent to France for her upbringing, while back in Scotland her mother assumed ever greater powers, becoming Regent on her daughter's behalf in 1554. Many French had followed her to Scotland. There was a large French garrison at Leith. In 1558, Mary of Guise contrived her masterstroke, arranging for her daughter to marry François, the heir to the French throne, who the following year would be crowned François II. For a brief moment in history the Scottish and French thrones were united. But then everything suddenly fell apart when François and Mary of Guise both died in 1560. Resistance to French and Catholic influence had been building for a while as the Reformation gained ground in Scotland, and now a group of Protestant nobles, known as the Lords of the Congregation, seized the opportunity to rise in rebellion. When they turned to England, the 'Auld Enemy', for help, Elizabeth – recognising the strategic threat of a Scotland dominated by Catholic France – sent troops north of the border and forced the retreat of the French army from Scottish soil.

The experience deeply marked Elizabeth and her advisers. An intense concern for the security of her throne and of Protestant England became the *leitmotiv* of her reign. It led to an increasingly harsh regime for English Catholics; and an ineradicable suspicion of Mary, Queen of Scots, and her French connection.

In 1572, when our story takes place, Elizabethan England was again in serious danger, threatened by plot, rebellion and invasion. Three years previously, the Catholic earls of Northumberland and

Westmorland had led the Northern Rising, and celebrated the old Catholic Mass in Durham Cathedral. They had hoped for support from the Duke of Alba, Governor of the Netherlands, at that time a Spanish possession. The rebellion failed. Elizabeth responded with severity, executing hundreds of rebels, many of whom suffered the awful fate of hanging, drawing and quartering. She then passed laws seizing the assets of Catholics living abroad, and made all members of her Parliament swear an oath of supremacy.

At this point Pope Pius V intervened, promulgating a Papal Bull, *Regnans in Excelsis*. It declared Elizabeth a monstrous heretic and excommunicated her, along with anyone who followed her. Worse, it called for mass civil disobedience by English Catholics: 'We charge and command all and singular the nobles, subjects, peoples and others aforesaid that they do not dare obey her orders, mandates and laws.'

The call was heeded by a Florentine banker and zealous Catholic, Roberto Ridolfi, himself implicated in the Northern Rising. Ridolfi sought to put together a grand international conspiracy to unseat Elizabeth. Once again it relied on the intervention of Spanish troops from the Netherlands, who would disembark at Harwich. The plan embraced the King of Spain, the Pope, some English nobles – and Mary Stuart, Queen of Scots. The plot was discovered and thwarted. The Duke of Alba had in any case got cold feet, fearing that France would derive advantage over Spain if the half-French Mary secured the English throne.

Having discovered the tentacles of conspiracy once again reaching into Scotland, Elizabeth hardened her heart against Mary Stuart. Elizabeth and Mary were cousins through the Tudor line, with a common ancestor in Henry VII. This gave Mary a claim to the English throne. In fact, she was next in line, should Elizabeth die childless. In the eyes of Catholics she was already the rightful English sovereign, since they regarded Elizabeth as the illegitimate daughter of an unsanctified marriage. All this made Mary a magnet to Catholic plotters. In 1568 Mary had sought refuge in England after being forced to abdicate the Scottish throne by the Protestant Lords of the Congregation. Elizabeth had taken the precaution of putting her under house arrest, but after the Ridolfi affair, her imprisonment became harsher; and the Duke of Norfolk, England's senior Catholic nobleman, whom Mary was supposed to marry as part of the plot, was beheaded.

In 1572, as Henry Killigrew rode into Woodstock Palace, Elizabeth's strategy was based on two principles: to ensure the Protestant ascendancy in Scotland, thus removing the threat of Catholic Franco-Scottish invasion from the North; and to stop Spain from using the ports of the Low Countries and Northern France to mount an invasion (which the Spaniards came close to doing in 1588, the year of the Armada). Very soon, a third objective would be added in support of the first, namely, to remove Mary Stuart from the scene. Even from imprisonment, her continued existence as a lightning rod for Catholic plot and rebellion menaced not only the life of the Queen, but the very survival of Protestant England.

In plotting the defence of the realm, Elizabeth had four weapons at her disposal: her navy, her army, her spies – and her diplomats.

As long as there have been polities, there have been diplomats or envoys. They repeatedly make their appearance in classical history and, here and there, in the Old Testament of the Bible. Rulers need diplomats to convey messages in confidence to other rulers; to conduct negotiations; to gather information; to represent one state in another's territory and to look out for its interests there. In medieval Europe, diplomacy had often been conducted by churchmen. Ambassadors would be sent on special missions by princes, by the Pope, by the leaders of individual cities, or even by universities or trades guilds. As soon as the mission was over they were expected to return home.

By the sixteenth century, as sovereign princes began to tighten their grip over territories with clearly defined frontiers, they appropriated to themselves the right to send and receive ambassadors. Embassy became an attribute of sovereignty. Increasingly, ambassadors could be sent only from one ruler to another by bilateral agreement. From this emerged the practice of accreditation. When I was appointed Ambassador to Germany and then the United States, on each occasion, shortly after arriving, I presented my 'letters of credentials' from the Queen to the President. My formal authority as ambassador came not from the government but from the monarch.

The modern diplomatic career began to take shape in other ways during the sixteenth century, with the development of a permanent, professional cadre of diplomats and the posting of ambassadors to foreign capitals for prolonged periods. The universal and long-standing practice of granting ambassadors and envoys safe-conduct in the discharge of their duties began to evolve into a doctrine of diplomatic immunity. This was designed to protect the con-fidentiality of diplomatic communications as well as the person of the ambassador. History is full of stories of ambassadors coming to a sticky end when a vengeful ruler takes murderous objection to the message that the hapless diplomat has just delivered. Herodotus describes the rough reception accorded Persian envoys by the Athen-ians and Spartans in the fifth century BC. One of Henry VIII's ambassadors was threatened with a beating by the French King, François I. By contrast, in 1584, the Spanish Ambassador, de Mendoza, who was found to have been involved in the failed Throckmorton Plot against the Queen, was expelled from England, while Throckmorton himself was executed. To this day, expulsion remains the ultimate sanction against an ambassador found guilty of serious misbehaviour.

By the time of the Woodstock meeting, Killigrew was already known to the Queen as a diplomat she could trust. He had worked under Sir Francis Walsingham, Elizabeth's 'Complete Ambassador' and head of her secret intelligence service. Wal-singham was, with Burghley and Leicester, one of the Queen's closest and most trusted advisers. He was a master of sixteenth-century European politics, a prototype of the modern statesman and diplomat. His espionage network extended across Europe, above all in search of intelligence about Spain's intentions towards England. His agents were particularly active in Italy, which proved a good listening post for finding out what the Spaniards were up to. He grasped the importance of sea-power to England's security and prosperity. He was to be a prime mover in organising the naval effort that thwarted the Spanish Armada; and he encouraged and invested in the voyages of discovery of Sir Francis Drake and Sir Martin Frobisher.

In 1570, Walsingham had been sent as Ambassador to France. His instructions were to seek an alliance with the French in support of the Protestant Dutch revolt against Spanish rule. For a while, Killigrew was on his staff. The two men shared a powerful belief in a Protestant England, but the pragmatic Walsingham had no difficulty with the proposition that England should ally with a lesser Catholic power to thwart a bigger Catholic power, if that advanced England's security. It was truly a time when my enemy's enemy was my friend, a long-standing principle of diplomacy. He did however draw the line later in the decade when there was talk of his sovereign marrying the Catholic Duc d'Anjou – half her age and known affectionately as her 'frog'. To this day we do not know for sure whether Elizabeth seriously entertained the notion of marriage; her personal feelings apart, some of her advisers thought an alliance by marriage to the heir to the French throne would be a smart move against the main enemy, Spain. But the liaison was deeply unpopular in the country at large; and Walsingham, as ever thinking several steps ahead, saw a greater danger in Elizabeth's dying without an obvious successor while married to a Catholic French king. In the end, with apparently no hard feelings, Elizabeth sent the Duc d'Anjou away, to join what was already a sizeable army of rejected suitors.

In 1572, shortly before Killigrew's meeting with the Queen at Woodstock, shocking news from France had broken into the calculations of English diplomacy. Late at night on 23 August, the King of France unleashed an orgy of slaughter in Paris. Pressed by his overbearing mother to do something about the troublesome heretic Protestants, he ordered the assassination of their leaders. The first to go, Admiral Coligny, was dragged from his bed and murdered. His body was then pitched out of the window to the street below, where it was dismembered and the head sent to the Pope in Rome. Soon, the King's troops were joined by the Parisian mob, and the religious tensions which had been simmering for years exploded. Over the course of that night and the following day, St Bartholomew's Day, three thousand Protestants were massacred in Paris alone, and another ten thousand were killed in the rest of France over the weeks that followed.

Stories of the horrific atrocities quickly reached England: women and children had been murdered; a bookbinder had been burned alive; the River Seine was awash with rotting corpses. Burghley called it 'the greatest crime since the Crucifixion'. The killings sent Protestant Europe into shock, because in recent years Protestants in France had won an uneasy toleration. Now, it seemed that Europe's Catholic leaders had raised the stakes and henceforth the Counter-Reformation would assume the most extreme forms of religious persecution. There was consternation in London. What to do?

Walsingham's advice from Paris was unambiguous. The clear and present danger was Scotland. The time had come to close 'the postern gate' – England's vulnerable back door in the North. Scotland had been in turmoil since Mary Stuart had fled the country four years before. The Protestant party had replaced her with her infant son, James. There had been a series of regents, who had an unfortunate habit of dying violently. Scotland, like France, fell into a civil war between Protestant and Catholic factions. The latter wanted Mary back. Meanwhile young James VI – who would succeed Elizabeth on the throne of England in 1603 and would never see his mother again – was being given a strict Protestant education.

By 1572, the war had reached stalemate in Edinburgh. High above the town, the supporters of Mary were holed up in the well-nigh impregnable castle (Mary herself was imprisoned over two hundred miles away in England). There had been a time when some of Mary's supporters entertained hopes that Elizabeth might intervene to restore her cousin to the throne; those hopes had long since foundered as plot after plot against Elizabeth was uncovered in England, implicating Mary. If the besieged Catholic nobles were to receive help, it would come from France, the 'Auld' ally and the place where Mary had spent her youth. This, if it were to happen, would be an intolerable challenge to Protestant England.

Down below in the town were the troops of the Regency, mostly Protestant, led by the Earls of Mar and Morton, who wanted the Marian party to back down and allow them to rule as regents for young James. A ceasefire, known as the Abstinence, was in place. But it was fragile and due to expire soon. The Regency or King's party, the mirror opposite of their opponents, looked to the 'Auld Enemy' England for help.

It was a combustible situation, one which could lead England

and France into direct and expensive conflict, with an uncertain outcome. Elizabeth and her advisers considered the options. A French intervention had at all costs to be avoided. It was the hour of the diplomat: summon Killigrew.

As Killigrew entered the Queen's presence at Woodstock, her eye fell on a figure who was not immediately prepossessing. He was short and walked with a limp, nothing like the toothsome young men with whom Elizabeth liked to surround herself. She found him 'dull'. This judgement hardly did justice to his background, for he was descended from a Cornish family that had dabbled in piracy. His limp bore witness to his time as a soldier in France, when he was shot in the foot during the siege of Rouen in 1562. A diplomat of many years' standing, going back to the reign of Edward VI, he was fluent in French, Italian and Latin. He was probably known to Elizabeth before she ascended the throne, for he was well connected; his brother-in-law was Burghley. Most important of all, Killigrew was trusted.

In a tradition which persists to this day, Killigrew was issued with detailed written instructions, setting out the mission he was expected to undertake. The very word 'diplomat' – though it would not be used in English for another two hundred years – has its roots in the Greek word for document, *diploma*. It means literally a 'doubling', because an official document, letter of engagement or set of instructions would be folded in the middle.

For an ambassador, the most useful instructions are those which set out clear strategic objectives but which leave a fair degree of tactical discretion as to means. Unfortunately, foreign ministries have a tendency to be overly prescriptive, leaving little discretion to the head of mission. Quite often you will be asked to do or say something that makes no sense in the local context, leaving you to choose between challenging your instructions, or simply ignoring or changing the bits you do not like. The Nelsonian blind eye is nearly always the better option.

Nowadays, instructions will arrive by instant electronic message, though still referred to by the quaint name of 'telegram'. But this is not the full story. When I was Ambassador in Washington, I very rarely received a direct, written instruction from the Foreign Office. In fact, the Office sometimes gave the impression of not wanting to be disturbed at all. I recall complaining once about the complete lack of reaction to a number of embassy reports. This provoked an enraged response from the relevant Under-Secretary, who clearly resented the disturbance to his day-long siesta. On a subject like Iraq or some other important issue with the Americans, I would receive oral instructions over the secure 'phone – not from the Foreign Office, but from No. 10 Downing Street. Under Tony Blair, such calls were the foreign policy version of sofa government. Quite often these conversations would reveal differences between the two sides of Downing Street. There was often pressure on Renaissance diplomats to reveal their instructions to their hosts, as a dem-onstration of good faith. Used with care and only with trusted contacts, that can still be an effective way of doing business. It was a technique that I used from time to time in Washington, so as to extract the maximum information in return. With a close contact, I would engage in a comparison of our respective records of conversations between the President and the Prime Minister. Sometimes it was surprising how much they diverged. Direct contact between leaders over the phone or through video-conferencing is here to stay; but it is astonishing how it can give rise to misunderstandings. Quill pen and parchment had their advantages.

The Queen's instructions to Killigrew, drafted by Burghley, were designed to operate at two levels. Formally, he was required to work with the French Ambassador, Monsieur Du Croc, to restart the peace negotiations between the two Scottish parties and to bring them back from a resumption of hostilities. Behind the scenes, however, Killigrew was to spread the news of the recent atrocities in France, showing the French to be murderous and untrustworthy fiends who would not hesitate to impale Scottish babies on pikes.

It took Killigrew three days to cover the three hundred miles from Woodstock to Berwick, not bad going even with frequent changes of horse. Since I have never mounted anything after falling from a cow at the age of five, I am relieved that my incarnation as ambas-sador was in the age of the Rolls-Royce. Killigrew arrived north of the border on 11 September. Without pause, he rode straight to Tantallon Castle in North Berwick to meet the ailing Earl of Morton, a key man in the Regency party. Despite his exhaustion, Killigrew let himself be briefed on the situation by Morton until the early hours of the morning. He then rode the fifty miles to Stirling, to talk to the Regent himself, the Earl of Mar. The next few days were then spent making himself agreeable to leading figures on either side.

The role of an embassy in any country is to be on good terms with all parties, including those in opposition to the government, and to win their confidence. You never know who is going to be in power next. When I was a young Second Secretary in Madrid in the early seventies, my job was to build links to the political opposition to General Franco. If you do not create this kind of network, you find yourself in the position of the British Ambassador to Iran who failed to foresee the fall of the Shah in 1979.

After three days, Killigrew felt confident enough to report that 'it seems I am not misliked of by either party'. He put his networking to good use, and was equally diligent in discharging a further basic diplomatic task – to acquire information and to send it back to London. He wrote detailed reports to Burghley and Robert Dudley, Earl of Leicester (reputedly the Queen's lover, although ironically, some years before, Elizabeth had schemed to marry Dudley to Mary as a way of neutralising her), as well as some reports addressed to the Queen herself. These briefings covered conversations of interest, as well as Killigrew's own assessments of people's motivations and likely next moves. They also expressed his frustrations. His flattery and charming manner in the company of his hosts hid a deep distrust of the Scots. Behind their backs, he was blunt:

These men be so devilled and uncertain in their doings as I cannot tell what to write of them, but of this your honour may be assured, I trust no one no farther than I see with my eyes or feel with my fingers.

There are many nationalities of which this might be said. But, there is something about Scottish politics which to this day attracts venomous internecine rivalry. The only thing missing is the assassin's dagger.

Despite Killigrew's skilful diligence, he was having mixed success.

He held out little hope for his objective of resuscitating the peace talks. It seemed, he reported, that Mary's supporters in the castle were stalling with a purpose. The longer they dragged out the 'abstinences', the more time they gave the French to come to their rescue. He had better news regarding the impact of the St Bartholomew's Day Massacre, the details of which he had assiduously circulated. People were shocked and scandalised. Killigrew had given a full account of the massacre to his old contact, John Knox, the tub-thumping Presbyterian preacher and great misogynist.[1] By late 1572 Knox was old and dying, but with the last spark left to him, he terrified Protestant Edinburgh with stories of the slaughter, branding the King of France a 'cruel murderer and false traitor'. The tide of opinion turned against the French; and their ambassador, Du Croc, slunk home with his tail between his legs. It was a fine propaganda victory, akin to the success enjoyed by the late Sir Nicholas Henderson, one of my predecessors in Washington, who played a vital role in keeping American opinion behind us during the Falklands war 410 years later.

Yet the French threat remained very much alive. Killigrew learned that the Marian party in the castle had been receiving money from France and were boasting of the further help they expected at any moment. In early October, he reported:

They of the Castle be very jocund, and give forth tales as though their Queen should be at home shortly. What it means, I know not, but it appears there should be some threatening message sent from beyond the seas to her majesty to that end.

The time had come for Killigrew to pursue the notorious 'Third Matter' – a part of his mission so secret, so sensitive, so dark that it almost dared not speak its name. Though it would have formed part of the discussions during Killigrew's intimate audience with Elizabeth in the completely secure surroundings of Woodstock just before his departure for Scotland (the equivalent of today's 'secure speech' rooms in embassies, where electronic eavesdropping is unable to penetrate), nothing of it appeared in Killigrew's formal instructions from the Queen. There could be no paper trail leading directly to Elizabeth. Instead, it was committed to a separate document, possibly with an instruction to 'burn after reading', since the document is not to be found in the official State Papers. What we know of its contents comes from a draft in Burghley's hand, which was later found in his family archive at Hatfield House. The delicacy and difficulty of drawing up such an instruction are evident from the frequent instances of crossing-out and redrafting.

Burghley's instruction to Killigrew pressed an extreme course of action. It reflected the profound fear of Catholic invasion and conspiracy that now gripped Elizabeth and her advisers:

Where you are by other instructions directed, first, to treat both with the King's party, and the others of the Castle, for the better observation of the late accord for the Abstinence; and next that, secretly to inform some of the principal of either part, of the late horrible, universal murder in France, and thereupon to move them to have good regard to that State, that the like be not there attempted.

2. Although those Matters are of reasonable moment to move to cause you to be sent thither at this time; yet, upon a singular trust you are chosen to deal in a Third Matter, of a far greater moment, wherein all secrecy and circumspection is to be used, as your self consider that the matter requireth.

It is found daily more and more, that the continuance of the Queen of Scots here is so dangerous, both for the person of the Queen's Majesty, and for her state, and realm, as nothing presently is more necessary, than that the realme might be delivered of her; and though by justice, this might be done in this realm, yet for certain respects it seemeth better that she be sent into Scotland, to be delivered to the Regent and his party, so as it may be by some good means wrought, that they themselves would secretly require it, and that good assurance may be given, that as they have heretofore many times, specially in the time of the Queen's former Regents offered, so they would without fail proceed with her by way of justice; so as neither that realm nor this should be dangered by her hereafter, for otherwise to have her and to keep her were of all other most dangerous.

Within the ornate language and complex sentence structure of sixteenth-century English, there was a message of brutal clarity:

Mary Stuart, Queen of Scots, had become too dangerous to be allowed to live. But it would not be expedient to execute her in England, for this would attract the odium of all Catholic Europe. It was more than squeamishness on Elizabeth's part at having Mary's blood on her hands: there was a real taboo about one monarch executing another, and a blood relative to boot. Once embarked on the path of regicide, who knew where it might end?

Killigrew's mission was therefore to contrive matters so that the Protestant Scots of the King's party should do the deed themselves. It is hard to think of a more testing challenge for a diplomat. To succeed, and have the King's party request Mary's extradition to Scotland, Killigrew would have to persuade them that it was in their over-riding national interest to do so: either, explicitly, by offering inducements of one kind or another; or, subliminally, by planting the thought in their heads that it was their own idea to start with. Burghley left it to Killigrew's discretion how the plan was to be carried out. He was the man on the spot with the local knowledge and contacts. There was no point back-seat driving from London. Burghley did however stipulate that the plan must be carried out quickly, before the French could send more money or troops to Mary's aid; and that Elizabeth's name must be kept out of it.

Killigrew, as a fervent Protestant patriot, would not have been shocked. Though we have no evidence, he may well have played an active part in formulating the secret instructions. A few months previously, when the Ridolfi plot had been uncovered, he had written to Elizabeth from Paris. No one in France, he said, would blame Elizabeth for dealing with the Mary problem once and for all. God would be on her side, and 'accursed be whosoever should persuade your Majesty to fear or forbear that which God alloweth you to do'. The ideal for ambassadors has always been, through influencing debate at headquarters, to draft their own instructions. That is, in effect, what Killigrew did in the 'Third Matter'.

In the event, Killigrew decided to employ a go-between to put the idea to the key men in the King's party. His letters to Burghley and Leicester include regular updates on the progress of 'you-know-what' (or 'the matter they wot of', as he put it). But the plan ran into difficulties from the start. The leaders of the King's party, the Earls of Mar and Morton, were willing in principle, but their cooperation came with a price. Without military assistance from England, they were no more prepared to have Mary's blood on their hands than was Elizabeth.

This left Killigrew caught on the horns of a dilemma. He could not persuade the Regency to eliminate Mary without offering something of value in return. But what they wanted was the very thing that Elizabeth did not wish to provide. The risks and expense of armed intervention were too great. War was the very last resort.

Killigrew had no choice but to play for time. He proved good at it, constantly reiterating Elizabeth's support for the Regency, without committing her to anything specific. Fudge was the order of the day.

At the end of October 1572, things started to go badly wrong. The Earl of Mar died unexpectedly, leaving the King's party temporarily leaderless. Then the Regent's supporters approached Killigrew with a plan for dealing with Mary Stuart that involved a slow, cumbersome procedure of 'rendering' Mary to Scotland, under escort from thousands of English troops. Elizabeth's involvement would thus be advertised from the start. Though the plan went against the terms of his instructions, Killigrew's judgement seems to have deserted him. Perhaps it was the stress of having to play both sides of the Scottish divide; or perhaps he had come to believe that matters could not be resolved without England's armed intervention; either way, he blundered. Instead of rejecting the Regency's proposals, he sought to push things along in London by forwarding the details to the Queen and her councillors.

The reply was swift. Elizabeth was furious that Killigrew had evidently let slip to the Scots that she would aid and abet the elimination of her cousin. This was an age when the monarch's servants walked a fine line between royal approval and falling dramatically out of favour, and the consequences in the latter event ranged from banishment – if you were lucky – to the executioner's blade. On receiving his royal reprimand, Killigrew was so stricken by fear that he took to his bed, unable to eat, and shook with remorse. From his sickbed, he sent a painfully undignified letter to Burghley and Leicester, denying ever having let the cat out of the bag, and claiming the whole thing to have been a misunderstanding brought about by his 'Cornish English'. In his self-abasement, he even begged Burghley and Leicester to replace him with someone better, saying

in respect of my unableness to answer the expectations conceived of me and the necessity in my judgement of some fitter man for Her Majesty's service here, I am a most humble suitor to your Lordships (as I was also before this fault was laid to my charge) to be called home where I may serve in some other vocation more apt for my capacity than this.

Despite many an error of commission or omission, I never found it necessary to grovel to quite such a degree, though a little obsequiousness from time to time can do wonders for a career. I did once vomit and take to my bed, when, in an excess of zeal and speed, I ran over the two valuable Abyssinian hounds of Sir John Russell, Britain's Ambassador to Spain in the early 1970s. As for courts and courtiers, not a lot changes over the centuries. To work in today's Downing Street is to work in a claustrophobic court where advisers rise and fall in the Prime Minister's favour, while they fight like ferrets in a sack for advantage. To stay ahead of your rivals, it is important to have in mind at all times two golden rules: first, the old maxim from Justinian, the sixth-century Eastern Roman Emperor: 'What pleases the Prince has the force of law'; and, second, if you wish to avoid being cast into outer darkness, never take the Prime Minister at his word when he says that he doesn't want somebody who tells him what he wants to hear.

In Killigrew's case, the storm blew over and he kept his job. The plot to have Mary returned to Scotland for execution retreated to the back-burner. The urgent task, after Mar's death, was to ensure that the right man was appointed Regent and not to allow the Marians to take advantage of the hiatus at the top of the King's party. The Earl of Morton was Killigrew's candidate. He was strong, able, and well disposed towards England. But, again, Morton was reluctant to take the post without an unambiguous offer of aid from Elizabeth. This was still not practical politics in London, so once more, Killigrew was forced to retreat behind a diplomatic smokescreen of obfuscation and equivocation.

Realising that something more would be needed to keep Morton in play, Killigrew solicited a letter from Elizabeth that he could read out to the group of nobles who would appoint the new Regent. As before, it was long on general statements of friendliness and short on material support. But it was accompanied by a personal message for Morton, informing him that, were he to visit Killigrew in private, he would be told something of great importance. Excited at the prospect of a message of such significance that it could only be delivered in this manner, Morton called at the ambassador's residence that same night. There, he was given bad news: Killigrew had been taken ill. Of course, the messenger assured him, Elizabeth remained as supportive as ever of the Scottish King and whoever would be his next Regent, especially if it were Morton. If he could only wait a few days, the Earl could have his meeting with Killigrew and things would be sorted out to everyone's satisfaction ...

Killigrew's devious ruse paid off. Morton, persuaded that he could expect backing from England, accepted the role of Regent. The day after his appointment was announced, Killigrew made a marvellous recovery and was out and about again, admiring the results of his manipulations. He had finessed Elizabeth's dithering beautifully, and had engineered the best possible outcome for England.

This was fine as far as it went. But there was still stalemate in Edinburgh, and it could not be allowed to go on indefinitely. As the Scottish winter deepened, the temporary 'abstinences' between the two sides within and without the Castle walls were repeatedly extended, with the most recent ceasefire due to expire on 31 December. As Killigrew kept pointing out, every delay gave Mary's supporters new hope that the French would come to the rescue.

At 6 a.m. on 1 January 1573, the sound of cannon-fire broke the truce. The soldiers in the Castle had fired into the town below, signalling their rejection of the final peace terms offered by the Regent. Over the following days shot rained down on the town, killing civilians as well as the Regent's men. When a cannonball fell on the fish market, a number of hungry townspeople were killed as they ran to gather up the scattered fish. At one point the garrison made a bold sortie into the town and set fire to part of it. When the townspeople tried to put out the flames, they were picked off from the Castle walls.

Killigrew could no longer keep Regent Morton happy with vague promises. Diplomacy can, more often than not, achieve its ends by its own devices, but there are times when it needs an injection of muscle. Nowadays, that usually means going to the United Nations and getting a Security Council resolution to impose sanctions. From the time of the League of Nations in the 1930s (see Chapter 8), sanctions have generally shown themselves to be a blunt and ineffectual weapon. Sometimes, diplomacy needs to be backed by the threat, implied or overt, of force. However, for such a threat to work, it must be clear that the will exists to carry it out. There must be confidence that military means will achieve the objective without highly undesirable and unintended consequences. The 'Lang Siege', as an economic blockade, had not worked and showed no signs of working. The whole edifice of Killigrew's diplomacy risked collapse unless the Queen was ready to back words with deeds – namely guns and soldiers. It was by no means clear that this cautious, tight-fisted monarch would do what Killigrew wanted.

Diplomacy is not only about getting foreigners to do what you want. It is just as important to use your powers of persuasion back home: to get your government – or in this case, your Queen – to accept that you know best what is in the nation's interest. In January, Killigrew decided that there was only one thing for it. He got on his horse and made the journey back to England, this time in secret. It was a brave decision. Only a couple of months had passed since his silly mistake had earned the Queen's wrath, and he knew from personal experience how stubborn and wilful Elizabeth could be. Fortunately he soon discovered that he still had the trust of Elizabeth and her advisers. At last she was ready to accept that she simply could not afford not to act. This may not have been entirely due to Killigrew's powers of persuasion; intelligence reports from France had made it clear that troops were on their way (James Kirkcaldy of Grange, whose brother, William, commanded the Castle garrison, had recently been caught landing from a French ship at the nearby castle of Blackness with money, men and weapons). Killigrew returned to Scotland with a chest of 10,000 gold crowns to give to the Regent. Once he had reported to Elizabeth the results of surveys of the Castle, saying that it could be taken in a matter of weeks, she was ready to send cannon as well.

Two hundred and fifty years later the great Prussian military strategist, Clausewitz, made the obvious point that war was the extension of politics by other means. Obvious it may be; but not obvious enough for American and British leaders after they sent troops to Iraq and Afghanistan. Elizabeth, by contrast, was still not persuaded that diplomacy had achieved all it could, and instructed Killigrew to prepare the political ground for military intervention. Armed with English gold and the threat of English force, Killigrew set about further isolating the Marian party in Edinburgh Castle by bringing over two key Scottish nobles, the Earl of Huntly and Lord John Hamilton, to support young James VI.

He had less success persuading those in the Castle to accept terms. By the end of March, he could honestly say to Burghley that he had done his best. 'By your letters', he wrote, 'I see her Majesty's earnest charging of me. Nothing has been left undone that might reasonably be done to end this trouble without the Queen of England's forces.' The final terms he offered were stark. If the men in the Castle surrendered, they would be allowed to go free and keep their lives and property. If not, they would 'feel the cannon'. They were given eight days to decide. At this point there were only 150 men left within the Castle walls, and they would soon be running low on food, water, and ammunition. Still they refused to surrender.

On 25 April 1573, the help which Killigrew had dangled before the Scots for the past six months finally arrived. An army of 1,500 English soldiers entered Edinburgh with thirty-three pieces of artillery, including one large cannon captured from the Scots at the battle of Flodden Field in 1513. Killigrew himself picked up a shovel and helped build a couple of gun emplacements. He was expected also to meet some of the local costs of the expedition. In the sixteenth century, ambassadors regularly incurred large debts abroad in the course of carrying out their duties, for which they would expect generous recompense on returning home. Killigrew wrote to Burghley that 'for anything our men can want above the Regent's promise I will see it performed, and if any have cause to complain for ill-use, either in lodgings or victuals, let them come to me'.

By mid May, the Regent's soldiers were in place and the final chapter of the siege was under way. Edinburgh Castle occupies a magnificent defensive position. With sheer drops on three sides, there is only one way in or out. The Marian garrison could rely also on powerful cannon. But it took just eleven days of sustained artillery fire to achieve victory. The English guns were renowned for their accuracy. One scored a bull's-eye in the mouth of a Castle cannon. Parts of the Castle were entirely destroyed. Rubble blocked the wells, depriving the garrison of water. On 28 May, the garrison commander, Sir William Kirkcaldy of Grange, surrendered.

Killigrew found several smoking guns in the Castle. The rebels had been in correspondence with both the French and Spanish kings. There were incriminating letters from the Duke of Alba, the commander of Spanish forces in the Netherlands. Killigrew collected the evidence and sent it to London with the recommendation that the two leaders of the Marian party, Kirkcaldy of Grange and John Maitland, should hang. 'I think them now fitter for God than for this world', as he put it. The Queen agreed. Maitland escaped punishment: within a fortnight of the Castle's surrender, he died in gaol from disease, or possibly by his own hand. The other leader, Kirkcaldy, went to the gallows in August. Afterwards, his body was chopped into quarters and his head stuck on a spike over the entrance to the destroyed Edinburgh Castle. It was a strange fate for a man who had once been in the service of the Protestant English king, Edward VI.

The 'postern gate' to England clanged shut. Killigrew was rewarded with the grant of Lanrake Manor in Cornwall, a great boost to his financial security. At the end of June he was able to return, covered in glory, to his wife and children, who must have been more than a little concerned that he had disappeared for nine months without saying goodbye. But for the two royal cousins, Elizabeth Tudor and Mary Stuart, the moment of truth had only been postponed. Mary would remain Elizabeth's prisoner for another fourteen years. It was 1587 when Elizabeth finally steeled herself to order Mary's execution. By then there had been further Catholic plots involving Mary and war with Spain had become well-nigh inevitable.

There is much in this tale to offend the modern sensibility: capital punishment carried out in the most barbarous fashion; assassinations; pogroms; judicial murder; 'rendition'; torture; bribery; treachery ... But that was then and this is now. As a diplomat, Killigrew had done a good job – a job of which any diplomat today would be proud. He had rapidly adapted to his surroundings without going native; he had created networks of influence in both Mary's and the King's party; he had supplied high-grade information; he had deployed with some brilliance the tactic of masterly inaction while he waited for his sovereign to make up her mind; he had resorted, when necessary, to subterfuge and dissimulation without alienating his key Scottish contacts; and, if his judgement had gone awry on the matter of Mary's extradition, Killigrew was spot-on in pressing for action against Edinburgh Castle when he did. Above all, he never lost sight of his mission: the successful defence of the realm – Queen and Country – against Catholic conspiracy and attack, to which all else must remain subordinate. As today's First Minister of Scotland, Alex Salmond, remarked to me last year, 'Killigrew may not have been the person you'd want your daughter to marry, but he was a pretty successful and effective diplomat.'

Killigrew's near-contemporary, the English diplomat Sir Henry Wotton, once described an ambassador as 'an honest man sent to lie abroad for the good of his country'. The description fits Killigrew perfectly. And that is a compliment.

2

A JUST EQUILIBRIUM:
Castlereagh at the Congress of Vienna

In my diplomatic career I went to international conferences of every shape and size: European Councils, Commonwealth Conferences, G7 Summits, UN General Assemblies, Conferences on Security and Cooperation in Europe. You name it and I went to it. They were all, without exception, dark-suit affairs of uniform drabness. The ratio of concrete decision to hot air was invariably modest. I recall hours spent fighting sleep as one politician after another droned on.

The tedium can rot the finest minds. At a Commonwealth Summit in Nassau in 1985, the Cabinet Secretary, Britain's most senior civil servant and a member of Margaret Thatcher's delegation, told the No. 10 and Foreign Office spokesmen that they should inform the press of the creation by the conference of a special committee to study apartheid, under the chairmanship of the Foreign Secretary, Sir Geoffrey Howe. The special committee turned out to be the purest fiction, something that was not discovered until after the spokesmen had duly fed it to the press as the scoop of the day. The mortified spokesmen – who happened to be Bernard Ingham, the Prime Minister's press secretary, and me – had to grovel in apology afterwards to the reporters, who, as ever, saw conspiracy where there was only cock-up. When we sought to establish from the Cabinet Secretary – the very grand Sir Robert, now Lord, Armstrong[1] – how the blunder could have possibly occurred, he was unusually lost for words. We were left with the suspicion that he had nodded off and literally dreamed up the committee.

From time to time the boredom of these events would be

lightened by an exotic or historic location. Corfu and the Castello Sforzesco in Milan, for example, helped me through marathons of monotony, whereas Luxembourg and a weird, windowless concrete bunker in Cannes were living death. I recall attending a meeting in Vienna in 1986 of what was then the Conference on Security and Cooperation in Europe – a creation of the policy of *détente*, intended to lower tensions during the Cold War, but in reality a fairly useless organisation that specialised in long declaratory statements – and finding myself keenly aware that we were being observed by the ghosts of one of the most elaborate, colourful and important international conferences ever held. These diplomatic wraiths must have looked down in some bewilderment at the modesty and drabness of our efforts. For they had been present at the Congress of Vienna in 1814, the likes of which had never been seen before and would never be seen again.

In the winter of 1814 diplomats from all Europe poured into Vienna. So did kings, princes and dukes, attended by their wives, mistresses, courtiers, retainers, and general hangers-on. The Austrian Empire greeted them with lavish hospitality and an elaborate network of spies, all reporting to the Austrian foreign minister, Prince von Metternich. A fleet of specially assembled green coaches, emblazoned with the coat of arms of the ruling Habsburg dynasty and pulled by 1,200 white horses, conveyed splendidly dressed VIPs to a cornucopia of balls, dinners, skating parties, receptions, concerts, and hunting parties. The city's population swelled by a third.

Nowadays, the baggage train of an international summit will comprise, with significantly less bling, a couple of thousand journalists and as many security officials. Wives, and the odd husband, are paraded as political accessories; and mistresses are hidden or kept at home. The leaders themselves are placed in a kind of quarantine, sealed off from demonstrators and the public at large. London's G20 Summit in 2009 took place in the remote Docklands area, while the Germans have a preference for monstrous warehouses at permanent trade fairs on the outskirts of town. Heaven forbid that the leaders should come in contact with a normal human being! A sighting of a president or prime minister at these events has become a thing of the past. In 1960 I could stand on the pavement just opposite the French President's palace in Paris and watch Nikita Khrushchev arrive in an open-top car. To stand that close now would be to invite immediate arrest or worse.

The army of journalists, imprisoned in its own quarantine zone, is from time to time admitted to the presence of the leaders for press conferences. In between these carefully staged events, the spokesmen of each government roam among the journalists, scattering their seeds of slanted information and dropping particularly juicy morsels into the mouths of favoured reporters like herring for performing seals. The purpose of this highly competitive and tendentious activity is to underline the brilliance with which your leader has outwitted all the others and become the dominant figure at the conference. Taking particular care that the journalists conceal the source of their information, your briefing will sometimes rubbish other leaders and give information to their disadvantage. I had to do that once to a Canadian Prime Minister. The spokesmen of President Sarkozy of France are particularly good at this, and the French press are sufficiently chauvinist to swallow most of it. It is a measure of the cultural differences on the two sides of the Channel that British reporters tend to see it as a matter of pride not to believe a word they are told by the British briefers.

Vienna in 1814 was extravagantly different and blessedly free of journalists. The city was packed instead with flocks of tourists, who thronged the streets and ballrooms to gawp at the crowned heads and other celebrities. It was as if the pages of *Hello!* magazine had come to life and you could mingle with the rich and famous. There is something ironic about an age of aristocracy, with highly conservative values, that permitted a physical mingling of classes that would be unthinkable in today's *faux* egalitarian age with its cult of celebrity and VVIPs.

Ludwig van Beethoven, the Andrew Lloyd Webber of the day, composed a welcoming chorus for the opening of the Congress. Antoine Carême, the first celebrity chef, with a repertoire of two hundred soups, prepared the French Embassy's banquets. Tsar Alexander of Russia arrived from St Petersburg with his own wine cellar. Beautiful women of all levels of class and modesty turned out in their finest for the plethora of balls and receptions. Brussels on a wet Friday afternoon this was not. But the pomp, extravagance and frivolity of the conference fringe were more than matched by the seriousness of the matter at hand: to repair and stabilise a Europe ravaged by a quarter-century of war. It would take the Congress seven months to redraw the map of Europe. Though singed and torn by intermittent wars and outbreaks of violence, it would be another hundred years before the Vienna map was consumed in the flames of a general European conflagration.

When the Bastille fell in July 1789, marking the start of the French Revolution, it was the prelude also to a period of strife and instability in Europe not seen since the devastation of the Thirty Years' War in the seventeenth century. In France, the institutions of the Bourbon monarchy were swept away and the King himself, Louis XVI, beheaded. With the egalitarian ideas of the Revolution beginning to infect the rest of Europe, this act of regicide sent a thrill of horror through the European monarchs and élites. Having been at war with France on land and sea almost continuously since the beginning of the eighteenth century, there were many in Britain who welcomed the Revolution in its early days, either because they were sympathetic to its ideas; or simply glad to see an old enemy in distress. But soon the bloodthirsty excesses of the revolutionaries began to provoke revulsion, while the success of the French Republican armies against those European powers who sought to snuff out the Revolution was viewed with growing alarm. The British Prime Minister, William Pitt the Younger, had wanted to keep out of the Continental war, but the French invasion and occupation of the Netherlands posed such a strategic threat to Britain that he was left with no alternative but to intervene. In 1793 Britain took up arms against revolutionary France, embarking on a conflict that was to endure for the better part of a generation. Then, in 1799, Napoleon Bonaparte, already France's most successful general, seized the reins of French power. In an almost uninterrupted series of victories, he proceeded to smash the various coalitions ranged against him and carve up Europe as his ambition pleased. Napoleon was not to be seriously checked until his failed invasion of Russia in 1812.

Meanwhile, monarchs and princelings of the old order fell like ninepins.

The horrors of revolution and war left a lasting impression. In 1813, after Napoleon was finally defeated at the Battle of Leipzig, a huge and bloody encounter lasting several days, the Earl of Aberdeen, Britain's envoy to Austria, wrote to his sister:

For three or four miles the ground is covered with the bodies of men and horses, many not dead. Wretches wounded unable to crawl, crying for water amid heaps of putrefying bodies. Their screams are heard at an immense distance, and still ring in my ears. The living as well as the dead are stripped by a barbarous peasantry, who have not sufficient charity to put the miserable wretches out of their pain. Our victory is most complete. It must be owned that victory is a fine thing, but one should be at a distance.

Europe would not again see slaughter on this scale until the First World War.

Across Europe, it was not only the towns and countryside that were laid waste by the Napoleonic Wars, but the public coffers also. War had been a very expensive business. For Britain, the costs are estimated to have been proportionally more than those of the First World War. The nation's strategic contribution was through the Royal Navy and its control of the oceans. Britain's traditionally small standing army had been the war's poor relation, the Redcoats' main contribution being the Duke of Wellington's successful campaign against the French and Spaniards in the Iberian Peninsula. The army's finest hour came at the battle of Waterloo, which finally put paid to Napoleon. But, even here, it is doubtful that Wellington would have won his famous victory without the arrival in the nick of time of Marshal Blücher and his Prussians. Instead of trying to raise a large army to match those of its Continental allies, the British government's preference was to feed them subsidies. This had straitened the Treasury so much that the government had been obliged to introduce the country's first income tax and to suspend the redemption of paper money for silver.

Napoleon's defeat at Leipzig had led the following year to his abdication as Emperor and departure into exile on the

Mediterranean island of Elba. Seven months later, in November 1814, the victorious powers, led by the Big Four – Austria, Russia, Prussia and Britain – convened in Vienna to draw up a peace treaty. Top of the agenda: who would get what from the break-up of the Napoleonic empire. It is a law of diplomacy that the unity and common purpose of a victorious wartime coalition will start to bend or fracture under the stress of dividing the spoils. Yalta in 1945 is the most recent example. Vienna was another. Russia and Prussia wanted large increases in territory. Austria was determined to contain Prussian ambitions. Britain wanted a stable balance of power, with no one state dominant on the Continent. France, the vanquished power, at one point threatened with dismemberment, manoeuvred with consummate diplomatic skill between these clashing interests. As a result, the French ultimately emerged from the negotiations not only relatively unscathed; but, in an astonishing reversal of fortune, as party to a secret alliance with Britain and Austria against the expansionism of Russia and Prussia. It was a master class in how to turn negotiation from weakness into an advantage.

Into this diplomatic cockpit stepped Britain's representative, the Foreign Secretary: Robert Stewart, Viscount Castlereagh. Ranged before him were the eccentric and religiously obsessed Tsar Alexander of Russia; the highly experienced and accomplished Prince von Metternich of Austria; the much less impressive Prince von Hardenberg of Prussia, who was to be outwitted by Metternich; and the Great Survivor himself, the wily Talleyrand of France, whose long career covered four kings, one emperor and a revolution. In the twilight of his years, this legendary diplomat was to become French Ambassador to London. More than anyone else, it is Talleyrand who has given French diplomacy its deserved reputation for skill, finesse and brutal cynicism.

Castlereagh arrived at the Congress with three very great advantages. The first was that Britain had come triumphantly out of the Napoleonic Wars, the one true global superpower. It was the biggest geo-political player in town. It had come a long way since the days of Henry Killigrew. The second was Castlereagh's professional temperament and talent. As Britain's representative, he would automatically occupy a pivotal place at the Congress, but this would be of little use unless he knew how to exploit it. Fortunately for Britain, Castlereagh brought to the negotiating table a calm, clear-headed pragmatism, allied with the ability to win widespread respect through his courtesy, tact and integrity. He was also experienced in the art of negotiating with the Europeans. Third and last, Britain had no territorial claims on Continental Europe, which played to Castlereagh's strengths as an honest broker. All this proved to be a winning combination.

Castlereagh was a hard-working, domesticated man of sober habits, who drew strength from his happy marriage and hobbies of gardening, reading, singing, and playing the cello. It had not been ever thus. Castlereagh had an impulsive, angry side to him. In 1809, when he was head of the War Office, he discovered that his rival George Canning, the Foreign Secretary, had been plotting to oust him from his job. Not satisfied with Canning's resignation, Castlereagh offered his own and then challenged his adversary to a duel with pistols. They met on Wimbledon Common, and managed to miss each other with their first exchange of fire. They could honourably have left it there, but Castlereagh insisted on another exchange. With this second shot he wounded Canning in the thigh, while Canning succeeded only in shooting a button off Castlereagh's coat. Even by the standards of the day, this violent altercation was scandalous; and Castlereagh's political career went into eclipse for several years.

By the time of the Congress of Vienna, Castlereagh had not only smoothed the edges of an earlier impulsiveness, but had moderated also a youthful radicalism. As a young man, Castlereagh had sympathised with American revolutionaries and Irish nationalists. Robert Stewart came from an Anglo-Irish family of landed gentry and in his early years was immersed in the life and politics of Ireland. He is even recorded to have drunk a toast to 'the rope that shall hang the king'. Born in June 1769, he was twenty when the French Revolution broke out. That Wordsworth's evocative lines 'Bliss was it in that dawn to be alive, / but to be young was very heaven' must have struck a chord with the young Robert Stewart is an irresistible conclusion.

The tough, experienced Castlereagh of 1814 was very different from the callow youth of 1789. A few years after the Revolution, just before the king was guillotined and the Terror began in earnest, Castlereagh travelled in France and Belgium. The scales fell from his eyes as he saw the repression and chaos that the Revolution had brought. He went into politics in a serious way, gaining his first seat in Westminster at the age of twenty-four and a place in Cabinet at thirty-three. He turned into a Westminster politician through and through. There can be no surer way to burn off youthful idealism. In its place came a careful realism and a clear understanding that politics is the art of the possible. Translated into foreign policy, this meant that Castlereagh would place a premium on peace and stability.

Castlereagh arrived in Vienna with a plan in his pocket. The government's aims for the end of the Napoleonic Wars had been established for some time. William Pitt the Younger had set them out in a memorandum in 1805. France must give up the territories it had conquered and return to its borders as they were before the Revolution. Then, steps must be taken to contain France and ensure that it could never again lay waste to Europe. This would be achieved by redrawing the map of Europe in such a way that a robust balance of power would be created, in which no one state would be dominant. Proposed measures included strengthening an independent Netherlands; restoring Spain, Portugal and Sicily to their rightful monarchs; and keeping a balance within a balance between the rival German powers of Austria and Prussia, so that neither could itself prove a threat to European peace. This last point proved in the end to be beyond diplomacy's reach. The Vienna Congress could do no more than delay the day of reckoning between Prussia and Austria. In 1866 Prussia emerged victorious from a short war against Austria and then went on to thrash Napoleon III of France in 1870. To the humiliation of France, the German Empire was proclaimed at the palace of Versailles. The title of European bogeyman passed from France to Germany.

The point in the Pitt memorandum, which perhaps had the greatest resonance with Castlereagh, was the proposal to set up a system to keep the peace. According to Pitt, the aim would be 'to form, at the restoration of peace, a general agreement and Guarantee for the mutual protection and security of different Powers, and for re-establishing a general system of public law in Europe'. Of course, said Pitt, making the necessary territorial adjustments would go a long way to sorting out Europe's problems:

But in order to render this security as complete as possible, it seems necessary, at the period of a general pacification, to form a Treaty to which all the principal Powers of Europe should be parties, by which their respective rights and possessions, as they then have been established, shall be fixed and recognised; and they should all bind themselves mutually to protect and support each other, against any attempt to infringe them: It should re-establish a general and comprehensive system of public law in Europe, and provide, as far as possible, for repressing future attempts to disturb the general tranquillity; and above all, for restraining any projects of aggrandisement and ambition similar to those which have produced all the calamities inflicted on Europe since the disastrous era of the French Revolution.

This was extraordinarily far-sighted and sophisticated. Pitt gave a rigorous focus to Britain's national interest, but within a vision of collective European security, which is strikingly modern. Though Pitt gets no credit today in an age when history is disdained, his plan has resounding echoes in the creation of the European Union, the Organisation for Security and Cooperation in Europe and NATO. There are things in the Pitt plan which would not be out of place in the UN Charter. It is a rebuke to modern politicians, who condemn the diplomacy of the time as an exercise in cynical power-broking.[2] It is a rebuke also to those who believe multilateral diplomacy to be a modern invention, the consequence of the coming into being of the so-called post-modern state. Multilateralism is now, as it was then, an arena for the reconciliation of national interests. But those who ignore history are condemned to reinvent the wheel.

Pitt had a further insight of profound importance to Castlereagh. This was that, however much public opinion in Britain might be baying for French blood, European peace would not be served by punishing the French with harsh reparations. If the Pitt principle had been followed in the treatment of Germany at the end of the First World War, who knows how much horror and bloodshed might have been avoided. Humiliation as a force in international affairs is much underestimated. The desire to right historical wrongs never seems to lessen with the passage of time. It lurks today, for example, in the shadows of Chinese, Russian and Iranian foreign policy towards the West.

Castlereagh stuck closely to the Pitt plan when negotiations were joined. It was a given in the British government that this was the blueprint for a peace that would last. As the former Prime Minister, Lord Grenville, put it in a House of Lords debate in 1813, there could be 'neither safety nor peace for England ... but with the safety and peace of Europe'.

Some elements of the plan, such as the creation of an independent Netherlands and Switzerland, had already been achieved in the first Treaty of Paris, which had brought hostilities with Napoleon to a formal conclusion in May 1814. The clock had been turned back with the return of the French to their pre-Napoleonic borders and the restoration of the Bourbon monarchy in the uninspiring shape of Louis XVIII. But there was much still to do to ensure a Europe which would not entangle Britain, militarily and financially, in its quarrels. Ever since the sixteenth century there has been a tension in British foreign policy between its blue waters and European vocations, the natural consequence of our island geography. In 1814, we were sick of Europe and eager to exploit, without further European distraction, the riches awaiting us in our far-flung empire.

The lasting peace was to be achieved by something close to Pitt's system of collective security, as elaborated in negotiation by Castlereagh. Just before the Congress began, Castlereagh explained his thinking to his companion, Lord Ripon, who took a note of their conversation:

In the course of our journey from Frankfort to Bâle [Basel], he stated to me that one of the great difficulties which he expected to encounter in the approaching negotiations would arise from the want of an habitual confidential and free intercourse between the Ministers of the Great Powers, as a body; and that many pretensions might be modified, asperities removed, and the causes of irritation anticipated and met, by bringing the respective parties into unrestricted communications common to them all, and embracing in confidential and united discussions all the great points in which they were severally interested.

One of the novel achievements of the Congress was to be precisely the establishment of a regular schedule of European conferences, of which Vienna would be the first. It proved to be an idea ahead of its time and would collapse in due course under the weight of national rivalries, but it formed a template for the twentieth century. Before this new framework could be launched, there had first to be agreement on the content: what kind of territorial settlement would the congress system monitor and uphold? At Vienna, Europe's rulers had to work through the fall-out from twenty-five years of war: hundreds of claims and demands, some big, some small, and many mutually irreconcilable. The most difficult and potentially dangerous lay in Germany. Here the situation was akin to a herd of elephants. Austria, a long-established empire with a strong sense of its own importance, was the old bull elephant who saw himself as the leader of a herd of princely and other German states. But the old bull's position was under threat from an ambitious, aggressive and younger rival – Prussia. Metternich was determined to contain Prussian ambition. The Prussians, for their part, wanted not only more territory in Germany but a kingdom that was more geographically coherent, not split in two, as it was, with a small corridor connecting the parts; they had set their sights on Saxony. Some feared the possibility of Prussia, Austria and the other German states doing a deal to unite and dominate Europe as France had done.

Another bull elephant to be satisfied was Russia. Having made a massive contribution to Napoleon's downfall, second only to that of Napoleon himself, the boorish, bullying Tsar Alexander wanted his slice of the cake in Poland. The Poles, not unnaturally, disagreed and wanted to run their own country, as they had done until recently. So began a period in Poland's unhappy history when its frontiers were to expand and contract like a concertina at the whim of German and Russian aggression.

Then came the smaller fry and the lesser issues. Austria wanted to keep its gains in Northern Italy; the Pope wanted the Austrians out of the Papal provinces; Denmark wanted compensation for having lost Norway; Norway wanted its independence from Sweden; the Jews wanted to keep the equal rights they had been given by Napoleon; the Knights of St John wanted to go back to Malta, which now belonged to the British; Switzerland was determined to stay neutral whatever happened; and the Continent's waterways had to be regulated. It was, as Rich Armitage, Deputy Secretary of State to Colin Powell, used to say to me in trying times, 'a soup sandwich'.

Castlereagh was undaunted, having spotted a way to hack through the undergrowth of claim and counter-claim. The 1814 Treaty of Paris, signed in May, had included a secret article which stipulated that the Big Four alone would have the final say in how Europe was to be remodelled. In other words, most of the delegates to the Congress were to be excluded from the decision-making process.

This was both a political and organisational decision. As Castlereagh himself said, 'in so large a Confederacy an equality and community of Council is utterly incompatible with the march of business.' There are several parallels today. Very large and cumbersome conferences, with complex agendas, need to discipline debate if agreement is to be reached. The vast international trade negotiations, conducted under the auspices of the World Trade Organisation (WTO) and embracing almost every country in the world, can last for years. The current 'Doha Round' started in 2001 and is still going on. To try to bring this kind of conference to a successful conclusion, the chairman will create an inner group of nations to whom the rest of the participants delegate negotiating powers. There is something similar at the United Nations, where the General Assembly, comprising all 192 member-states, will pass resolutions, but executive action on matters of peace and security is the preserve of the 15-member Security Council. At those conferences where all the presidents and prime ministers present expect to speak – such as the G20 meeting in London earlier this year – months of pre-cooking ensure that the issues left to be resolved on the day are reduced to the minimum. A 20-nation conference is not that large by modern standards, but if each delegation leader makes a modest fifteen-minute introductory statement, that is five hours gone before you even get into the meat of the matter; and at least half of the speeches, in my experience, will exceed the fifteen-minute limit.

Unlike today's UN or WTO, the Paris Treaty arrangement was a clandestine affair. Talleyrand of France knew about it, but, as the defeated power, had no choice but to acquiesce. The other nations at Vienna had no idea that they were to be excluded. As Castlereagh explained later in a Circular Despatch to all British diplomats:

Although the object of this transaction has been equally to provide, in liberality and in justice, for the interests of all Powers, whether parties to these deliberations or not, you will perceive that the conduct of these negotiations has necessarily fallen into fewer hands, and has almost exclusively been managed by the four principal States, whose efforts and whose resources have chiefly been instrumental in subduing the revolutionary power of France.

As a result, there was never a plenary session which all the participants attended; or, as Friedrich von Gentz, secretary to the Austrian Prince Metternich, put it, the Congress never actually met until the *Acte Finale* was signed.

The absence of formal sessions has never put a stop to diplomacy. So much has always been done informally. Diplomats get a bad name for engaging in what is seen as self-indulgent socialising at glamorous receptions, dinners and the like. When I was Ambassador in Washington, I was warned by a friendly journalist that I was going to be 'turned over' by the *Guardian* correspondent for being too 'social'. But 'socialising' with a purpose is an essential tool of the diplomatic trade. Put a dozen diplomats in the same room, and relationships are being created, information traded and deals struck before you can say Metternich. All of this activity informs and nourishes the formal diplomacy and negotiation.

This is what happened in Vienna by a process of spontaneous human combustion. The place was stuffed with diplomats, politicians, gossip-mongers and spies. The city became a vast *Exchange and Mart* for diplomatic intelligence. It gave those who were shut out from the magic circle of the Big Four the opportunity to try to influence the course of negotiation by pressing their case at every kind of social occasion. How many times did I return to the embassy to report to London a private, but significant, conversation with one or two diplomats in the corner of a room as a black-tie reception swirled around us? No doubt they did the same. I always found the intimate one-on-one lunch the most effective means of establishing a necessary relationship or of getting a decision to go Britain's way.

During the week of St Patrick's Day, Washington becomes an Irish town, flooded by visitors from the north and south of the island. The city is well-nigh paralysed by two days of partying and celebration, much as Vienna must have been. From the outside it looks, and, to a degree, is, an exercise in self-indulgence and excess. Because Northern Ireland is part of the United Kingdom, the Embassy in Washington cannot stand aloof from the celebration of the Irish saint. We would give a lunch, our largest social event of the year, with well over a hundred guests. There was only one really serious criterion for choosing the guest list: it would be a lunch that did not recognise any partisan, community or religious divide. They all came, Protestant and Catholic alike. By the end, it would become a pretty rowdy affair, wholly indifferent to sectarian division. You could never tell what effect this event, and the many organised by the Americans and the Irish Embassy, had on the peace process. But if they could lunch and drink together, they could live together – and for some of the Irish leaders, that was a lesson that had to be learnt at the British Embassy in Washington.

The informality of the Vienna Congress was a new diplomatic phenomenon for a profession that was encrusted with strict rules of behaviour and precedence. Time-honoured diplomatic etiquette took a battering. At receptions in the Hofburg Palace, the Imperial residence, the Austrian protocol officers gave up trying to seat the multitude of visiting monarchs in order of precedence. Instead, they drew up the seating plan on the basis of age. The insignificant, but elderly, King of Württemberg had the unusual experience of looking down on the Emperors of Russia and Austria. These things matter even today. Most governments still have protocol officers. I have seen a Spanish grandee walk out of a dinner at the British Embassy in Madrid because he considered that he had been seated beneath his station.

The truly astonishing, even revolutionary, aspect of this most conservative of conferences, however, was the levelling of the social classes at the elaborate fringe events. The like has never been seen since. Security and police cordons had not yet been invented. The pomposity, arrogance and self-importance of pin-headed celebrities were yet to come. Most events were open to all. Thousands of Viennese and foreigners of all classes turned out to see and be seen at the bigger balls. Huge crowds would go to the famous riding school with its myriad lanterns. Here and in the streets of Vienna, the lowly could rub shoulders with the cream of European society. The sex trade was at full throttle. (That usually happens at international conferences: I recall a big meeting in Kuala Lumpur between European and Asian leaders during which hotel massage parlours could not cope with the demand from conference delegates.) A Russian officer described the Austrian capital thus:

It is impossible, when talking of the good and the bad characteristics of the inhabitants of Vienna, not to mention the unbelievable depravity of the female sex of the lower orders, victims of which one meets at every step in great quantities, among them girls of no more than fourteen years of age, daughters of city employees.

For most of the grandees in town it was a case of being able to resist anything but temptation. The Grand Duke of Baden was fond of hosting orgies with the Hereditary Prince of Hesse-Darmstadt, for which girls were brought in from the streets. But in the cheerfully mixed social atmosphere of the Congress, women of all classes were fair game. Tsar Alexander – founder of the Holy Alliance of religiously conservative powers – was an enthusiast in this regard, undaunted by the repeated rejection of his unsubtle approach. At a ball, he pounced on the Countess Szechenyi when her husband was dancing with someone else. The Tsar commented on the Count's absence, intimating that 'it would be a great pleasure to occupy his place for a while'. The Countess knocked him back with 'What do you take me for, a province to be invaded?' It must have been a challenge at such times to maintain one's belief in the divine right of monarchs.

For the more astute and better-connected women, there were opportunities to become significant players in the diplomatic game. It was already a well-established convention of the time that powerful women should conduct *salons*, bringing together the great and good of the day. Partly this was for networking, partly for intelligent and interesting debate, partly to allow the hostess to have her pick of famous lovers. The Swiss Madame de Staël, a life-long opponent of Bonaparte, was the most famous of the day, taking numerous lovers from the glittering cast of writers and intellectuals who passed through her *salon* near Geneva. At Vienna there was a ferocious struggle for supremacy between the two top social lionesses, the German Wilhelmine, Duchess of Sagan and the Russian Princess Bagration. Sagan, who had started an affair with Metternich the previous year, was also his political and diplomatic *confidante*. Bagration, the widow of a Russian war hero who had fallen at Borodino, was mistress to Tsar Alexander. Each held a highly influential *salon*. Each was prodigiously promiscuous. Sagan also slept with the Tsar; while Bagration bore Metternich's love child. The Russian was known around town as the 'White Pussy Cat' and the 'Naked Angel' in homage to her habit of wearing transparent white muslin dresses. The politico-erotic mix was further enriched by Sagan's younger sister, Dorothea, taking up with the much older and rather decrepit Talleyrand, despite, of all things, being married to his nephew.

Sexual merry-go-rounds at this level inevitably go political. Sagan and Bagration were lodged in the same building. Tsar Alexander, so the story goes, climbed the stairs one day and knocked not on Bagration's door but Sagan's. She let him in. Soon it was the talk of the town. Metternich's embarrassment was not only personal, but political. He, with Castlereagh, was the principal opponent of Russia's demand to have Poland.

Discretion is diplomacy's ally, pillow talk its enemy. Vienna was a pullulating mound of gossip and rumour not least because too many confidences were being whispered to too many mistresses in those dangerous moments of post-coital relaxation. Indiscretion is driven by people who want to show that they are in the know. In Vienna, as anywhere, knowledge was power. The Austrian Chief of Police, Baron von Hager, could not have hoped for a richer diet of information. He ran a huge spy network, recruiting informants from among the maids and drivers who served the different delegations, and reported to the Emperor each day. The

Austrian postal service was as dedicated to its task of intelligence gathering as it was to the job of delivering the mail. All letters were opened and read. There was no sense that diplomats' correspondence should be sacrosanct in any way. Couriers' bags were emptied when they changed horses; and the letters opened, copied, and replaced in secret. The British delegation appears to have posed a problem for Hager; who complained that 'the British mission, owing to excessive caution, has engaged two housemaids of its own. Before I can get at the waste-paper which they throw into the baskets I must see whether I can count on these two women.'

It was only to be expected that Castlereagh would run a tight ship. He was alive to the wiles of foreign espionage. He had the self-confidence and experience to handle a complex negotiation. He had good, capable staff. Most important of all, as I know from my own experience, he had the support and partnership of a devoted wife, Emily. They had been married for thirty years, and in love throughout, writing fond letters to each other whenever Castlereagh's business forced them apart. Here is an example from early in their marriage, in November 1794:

I cannot retire to rest, Dearest Dr Wife, though a good deal fatigued, without sending you my blessing. Every stage that moves me further from you adds to my regret and makes the time which is to elapse before I again cross the Channel seem of intolerable duration. Perhaps the noise and bustle of London may dissipate the anxiety of separation which reflection uninterrupted dwells on with real pain. My day now passes without an event. I roll on from daybreak till long after the light is gone and, except the relief of reading, I have nothing to divert my thoughts from the loss I have sustained. Tomorrow I shall endeavour to sleep at Newark. I shall then be 126 miles from London: the night after, probably at Biggleswade, – the Almighty protect you, Dearest of friends.

Ever your most devoted

Robert

Castlereagh was dogged by rumours of homosexuality, which have never been substantiated. Whatever the truth, he and his wife were by every account extraordinarily close. His devotion to

Emily, reinforced by a powerful self-discipline, kept him out of scandal's way in Vienna. In contrast to the debauchery around him, Castlereagh liked to relax in a more wholesome manner, by singing hymns accompanied on the harmonium. Emily, who joined her husband in the Austrian capital, was herself the subject of much bitchy comment. Then as today, the personal appearance and fashion sense of diplomats' wives at social events would be discussed and dissected at length. Emily, unfortunately, was no oil painting. She was overweight (from the portraits of the time most women look plump by contemporary standards), and was cheerfully oblivious to the fact when choosing her garish wardrobe. Prince von Schwarzenberg, Prussia's representative, recoiled in horror at the sight of her: 'She is very fat and dresses so *young*, so *tight*, so *naked*.' Just as English women of every shape, size and age recently considered it fashionable to expose the belly, so in 1814 their predecessors displayed, with the same aesthetically blind enthusiasm, acres of leg and bosom. The Europeans thought English bad taste the result of being cut off from Paris fashions during the long years of war. When the peace talks moved from Vienna to Paris in 1815, a stylish Parisienne was heard to sneer, as Lady Castlereagh went past, that, 'England is renowned for beautiful women; but when they are ugly, they don't do it by halves!'

Even if aware of the criticism, the magnificent Emily Castlereagh seems to have been undaunted by it. She was fond of outlandish headgear, sporting gaudy multicoloured ostrich feathers and, on one notable occasion, improvising a headdress from her husband's Order of the Garter. He, however, did not show himself the least embarrassed by his wife's eccentric fashion sense. The Castlereaghs may have lacked the glamour of the Continental European peacocks and fashion plates; but they always appeared, as the French say, *bien dans leur peaus* – at ease with themselves. One of Baron Hager's spies reported that

there is much laughter at Lord and Lady Castlereagh, who are seen every-where in the streets and the shops, walking arm-in-arm, and who go into every single shop, have everything the establishment contains shown to them, and then leave without purchasing a single item.

The two were inseparable; and whatever his business, Castlereagh hated to travel without her. I can well understand. I was less effective as a diplomat without Catherine at my side. We were a partnership in the United States, as the Castlereaghs had been in Vienna. After all, at a diplomatic dinner, Emily Castlereagh would always be seated between two men. If they were significant players at the Congress, it would be her opportunity, not her husband's, to find out their latest thinking. Catherine did the same in Washington; and many of her conversations found their way into my reports to London.

The Vienna routine must have been crushing. Most evenings would involve a dinner, followed by a ball, after which Castlereagh would work into the night. One of his right-hand men, Edward Cooke, suffered a breakdown from overwork. Castlereagh was conscientious and effective, drafting all important notes himself, and replying speedily to correspondence. He rose at 5 a.m. in summer and at 7 a.m. in winter. The lack of sleep was bad enough, but Castlereagh had another cross to bear. He shared with many British men a disabling lack of dancing skills. Nowadays, that does not matter too much, since diplomatic balls are few and far between. In 1814, however, it was a serious social and professional disadvantage. The sight of his skinny legs flailing around during a waltz was to some a hideous spectacle. This was not for lack of trying. An Austrian spy reported that Castlereagh practised his waltz with a chair.

Castlereagh was ideally suited to the informal diplomacy of the Congress. He later explained to the American diplomat Richard Rush that he preferred 'to treat of business in frank conversations; a course which saved time and was in other ways preferable as a general one to official notes'. Castlereagh's sober and agreeable manner earned him the trust of his fellow delegates as a fair man in negotiation. On first meeting him, Prince Metternich was immediately impressed, writing to his lover Wilhelmine that he felt as though he had been working with Castlereagh all his life. 'He is cool and collected,' he enthused, 'his heart is in the right place, he is *a man*, and he keeps his head.' His colleague Lord Ripon commented in similar vein on his negotiating technique:

the suavity and dignity of his manners, his habitual patience and self-command, his considerate tolerance of difference of opinion in others, all fitted him for such a task; whilst his firmness, when he knew he was right, in no degree detracted from the influence of his conciliatory demeanour.

The Prussian soldier and military strategist, Karl von Clausewitz, admired Castlereagh's approach, comparing it favourably with Prussian diplomacy. The British, he said, 'do not seem to have come here with a passion for revenge ... but rather like a master who wishes to discipline with proved coldness and immaculate purity'.

Put all these comments together and you have a portrait of the model British diplomat: formidably well prepared and hard-working; an accomplished networker; calm, judicious and fair and seen as such; tough when the need arises; and always with an unwavering focus on the national interest.

By the end of 1814, Castlereagh's diplomatic skills were being tested to the limit. The negotiations were at crisis point. The Big Four were in deadlock over the two biggest issues of the Congress: the division of Saxony and Poland. Matters were complicated by ideology. The newfangled ideas of nationalism and self-determination were taking hold. For the old guard, particularly the multi-ethnic Austrian Empire, nationalism was a dangerous threat. For liberals it was a moral crusade. National feeling was particularly strong in Poland; but neither Prussia nor Russia wanted an independent Poland between them. Tsar Alexander, whose passion to absorb Poland was undiminished, offered the Poles the inducement of a constitution of their own, protesting that they would merely share a ruling family with Russia. Prussia, which also had claims on Poland, was ready to abandon them in return for Saxony. Britain and Austria were determined to limit Russian and Prussian ambitions. As the negotiations wore on, the Prussians began to sabre-rattle. On New Year's Eve, they issued an ultimatum. If the Congress rejected the Prussian claim on Saxony, it would, said Hardenberg, mean war.

Castlereagh then did what every diplomat must be ready to do when the need arises – he threw off the 'Mr Nice Guy' image and began to play it rough, announcing that the Congress would have to be abandoned. Then, early in 1815, he engineered a secret alliance between Britain, France and Austria, with a number of smaller states brought into the fold as well. At the same time, the so-called War of 1812 between Britain and the United States came to an end; this was particularly good news from Castlereagh's point of view because the cessation of hostilities in the Americas would release significant naval and military resources for the European theatre. When rumours of the secret alliance emerged, Prussia and Russia realised that the game was up and they returned to the negotiating table.

It was an audacious masterstroke, executed by Castlereagh without prior reference to the government in London. There are occasions when diplomacy will not work unless backed by the credible threat of force. 'Credible' means that there is no doubt that force will be used if it is the only way to achieve diplomacy's goals. In 2003, Saddam Hussein would have folded his cards, had he not believed that the French and Russians would save him from Anglo-American attack. Castlereagh had defused the situation by making plain that he meant business. It was a tribute not just to his skills and strength of character; but to the pragmatism that is the hallmark of effective diplomacy. Russia and Prussia had been faced down by a coalition in which France, the enemy of twenty-five years, and the very reason why the Congress was necessary, had been accepted in alliance by Britain and Austria.[3] It was also a tribute to Britain's strength. Just as, following the Second World War, the United States became the 'indispensable nation' – to quote a former US Secretary of State, Madeleine Albright – for the success of almost any international arrangement, this was to be Britain's destiny for the remainder of the nineteenth century.

Over the following weeks, negotiations moved to their conclusion. Castlereagh was in the thick of it. Despite the crisis with Russia and Prussia, he managed to remain on good terms with all parties, even when he was pushing unpalatable propositions down their throats. By the middle of February, the deal was done: Prussia got about half of Saxony; and Poland (with the exception of Cracow, which was given the status of a free city) was split between Prussia, Russia and Austria. Castlereagh could start to think about packing up and going home. It was a very British diplomatic victory.

Meanwhile, back in Vienna, social life had also come to something of a climax. Party planners were in permanent search of ever more exotic novelties to satisfy Vienna's jaded and lascivious palates. November witnessed an event known as the 'Carousel': a medieval tournament re-enacted in the famous riding school, to allow the resting veterans of the Napoleonic Wars to display their equestrian and martial skills. This homage to the age of chivalry allowed every sartorial indulgence. The knights were dressed in gorgeous costumes and broad-brimmed, feathered hats, as they sliced dangling apples in feats of showy swordsmanship. The women adorned their period costumes with jewellery of every kind, each in fierce competition with the rest to shine the brightest. Afterwards, there was the usual magnificent banquet, dancing till dawn, and who knows how much urgent coupling and debauchery as the sun rose over Vienna.

In January 1815, as Europe stood on the edge of war, the VIPs and their wives were pulled to the palace of Schönbrunn in thirty-two luxurious sleighs by horses sporting ostrich feathers. The first sleigh held an orchestra, the last a Turkish ensemble. When they reached Schönbrunn, the party was treated to an ice spectacular, which included a particularly skilled dancer who carved into the ice with his skates the monograms of the various European rulers. As usual, on return to Vienna, there was a ball.[4]

The nearest my wife and I got to a Vienna-style extravaganza was the Red Cross Ball in Palm Beach, Florida, an annual event for charity which attracts a well-heeled social élite. It is a white-tie, wear-your-medals event. Ambassadors are invited. At the sound of trumpets, each ambassadorial couple is escorted into the vast ballroom of the Breakers Hotel by a US Marine in full dress uniform, to be announced to, and applauded by, the throng. While this is going on, you are blinded by an intense searchlight. The year we attended, the great American singer, Tony Bennett, was to provide the entertainment. He had got some way into his set when people started dancing. You do not dance when Tony Bennett sings. He stormed off stage, walked out on to the beach and, despite the pleadings of the *grande dame* who hosted the ball, declined to return.

By early 1815, many were getting impatient with the frivolity of Vienna. The Prince de Ligne was heard to say that '*Le Congrès danse et ne marche pas'* (the Congress is dancing, but it's not working). As for Castlereagh, his own contribution to the social whirlwind was frugal and minimal: when the British threw a ball, Lady Castlereagh's things had to be moved out of her bedroom to make room for the dancers. There was never any risk of Castlereagh getting into trouble over his expenses. He was, however, in trouble on another front.

The French Revolution had opened a Pandora's Box, from which flew the spirits of nationalism and self-determination. 'Liberty, Equality, Fraternity', though grossly traduced by Napoleon, had gained a hold on the political thinking and imagination of wide sections of European public opinion. A liberal European politics was born, which reviled the Congress of Vienna and the settlement it produced. For those infected by the new thinking and its emphasis on liberty, the restoration of *anciens régimes* was too much to bear. Castlereagh was well aware of the criticism to which he was subject in Parliament and press. He was taking fire from two distinct directions. There was a significant body of public opinion which wanted to exact vengeance on France, whereas Castlereagh wanted to ease the French back into the fold better to contain them. Then there were the radicals and Whigs, who identified with the weaker parties at the Congress. They felt that Britain was riding roughshod over the wishes of peoples like the Poles and Norwegians. The Whig MP, Samuel Whitbread, put it this way in a Commons debate in November 1814:

The rumours were that the Emperor Alexander had strenuously contended for the independence of Poland and that he had been opposed in his benevolent views by the British ministers ... We now live in an age when free nations are not to be sold and transferred like beasts of burden; and if any attempt of the kind was made the result would be a bloody and revengeful war.

Castlereagh sought in vain to convince domestic opinion otherwise. It was not that he opposed the existence of an independent Poland; it was simply not practical in political terms. Too many Great Powers had refused to countenance an independent Poland. 'Such a plan', said Castlereagh to the House of Commons in March 1815, 'could

not be carried into effect without the complete and general con-
currence of all the parties interested.'

Castlereagh was an arch-proponent of the 'realist' school of diplomacy, which takes the world as it finds it, not as it might wish it
to be. He saw this as simple common sense (I think that he would
be surprised to belong to a school of diplomacy). To succumb to
the pathetic fallacies of the idealist school was to promote solutions
that were inherently unstable and would most likely lead to war.
Poland in 1815 was a *locus classicus*. An independent Poland would
be a permanent temptation to Russian aggression: it would be a
destabilising force in the heart of Europe. A Poland divided into
agreed spheres of influence would not. Ergo, however much
Castlereagh might personally sympathise with the Polish predicament, they could not be independent if Russia and Prussia would
not have it.

For Castlereagh, the goal for Britain was a stable, long-term peace,
which would not give rise to costly entanglements in European
disputes. As George Canning, Castlereagh's erstwhile rival, succinctly put it a few years later: 'our true policy had always been not
to interfere except in great emergencies and then with commanding
force.' Poles today, heavily bruised by history, may say that this is
the mentality that led to the appeasement of Hitler and the shame
of the Munich Agreement. On the contrary: in 1815 the aggressor
had already been defeated at great sacrifice. The proper parallel for
Vienna is the meeting of the Great Powers at Yalta in 1945, where
there was no gainsaying the contribution of the Red Army to the
defeat of Hitler; and where there was no alternative to giving Stalin
a share of the spoils. Diplomacy, too, is the art of the possible. A
deal had to be brokered with the main parties if it were to stick;
and, as Castlereagh put it, that meant that 'in its very nature it must
be conservative'.

To more idealistic observers, all this was pretty repugnant. Friedrich von Gentz commented that 'the real aim of the Congress was
the dividing up between the victors of the spoils stolen from the
vanquished', articulating an impression of the Congress of Vienna
which was widespread among liberals and has remained so to the
present day. Over a century later, when statesmen met at Versailles
to put Europe together again after the First World War, the US

President, Woodrow Wilson, a classic idealist, said he hoped 'no odour of Vienna' would hang over the conference. More recently the Labour Foreign Secretary, David Miliband, declared that 'Europe cannot have its destiny settled on the basis of the Congress of Vienna'. What a pity! Vienna, with its concern for spheres of influence and Castlereagh's 'just equilibrium' between powers, gave us ninety-nine years without a general European war; Versailles and the hobbled League of Nations, twenty-one. The disdain of today's callow politicians for the achievements of Castlereagh are in any event the purest hypocrisy. Despite facile rhetoric to the contrary, there is not the slightest chance that the Ukraine and Georgia will be admitted to NATO, because, if the politicians had the candour to admit it, both lie in Russia's sphere of influence.

If the Congress of Vienna in plenary session would have been the rough equivalent of the UN General Assembly, then the Quadruple Alliance was supposed to be its Security Council. The agreement to create the Alliance was signed in Paris in November 1815. It bound Britain, Prussia, Austria and Russia to secure Europe against a future resurgence of French aggression and to uphold the decisions of the Congress. What constituted aggression, and what exactly would be done about it should it arise, was left deliberately vague. Each agreed to put 60,000 men in the field, in the event of such an emergency. The signatories were to meet at regular congresses. In 1818 France was admitted as a full member, so completing the process of French rehabilitation. This changed the Alliance's rationale and marked the beginning of the end for the congress system. The last meeting was in 1822 at Verona, by which time Britain was keen to extract itself.

The Quadruple, now Quintuple, Alliance had in effect been taken over from within by the parallel Holy Alliance, also created in 1815, at the behest of the increasingly odd Tsar Alexander. This comprised Russia, Austria and Prussia, three-quarters of the Big Four. It was ostensibly dedicated to the propagation of religious values as the basis for peaceful international relations. In practice, thanks in particular to the influence of Metternich, it quickly became a reactionary instrument for the return of genies to bottles: nationalism, democracy and self-determination, wherever they appeared. Louis XVIII of France, the most conspicuous member of the restored

European *ancien régime*, found this immensely congenial. The Tsar pressed Britain to join. But the British were having none of an alliance which preached a divine right of intervention anywhere it pleased. The Holy Alliance was, said Castlereagh, a 'piece of sublime mysticism and nonsense'. It was worse. If troops of the three member-states were to tramp at will around Europe in the name of religion, the careful balance of power established at Vienna would be wrecked. As it was, the Holy Alliance destroyed the Quadruple Alliance, by forcing Britain's withdrawal. As Castlereagh put it:

In this Alliance as in all other human Arrangements, nothing is more likely to impair or even to destroy its real utility, than any attempt to push its duties and obligations beyond the Sphere which its original conception and understood Principles will warrant: ... It never was ... intended as an Union for the Government of the World, or for the Superintendence of the Internal Affairs of other States.

Castlereagh warned the Tsar of the dangers for a statesman 'permitted to regulate his conduct by the counsels of his heart instead of the dictates of his understanding'.

Britain broke with her allies over the issue of French intervention in Spain, where Louis XVIII wished to help the royalists against liberal revolutionaries. The British (and the Americans) took even greater exception to plans by the Holy Alliance to intervene in the rebellious Spanish colonies of America. London made plain that the Royal Navy would not let this happen; and a British Admiral became a hero of Chilean independence. With the death of Alexander in 1825 the Holy Alliance duly ran out of steam.

After a generation fighting Bonaparte on land and sea, Britain was ready for a little Splendid Isolation. It had the power, the wealth and the navy to be able to set the terms of its relationship with the Continental European powers. More than any other European figure, the Tsar, with his meddling, autocratic and barmy instincts, confirmed to Britain the wisdom of standing aloof from European quarrels and intervening, as George Canning had said, only in 'emergencies'. Canning, who succeeded Castlereagh as Foreign Secretary in 1822, put it even more pungently when he commented:

... intimately connected as we are with the system of Europe, it does not follow that we are therefore called upon to mix ourselves on every occasion, with a restless and meddling activity, in the concerns of the nations which surround us.

Castlereagh and the Royal Navy gave Britain a century of peace and prosperity. His genius was such that no 'emergency' arose until 1914, except, perhaps, for the mid-century aberration of the Crimean War against Russia. In the first decade of the twentieth century, Splendid Isolation was abandoned in favour of alliances with France and Russia to confront the growing threat of Imperial Germany.

Today, the notion of isolation, splendid or otherwise, is considered a bizarre anachronism. It is a given across the political and administrative class of the United Kingdom that our prosperity and security can be assured only by giving up vast chunks of our sovereignty in the interests of alliances in Europe and with the United States. Would Castlereagh recoil in horror at this degree of entanglement? Or would he, with his pragmatism and keen sense of the possible, acknowledge that Britain has no other choice? My guess is that, if given the Foreign Office once again, he would go back to basics: turn his rigorous and unsentimental gaze to the matter of the national interest and conclude that Britain has far more room to manoeuvre in international affairs than our under-confident foreign policy allows. After all – pass the smelling salts – if France can do it, so can we.

On returning home in 1815, Castlereagh told the Commons with justifiable pride that 'never before was so much accomplished for Europe, and that we never had in our history a fairer prospect of bright days of continued happiness than at the present moment, if they be not clouded by new and unforeseen calamity'. He had largely achieved the objectives of the 1805 Pitt Plan.

He had also managed to persuade the Great Powers to support a point of humanitarian principle for which there was enthusiastic public support in Britain: the abolition of the slave trade. The other powers were extremely reluctant. But Castlereagh got his way, with a Congress declaration proclaiming slavery to be 'repugnant to the principles of humanity and universal morality', and expressing the 'wish of putting an end to a scourge which has so long desolated

Africa, degraded Europe, and afflicted humanity'. It may not have gone as far as many reformers would have liked, but it shows Castlereagh as willing to insist on a humanitarian principle as on a 'just equilibrium' in dividing the post-Bonaparte spoils.

In his lifetime Castlereagh's achievements received scant recognition. He won the undying hostility of liberal opinion and beyond. This was sharpened by his being a member of a government which introduced various repressive measures against radicalism. It was on Castlereagh's watch as Leader of the House of Commons (he was Foreign Secretary as well) that the Peterloo Massacre took place in 1819 in Manchester, when cavalry charged into a rally for parliamentary reform, killing several demonstrators.

Castlereagh had worked himself into the ground for Britain, and possibly into mental illness. In 1822, his behaviour became increasingly erratic and worrying to his friends. Paranoid, fearful, and ridden with self-doubt, in August of that year he confessed to one of his staff: 'I am . . . quite worn out; and this fresh responsibility is more than I can bear.' A few days later, on 12 August, he found the only weapon which had not been removed by his doctors – a penknife in a drawer – and killed himself with it. His death was greeted with public jubilation.

In obituaries, obloquy and derision were poured on his head. *The Scotsman* summed up the general consensus: Castlereagh would 'long be connected with tyranny abroad, and all that was slavish and oppressive at home'. Byron composed an epitaph of exemplary scorn:

> Posterity will ne'er survey
> A nobler grave than this:
> Here lie the bones of Castlereagh
> Stop, traveller, and piss!

At Castlereagh's funeral in Westminster Abbey, a crowd booed his coffin. In the countryside, church bells rang in celebration.

Castlereagh's reputation had been overwhelmed by the troubles of post-Napoleonic Britain. Twenty-five years of war had engendered enormous deprivation. There was widespread unrest and dissatisfaction – fertile ground for radical and reformist ideas – which led in turn to pressure for parliamentary reform and extending the suffrage. This would come, ten years after Castlereagh's death, in the Great Reform Act. But his government, hopelessly out of touch with public opinion, had reacted to reform in a snarling, defensive crouch. Stability and conservatism worked at Vienna; but would not do for London or Manchester. When Castlereagh died, it was as if all of England's accumulated resentments and frustrations found their outlet in his vilification.

Posterity has been much kinder. In the twentieth century his reputation began to enjoy the renaissance that it deserved. A former Foreign Secretary, Lord Hurd, described him recently as 'our first great Foreign Secretary'. William Hague, the Shadow Foreign Secretary, credits Castlereagh's work at Vienna as 'one of the most successful post-war negotiations, perhaps the most successful, in the whole history of diplomacy'. Perhaps we should go abroad for a more objective evaluation. Henry Kissinger, the master of twentieth-century *realpolitik*, wrote his doctoral thesis on Castlereagh and Metternich; and then expanded it in his magisterial *Diplomacy*. Castlereagh emerges from Kissinger's pages 'a wizard of the Western world', as the Foreign Office used to call Kissinger himself when he was in charge of US foreign policy.

Let the last word go to another American, Castlereagh's friend, Richard Rush, who said in posthumous tribute:

British in all his policy and projects ... always self-possessed, always firm and fearless, his judgement was the guide of his opinions, and his opinions the guide of his conduct, undaunted by opposition in Parliament or out of it.

3

KEEPING UP WITH THE JONESES:
Our Man in Washington and the Nassau Deal

In late December 1962, two government aircraft converged on the Bahamas. One, flying from the east, carried the British Prime Minister, Harold Macmillan. The other, flying from the north, carried the President of the United States, John F. Kennedy. One of Kennedy's travelling companions was the British Ambassador to the United States, Sir David Ormsby-Gore. They were on their way to a summit meeting that would decide the course of Anglo-American relations well into the twenty-first century.

On the British side, the stakes could not have been higher. Britain's status as a power of the first order, and the survival of Macmillan's government, depended on the outcome. On the American side, the challenge was less urgent, but profound nonetheless. How should the Western superpower seek to organise the transatlantic alliance in the depths of the Cold War; and where did nuclear weapons fit into the equation? For the Americans there was a further consideration. Just what should be the nature of their relationship with Britain? A victorious, if fractious, alliance in the Second World War had deteriorated badly since 1945. Should Britain now be treated as just one among several big European powers like France and the rehabilitated Germany? Or should there be something special and exclusive about the relationship; and, if so, did this merit giving the British the nuclear weapons system that they so desperately wanted?

The British believed that, without an independent nuclear deterrent, the very core of their national security was in jeopardy. Their advantage in the tough four-day negotiation that followed would lie in their single-mindedness, a rare quality in the more recent history of Anglo-American negotiation. Though some in Kennedy's team were firmly opposed to Britain's pretensions, others, including Kennedy himself, were more open to persuasion. Macmillan and Ormsby-Gore played to this advantage with extraordinary skill and persistence; and in the end, they got their way. But, with the benefit of half a century's hindsight, was this triumph of diplomacy hollow? Britain may have secured its position at the top table of great nations, but was it a Faustian bargain that has required ever since the sub-ordination of Britain's security policy to that of the United States?

Harold Macmillan's reading matter on the long transatlantic flight was Gibbon's *Decline and Fall of the Roman Empire*; an appropriate choice for the Prime Minister of a country that had fallen a long way since the apogee of its imperial glory. Two world wars within thirty years had knocked the stuffing out of Britain's economy. The 1960s would see Britain grant independence to many of its colonial territories. The Empire was in full dismemberment as it turned into a Commonwealth of Nations. Macmillan had himself preached the 'wind of change' in a famous speech made in South Africa.

The years since 1945 had been rough. They were marked in par-ticular by fierce disagreements with the United States. The nego-tiations with Washington just after the war for a loan had been hard-fought and acrimonious (the loan was finally paid off at the end of 2006). In 1956, the US had humiliated Britain by pulling the plug on the ill-starred Franco/Israeli/British expedition to seize the Suez Canal from Egypt, marking the end of Britain's independence of action in the Middle East. It was a brutal reminder of how the baton of global power had passed from the British to the Americans. The crisis had driven the Conservative Prime Minister, Anthony Eden, from power, as his health cracked under the strain. Macmillan stepped into the breach.

By 1962, Supermac, as he had once been called, was himself in political decline. His slogan for the 1959 election – 'You've never had it so good' – was a distant memory. Unemployment stood at 800,000, the highest since the end of the war. Seven Cabinet min-isters had been sacked in the 'night of the long knives', a drastic reshuffle that looked like panic in the face of economic crisis. The government was losing by-elections. Within less than a year Macmillan would have resigned. He was hardly going into the Nassau negotiations from a position of strength.

The same could not be said for the occupant of Air Force One. The youthful, charismatic President John F. Kennedy had just successfully navigated the Cuban missile crisis. By facing down the Soviet leader, Nikita Khrushchev, and forcing him to withdraw missiles stationed in Castro's Cuba, Kennedy was generally judged to have saved the world from nuclear war. He was leader of the most powerful nation in the world, a man at the height of his powers and self-confidence. Negotiating with the friendly Brits was hardly in the same class. But with the customary insularity that afflicts even the most sophisticated Americans, the US administration had failed to grasp what was at stake for their old wartime allies. It was the number one task of the lone British official aboard Air Force One to get that message across to the US President.

Sir David Ormsby-Gore, who had arrived in Washington as Her Britannic Majesty's Ambassador to the United States of America in 1961, was perfectly suited to the task. He was a political appointee, that is to say, someone not from the ranks of the career Diplomatic Service. By and large, it is not the British custom to award political appointees with embassies and high commissions, but the Washington Embassy has been something of an exception with a handful of political appointments since the Second World War: Peter Jay, John Freeman, Lord Cromer. This is in contrast to the American practice, which, with each change of president, distributes ambassadorships as a political reward to big-ticket fundraisers and the like.

The Washington Embassy is the best job in the Diplomatic Service; and Ormsby-Gore was more than a match for the distinguished pedigree of those who had preceded him. This included Sir Ronald Lindsay, who held the job for almost a decade in the 1930s and was the first to occupy the magnificent house on Massachusetts Avenue, designed as residence and offices by the most renowned British architect of the time, Sir Edwin Lutyens. Lindsay kept a diary as he and his wife moved in, in June 1930. For those who have had trouble with builders, it may come as some consolation that even the most august residences are not immune to teething problems. Lindsay recorded that

Not a door ... has a fly screen. One third of the windows are still without screens ... sleep is impossible because the rooms are full of flies and mosquitoes, and rats run about behind the wainscoting when they are not actually galloping through the ballroom ... This morning, after a sleepless night, when I tried to leave my bedroom, I could not get out, as the door had jammed during the damp night. Servants were summoned and hurled themselves against the door, thereby liberating me ... the house is black with flies, and their dead bodies adorn our food.[1]

Ormsby-Gore had a thorough grounding in international affairs from his years as Under-Secretary and Minister of State in the Foreign Office, but it was his connections that made him stand out. He had the closest personal relationship with a serving US president since diplomatic relations were first opened in 1791. The *Sunday Times* correspondent in America, Henry Brandon, thought that his relationship with Kennedy was 'unique in the annals of British ambassadors in Washington'. Roy Jenkins, writing Ormsby-Gore's entry in the *Oxford Dictionary of National Biography*, commented that this 'was a wholly exceptional social position for any ambassador. It made Ormsby-Gore almost as much an unofficial adviser to the President as an envoy of the British government.' Ormsby-Gore and Kennedy had become friends as young men before the war, when the latter's father, Joe, had been US Ambassador to the Court of St James. To be a close family friend of an executive head of state is for an ambassador the Holy Grail, for it guarantees access, information and influence beyond the dreams of other envoys.[2] It helped also that Ormsby-Gore was Macmillan's nephew by marriage (and that one of Kennedy's sisters married a nephew of Macmillan's wife, Dorothy). Some charged Macmillan with nepotism. But this was beside the point. If a British prime minister wants to influence an American president, it would be perverse to the point of madness to ignore an ambassadorial candidate with the connections and qualifications of David Ormsby-Gore.

Ormsby-Gore had another quality of inestimable value: he could 'speak American'. This is an instinctive attribute, which cannot be learned in some language school. It combines a hard-to-define combination of attitude and idiom, which makes it much easier to win the confidence of Americans. The former head of the US Chamber of Commerce, Bill Archey, was making the same point when he once said to me that visiting British dignitaries could be divided into two types: those who needed a laxative and those who did not. Nothing puts an American back up faster than a sense of being patronised or preached to. The tough right-wing nationalist John Bolton, who was US Ambassador to the UN in the last years of President George W. Bush, waxes vitriolic about the British in his memoirs, taking an especially violent dislike to his UK opposite number, Emyr Jones Parry. By contrast, Tony Blair, who spoke perfect American, could have become US President, had he been born in the States. After a speech to a vast audience in Chicago in 1999, the British Prime Minister was greeted with cries of 'Blair for President!' (this was after Bill Clinton had been disgraced by the Monica Lewinsky affair).

Ormsby-Gore was in no need of a laxative. He wore his ambassadorship lightly. He endeared himself to Kennedy and other senior Americans with a relaxed charm and sense of humour. His light touch would emerge from time to time in his official communications. He once reported to London that 'I had to dash ahead of the President on to his plane because, as you know, it moves off the second he walks through the door. His valet has been left behind three times on the last four flights.' Little had changed in my time: Cherie Blair's French hairdresser was once left behind at Camp David, the President's retreat where the Blairs had been staying, because he missed the helicopter back to Washington. This was not, I recall, a matter of Ormsby-Gore-style levity. Instead, an atmosphere of Borgia-like recrimination prevailed among the Blair courtiers as they hunted for someone to blame.

Ormsby-Gore's access was peerless; his opportunities to influence American thinking extraordinary. It underlined the wisdom of Macmillan's choice. He was present at meetings of the National Security Council during the Cuba Missile Crisis; the Ormsby-Gores even had spaces reserved in the President's nuclear shelter in the Appalachians. As Ted Sorensen, Kennedy's speechwriter and Special Counsel & Advisor, told me in an interview for the companion television documentary: 'There was a paper I needed to deliver quickly to the President,' he recalled, 'and I was told he was at dinner over in the Residence. I went over to the dining room and the President and Jackie were sitting there with David Ormsby-Gore.' Other members of the Kennedy administration reported the American Secretary of State's resentment at the British Ambassador's closeness to the President.

No British Ambassador and his wife have since enjoyed a relationship of such intimacy with the President and First Lady. While all of us have had easy access to members of the so-called Principals' Committee – the Vice-President, the National Security Advisor, the Chief of Staff, the Secretary of State, the Secretary for Defense, the head of the CIA and so on – our contacts with the President have been more sparing. The only Ambassador, who, to my knowledge, could rival Ormsby-Gore's contacts with the White House was the Saudi Prince Bandar, who was a friend of the Bush family and in post for almost a quarter of a century.

Access can sometimes be too much of a good thing. A hostile American reaction built up to Margaret Thatcher's closeness to Ronald Reagan. After Reagan left office in 1989 to be replaced by George Bush Senior, a deliberate effort was made by the new administration to put some distance between it and Thatcher, whose influence was considered to have become too great. Thatcher and Bush were never especially close; and, more important, disagreed over German unification, to which she was viscerally opposed. For a while, the Americans saw Germany as a more important European player. Something of the old intimacy was only restored when America and Britain joined forces in 1991 to drive Saddam Hussein out of Kuwait in the first Gulf War.

The Ormsby-Gores enjoyed a special relationship with the Kennedys, as did Margaret Thatcher with Ronald Reagan and Tony Blair with Bill Clinton and George W. Bush. But as a concept defining the nature of British-American relations, the phrase 'Special Relationship' owes more to mythology and rhetoric than to reality. It was unknown before Winston Churchill and his wartime collaboration with President Roosevelt. From the American Revolution until the Second World War, to have suggested that relations between London and Washington were especially warm and close would have caused astonishment in the two capitals. The period was marked as much, if not more, by mutual suspicion and hostility than by intimate friendship between the governments. The negotiations in the 1920s to limit naval armaments were at one point so acrimonious that the Americans drew up plans for the possibility of war with Britain. The alliance against the Axis powers did much to change that; and there developed a habit of easy, pragmatic cooperation, which in my time conferred on the Embassy in Washington a degree of access to the US administration unrivalled by most other missions (the regular monthly meetings of EU heads of mission in Washington tended to be an exercise in getting the British Ambassador to spill the beans on what he had found out from his American contacts).

However the wartime alliance did not mean that the national interests of America and Britain would converge for all eternity. On the contrary, in the last sixty years major differences of view between Washington and London have cropped up regularly. Seen as a line on a graph, the British-American relationship since 1945 has to be drawn as a sequence of peaks and troughs. Macmillan and Kennedy represent a peak as a result of the meeting in Nassau; a few years later Harold Wilson and Lyndon Johnson fell into a trough, with neither liking the other and Wilson refusing to send troops to Vietnam. Wilson himself preferred the phrase 'close relationship' and his successor, the Europhile Edward Heath, the 'natural relationship'.

It is fine for British and American politicians to deploy 'Special Relationship' as a rhetorical device to embellish speeches and press conferences, but it becomes a problem if, as is increasingly the case on the British side, you start to believe your own propaganda. I discouraged the use of the phrase in the Embassy because it placed a burden on the relationship, one that it could not carry: it raised unrealistic expectations, exaggerated the identity of interest between the two countries, and, as was especially the case when Tony Blair was Prime Minister, it became an end in itself, crippling the British ability to express an independent view that could be at variance with that of the Americans. Things have got worse recently, with the obsequious grovelling to President Obama of British (and European) politicians eager to catch some of his stardust. The

United States is Britain's most important ally and partner; and will remain so for the foreseeable future. Managing relations with a larger and more powerful ally is often a more complicated affair than dealing with adversaries. By and large, the invocation of the 'Special Relationship' is a burden, not a help, in this endeavour.

The first deployment of 'Special Relationship' is generally attributed to Churchill's 1946 speech at Fulton, Missouri, when he coined another famous phrase, 'Iron Curtain', to characterise the division in Europe between the communist East and the democratic West. But his reference to a special relationship was itself an echo of something he had said several months earlier in the House of Commons about British-American cooperation on nuclear matters, the very issue at the heart of the Nassau meeting:

May I in conclusion submit to the House a few simple points which, it seems to me, should gain their approval? First, we should fortify in every way our special and friendly connections with the United States, aiming always at a fraternal association for the purpose of common protection and world peace. Secondly, this association should in no way have a point against any other country, great or small, in the world, but should, on the contrary, be used to draw the leading victorious Powers ever more closely together on equal terms and in all good faith and good will. Thirdly, we should not abandon our special relationship with the United States and Canada about the atomic bomb, and we should aid the United States to guard this weapon as a sacred trust for the maintenance of peace. Fourthly, we should seek constantly to promote and strengthen the world organisation of the United Nations, so that, in due course, it may eventually be fitted to become the safe and trusted repository of these great agents. Fifthly, and this, I take it, is already agreed, we should make atomic bombs, and have them here, even if manufactured elsewhere, in suitable safe storage with the least possible delay. Finally, let me say on behalf of the whole House that we wish the Prime Minister the utmost success in his forthcoming highly important visit to Washington.[3]

By the time Harold Macmillan crossed the Atlantic in December 1962, the nuclear core of Churchill's notion of a special relationship was threatening melt-down. In 1960, Macmillan had struck a deal with Kennedy's Republican predecessor, President Dwight D.

Eisenhower, to purchase the Skybolt air-to-ground missile, which would be fitted to the British 'V' bomber force[4] with a nuclear warhead. In return, the Americans would be given Holy Loch in Scotland as a base for their nuclear submarine fleet, equipped with the Polaris missile. This looked a good deal to Macmillan. Britain could abandon the costly and ineffectual development of its own nuclear missiles, Blue Streak and Blue Steel; it would not have to pay Skybolt's development costs; the life of the V bombers would be extended; an independent nuclear deterrent would be assured for the foreseeable future; and the relationship with the US would be pulled out of the doldrums.

By 1962 the deal had started to unravel. Skybolt was not working. Its development had run into technical difficulties. Costs had escalated. There were hints from the American side that the project might have to be cancelled. At a White House lunch in January for the British Minister of Aviation, Julian Amery, Kennedy was heard to ask whether the Skybolt project could ever be made to work, adding that 'one should not bank on it too much' – a remark which came as a great shock to Amery. As 1962 wore on, signs that the Americans might abandon Skybolt proliferated. Early in November matters came to a head. Robert McNamara, Kennedy's Secretary of Defence, came to see Ormsby-Gore. McNamara said that he had been reviewing the American defence budget for 1964, and the Skybolt programme had been giving him 'particular concern'. With tests of the missile continuing to fail, costs had spiralled from the original estimate of $200 million to $492 million, and looked set to rise still further. Delivery dates were slipping. Skybolt might have to be cancelled. After all, the Americans had other and better delivery systems in their nuclear arsenal. Ormsby-Gore takes up the tale in his reporting telegram to London:

I said I was sure he would realise that a decision to abandon the Skybolt programme would be political dynamite so far as the United Kingdom was concerned. . . . I must tell him that the repercussions of such a decision by the United States would be extremely grave. A major part of the United Kingdom's defence policy would be in ruins which would have serious internal political implications. Our military posture, not only in Europe but in other parts of the world, would be radically changed and Anglo-

American relations would be put under the severest strain. I feared that there would be people who questioned the United States' motives in arriving at this decision. They would say that this was a means of bringing pressure upon the British Government to abandon their independent nuclear deterrent.

'Political dynamite' was no exaggeration. The demise of Skybolt would mean the demise of the independent nuclear deterrent. That in turn would lead, as Churchill had warned in 1945, to Britain's exclusion from the club of serious world powers. The blow to Macmillan's personal authority and prestige would be immense. His government was already in serious political difficulty. There would be no *quid pro quo* for the US submarine base at Holy Loch, which had already enraged the vociferous anti-nuclear movement, including inside the opposition Labour Party. Ormsby-Gore's warning to McNamara of a crisis in Anglo-American relations was no exaggeration either. The history of cooperation between London and Washington on nuclear matters was already troubled. Britain had worked closely with the Americans during the Second World War on the Manhattan Project, contributing significantly to the development of the American atomic bomb. Britain's reward was the passage in 1945, during President Truman's administration, of the McMahon Act, which had forbidden US cooperation on nuclear technology with even the closest allies. This rankled hugely in the UK, where the government felt impelled to develop its own nuclear weapons – ironically, as much to insure against the unreliability of the US as an ally as to deter enemies. Things looked up again under Eisenhower; and the 1958 US/UK Mutual Defence Agreement had gone a long way to repair the situation, by restoring nuclear cooperation. But if Skybolt were cancelled, the boulder would roll back down the hill.

Since the end of the war there had been those in Washington who were hostile to Britain having its own nuclear weapons system. There were worries about proliferation; and many believed that Britain's days as a world power were over. McNamara himself was in this camp, arguing that 'limited nuclear capabilities, operating independently, are dangerous, expensive, prone to obsolescence and lacking in credibility as a deterrent', and that 'the creation of a single additional national nuclear force encourages the proliferation of nuclear power with all of its attendant dangers'. It was a shot across British and French bows.

A week after sending his report of the conversation with McNamara, Ormsby-Gore received Macmillan's instructions. He was to secure agreement from the President on three points: that the press should hear nothing more about problems with Skybolt until the leaders had spoken; that the President should make no decisions on the matter before discussing it with Macmillan; and that this discussion should take place as soon as possible. Macmillan proposed a telephone conversation with the President.

The telephone in diplomacy is a two-edged sword. You cannot do without it; and diplomacy without instant electronic communication is nowadays unthinkable. To a degree this has limited an ambassador's freedom of action. In the days of Killigrew and Castlereagh (though the latter had the considerable advantage of being a senior member of the government) advice, instructions and reports could take weeks to reach their destination. This meant that the man on the spot had to make extensive use of his initiative. Nowadays, if the government so chooses, it can keep an ambassador on a very tight rein. But instant communication can have certain benefits, too, allowing a head of mission to influence a policy debate in London in almost real time, occasionally attaining that ambassadorial nirvana where, in effect, you get to write your own instructions.

Direct communication between leaders raises a different category of issues. In my experience, phone conversations are as likely to create confusion as to bring clarity, especially where complex matters of substance are under discussion. This is partly because leaders tend to work from simplified briefs for these conversations, which fail to capture some of the detailed but essential points. I was told that Tony Blair insisted on working off one side of paper. It can be very difficult for advisers, who know the detail, to inject necessary points into a phone conversation, though they are, of course, listening in so as to take a record. There is also a problem about not being able to see the other person: the light in the eyes, the facial expression, the body language, all of which are essential to weighing up accurately the impact of your own words and what your next move should be. As an American official said to me once: some people give good phone, others don't. In Washington, I discovered from time to time that the White House had drawn a somewhat different conclusion from a phone conversation between President and Prime Minister than had Downing Street.

Video-conferencing has helped to overcome some of these problems. A link was set up between London and Washington just after I retired in 2003. But the electronic screen creates its own barriers; and is no substitute for two people facing each other across a table. All these difficulties are compounded when leaders and officials think that different forms of direct electronic communication remove the need to consult and inform the diplomats on the spot. That is the road to miscalculation and loss of indispensable political context.

Ormsby-Gore wanted to play to Macmillan's strengths. He knew also that, when you have a big gun, you can use it to best effect only once. So, he advised against a telephone conversation, on the grounds that Macmillan would be at his most effective in a face-to-face meeting with Kennedy, where he could deploy all his formidable powers of persuasion. In his report to Macmillan of 21 November, Ormsby-Gore confirmed that the President was content to put a stop to press briefings on Skybolt and to postpone decisions until after talks with Macmillan. In any case, the long Thanksgiving holiday was upon them and Kennedy was unlikely to take any further briefs on Skybolt during the break. Thereafter, he might even make contact himself. This fitted well with Ormsby-Gore's plan to save his trump card, the Prime Minister's personal presence and persuasiveness, for a face-to-face meeting towards the end of December at Nassau in the Bahamas.

It was to be a tense wait. Kennedy's undertaking notwithstanding, the intervening four weeks were plagued with uncomfortable indiscretions from the American side. This put pressure on Macmillan to demonstrate that he was not about to be let down by his American friends. In late November, the *Daily Express* ran a front-page story (possibly planted by the Labour Party) alleging that a 'lobby' within the US State Department was pressing for Skybolt's cancellation so as to prevent Britain acquiring an independent nuclear deterrent. Then came Acheson's dismissive speech about Britain losing an

Empire and not finding a role in the world. Finally, on 11 December, a week before the Nassau meeting was due to begin, McNamara himself came to London to meet the British Defence Secretary, Peter Thorneycroft. His visit was heralded by British press speculation that McNamara was about to strike Skybolt from the defence budget. To the consternation of the British government, McNamara seemed to confirm these suspicions in a prepared statement delivered to the British press on his arrival. Among other things, he stated: 'in Washington ... we are taking a very hard look at all of our programs. This includes Skybolt ... it is a very expensive program and technically extremely complex. It is no secret that all five flight tests attempted so far have failed and program costs have climbed sharply ...' It was also reported that the projected costs for Skybolt had reached an astronomical $2,800 million. As *The Times* put it the next day, 'If Mr Robert McNamara, the United States Secretary of Defence, was not sounding the death-knell of the Skybolt missile when he arrived in London yesterday, it was hard to see what else he was doing.'

There was by now a large measure of mutual misunderstanding. The British failed to appreciate that Skybolt made little sense when the US had both the land-based intercontinental ballistic missile, Minuteman, and the submarine-launched Polaris missile. The Americans, for their part, had yet to grasp the existential importance to Macmillan's government of an independent nuclear deterrent; and the damage that would be done to British–American relations if the US were judged to have left Britain in the lurch. Thorneycroft sought to get the point over:

A decision to cancel the Skybolt would not only have grievous political consequences to me and to my party. It would not only be seized by the opposition for that purpose ... We, on our side, of course, always said you would never let us down. We had to say that because we put our reliance in you absolutely. Now they will be able to say that they were right and we were wrong ...

Moreover, the position is made harder by recent statements by American spokesmen concerning the independent British deterrent. A number of US spokesmen have made themselves heard on this subject recently. ... The British press, and many others will say the Skybolt decision is part of that policy. They will say this decision is really taken to force Britain out of having an independent nuclear deterrent. The recent speech by Mr Acheson will be seized upon to place this action in that context . . .

In summary, he told McNamara that 'to cancel this project tears the heart out of our relations'. It was an aggressive performance designed to impress both the Americans and a British press primed to accuse the government of unforgivable weakness. McNamara left London without agreement, still failing to grasp the essential importance of independence to the British.

The government was now seized by a very great sense of urgency. Thorneycroft and Lord Home, the Foreign Secretary, were espied pacing back and forth in the middle of an anxious exchange: 'Will they give it to us?' – 'My God, if they don't, the Government might fall.' On 14 December, four days before the Nassau meeting, Macmillan telegraphed Ormsby-Gore in Washington:

You will realise what a row SKYBOLT is causing. We must treat it calmly but it is no use trying to ignore the facts.

It seems I shall not have a chance of talking with you at any length before my conversations with the President begin. So I would be grateful if you would think over this problem. If I stick to the order of BATTING proposed, we shall get immersed in various FASCINATING problems involving Russia, India et cetera and perhaps not get to SKYBOLT until quite late then there will be the danger of an inconclusive discussion. So my inclination is to ask for it to be put at the top of the list like an emergency resolution at a conference. Do you think the President would object to this? If so how strongly?

My difficulty is that if we cannot reach an agreement on a realistic means of maintaining a British independent deterrent, all the other questions may only justify perfunctory discussion, since an agonising reappraisal of all our foreign and defence policies will be required.

The Nassau meeting was formally the sixth in a series of summits between the American, Canadian and British leaders, at which world problems were discussed. The challenge for Macmillan and Ormsby-Gore was to convert it into an emergency bilateral meeting with Skybolt at the top of the agenda. But still the Americans did not seem to understand what was at stake for Macmillan. On the eve of the summit, Kennedy himself rubbed salt into the British wound. In a wide-ranging interview on television, he was asked about Skybolt and replied in a manner that could not have been more unhelpful to Macmillan:

we are talking about two and a half billion dollars to build a weapon to hang on our B-52s, when we already have billions invested in Polaris and Minuteman ... I would say that when we start to talk about the mega-tonnage we could bring into a nuclear war, we are talking about anni-hilation. How many times do you have to hit a target with nuclear weapons? That is why when we are talking about spending this $2.5 billion, we don't think that we are going to get $2.5 billion worth of national security ...

In other words, Skybolt was dead. The Americans gave Ormsby-Gore no warning of the President's remarks. Macmillan first heard of them on arriving in Nassau on 18 December. Henry Brandon wrote later of 'resentment and suspicion of American intentions such as I have never experienced'. George Ball, US Under-Secretary of State for Economic Affairs, described the British mood as 'grim'. Rene McColl, writing for the *Daily Express*, reported that the Americans had rebuffed British wishes to put Skybolt at the top of the agenda and were insisting on discussing instead the Katanga crisis in the Congo.

It fell to Ormsby-Gore to penetrate the British gloom. On 18 December, Kennedy flew to Nassau; as a mark of their close friendship, he invited Ormsby-Gore to accompany him on Air Force One. The British Ambassador used the time well. In a thirty-minute conversation he sought to impress on Kennedy the depth of British anxieties and the need for a firm public statement of support for an independent British nuclear deterrent. Professor Richard Neustadt, the American historian and expert on the presidency, who was also an adviser to Kennedy, later wrote a report on the Skybolt crisis. In describing how Ormsby-Gore finally managed to get Kennedy to understand the gravity of the situation for Macmillan, Neustadt says: 'the point was pure politics, not policy, not strategy, not dip-lomacy, not cost.' But Ormsby-Gore also made it clear that, if the

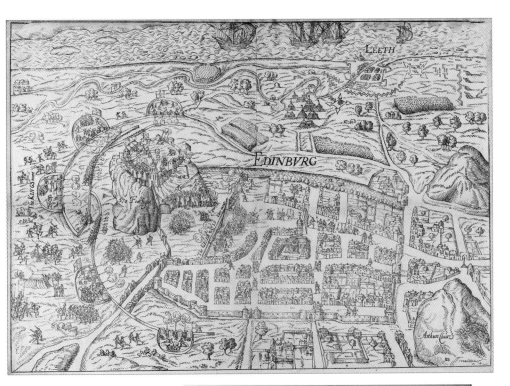

Edinburgh Castle, showing the siege and the fighting between Mary's followers and the Regent's party.
(The Edinburgh Room, City of Edinburgh Libraries)

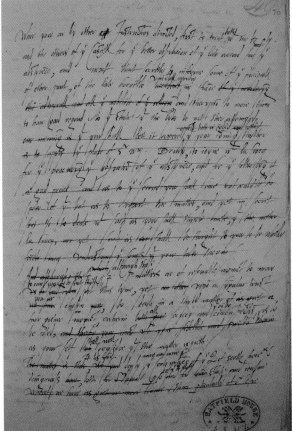

Burghley's draft of Killigrew's secret instructions, telling him to arrange the assassination of Mary Queen of Scots.
(The Marquess of Salisbury, Hatfield House)

A gruesome depiction of the St Bartholomew's Day massacre, by the Protestant artist François Dubois. Note the river full of corpses and the body of Coligny being hurled from a window.
(Scala)

MARIE
REINE
D'ESCOS
SE

Mary Queen of Scots by François Clouet, shown here several years before Killigrew was charged with getting rid of her.
(Bridgeman Art Library)

Viscount Castlereagh, the British hero of the Congress of Vienna. (Mary Evans Picture Library)

Lady Castlereagh, failing to cut a fashionable enough figure for the Europeans. (Mary Evans Picture Library)

A cartoon by Isaac Cruikshank mocking Castlereagh's duel with Canning in 1809, an undignified way to settle political differences. (Bridgeman Art Library)

The grand Carrousel of faux-medieval knights, just one of the many lavish
social events of the Congress.

Sir David Ormsby-Gore, British Ambassador to Washington and a close personal friend of JFK. (Getty Images)

ABOVE RIGHT: A test model of the Skybolt missile which was to cause so much tension between the US and UK. (Getty Images)

Prime Minister Harold Macmillan and President Jack Kennedy meet for vital talks at the Nassau Summit in December 1962. (Bahamas Historical Society)

Emperor Qianlong arrives at his 83rd birthday celebrations, as the British party await their reception. The scene was drawn by William Alexander, the artist who accompanied Macartney's embassy. (Bridgeman Art Library)

George, 1st Earl Macartney, first British envoy to China – if we discount poor old Charles Cathcart who set off first but never made it. (Mary Evans Picture Library)

Macartney's embassy receives an impressive welcome as it reaches
Chinese shores. (Mary Evans Picture Library)

The meeting of Macartney and Emperor Qianlong, as imagined by the
caricaturist James Gillray. (Bridgeman Art Library)

Sir John Bowring, Plenipotentiary and Chief Superintendent of Trade in the Far East and Governor, Commander in Chief and Vice Admiral of Hong Kong. (Mary Evans Picture Library)

The Emperor's subjects feed their habit in a Chinese opium den circa 1840. (Mary Evans Picture Library)

British press reported the cancellation of Skybolt as the US letting Britain down, there would be a huge wave of anti-Americanism in Britain, imperilling the whole relationship. This was a telling point when US relations with France and Germany were not at their best. By the time Kennedy arrived in Nassau, he and Ormsby-Gore had worked up a compromise proposal to put to Macmillan. This was the '50–50 deal': the US would continue to develop Skybolt, with the project's funding split equally between Britain and America. It was an encouraging sign that the Americans understood Macmillan's predicament and were willing to do something about it; and, thanks to Ormsby-Gore, it came from the top.

But Macmillan had already decided that if Skybolt was not good enough for the US, it was not good enough for the UK. He needed a different weapons system with the guarantee that Britain would have independent use of it. Polaris, launched from a new generation of nuclear-powered submarines and equipped with British nuclear warheads, fitted the bill. Macmillan had already had some preliminary discussion of this option with Eisenhower two years previously. Even if Skybolt had worked perfectly in tests, it would still have been inferior to Polaris. Macmillan's objective at Nassau was nothing less than a new agreement with the US to sell Britain the Polaris missile. In Macmillan's eyes, Britain's place in the world and his own political destiny depended on it.

As Air Force One landed, with Macmillan waiting on the tarmac to greet Kennedy, the Bahamas Band began to play 'Oh, Don't Deceive Me' – a musical choice which the US Under-Secretary of State, George Ball, assumed was no coincidence. The atmosphere for the talks could hardly have been less propitious. Macmillan's team had arrived in a state of near mutiny and bitter resentment towards the Americans. Thorneycroft, the Defence Secretary, was ready to walk out. After his talks with McNamara in London a week before, he felt that it would be better for Britain to be seen to take a stand than to be forced into a compromise to suit the Americans. There was still strong suspicion in the British delegation that the US objective was to deprive Britain of an independent deterrent. Ormsby-Gore had to point out that, even if the 50–50 deal was not good enough, it was not unreasonable; to storm out of the negotiations while this offer lay on the table would make the British look foolish and ungrateful. Undoubtedly it would not be difficult to spin it this way in the press. After some tense argument, Thorneycroft acquiesced. It sometimes falls to an ambassador to negotiate with the home team as well as the foreigners.

While Ormsby-Gore was keeping Thorneycroft and the rest of the delegation under control, the two principals were enjoying an intimate conversation alone. A few hours after arriving, before the start of the official talks, Kennedy called on Macmillan and the two of them went for a walk on the beach. They already knew each other well and had built a good personal and working relationship. To some they might have appeared an odd couple: the youngish, Democratic celebrity President and the sixty-eight-year-old Tory Old Etonian, of whom the American Ambassador to London had said, '[he] gives the impression of being shot through with Victorian languor.' But Kennedy, from his time in London when his father was Ambassador, was already well versed in the ways of the English upper classes. He liked Macmillan's dignity and old-fashioned charm; and admired and respected him for his extensive experience, including military service in the trenches during the First World War.

Thanks to his rapport with Kennedy, Macmillan may have been the only British politician or diplomat able to get away with the analogy of playing Greece to Kennedy's Rome, without giving offence. Try to use it today and most Americans will see it as intolerable British condescension. Kennedy, with his self-confidence and interest in history, was happy to learn from Macmillan. The British Prime Minister was, in any case, far more American than outward appearances might suggest. Like Churchill, he was half-American on his mother's side, and a staunch believer in a strong British-American relationship. During the Second World War, as Minister-Resident to the Allied Forces Headquarters in Algiers, Macmillan had been an adviser to General Eisenhower and the two had become close friends. It was a relationship which had served Macmillan well when Eisenhower became President; and he was keen to build a similar intimacy with Kennedy.

The result was an extraordinarily close relationship. Kennedy's Ambassador in London, David Bruce, commented that 'the frequency and frankness of their interchanges have few parallels in modern diplomatic intercourse'. Kennedy himself told the British journalist Henry Brandon: 'I feel at home with Macmillan because I can share my loneliness with him.' Later, after Macmillan resigned in October 1963, Kennedy was to say: 'In nearly three years of cooperation, we have worked together on great and small issues, and we have never had a failure of understanding or of mutual trust.'

After Kennedy's assassination, Macmillan repaid the compliment to his widow, Jackie: 'He seemed to trust me ... this is something very rare but very precious.'

Walks have played a prominent role in the diplomacy of the later twentieth century. In a famous 'walk in the woods' in Geneva's botanical gardens in 1983, the American (Paul Nitze) and Soviet (Yuli Kvitsinsky) negotiators tried in vain to strike an agreement on intermediate-range nuclear missiles. This led to a crisis in East–West relations, which contributed to a paranoid fear in Moscow at the end of 1983 that the US was about to launch a pre-emptive nuclear strike. It was not as dangerous as the Cuban Missile Crisis and is much less well known, but it was one of those occasions when the Cold War threatened to turn hot.[5] In 1986 at the Reykjavik summit, Reagan and Gorbachev, to the consternation of American and British officials, appeared to agree during a 'walk in the garden' to the unconditional elimination of all nuclear weapons (this teaches the lesson that to allow leaders to consort alone, without close advisers present, can sometimes lead to unpredictable and inadvisable results, a diplomat's nightmare).

Exactly what Kennedy and Macmillan said to each other in their walk on the beach was not recorded. Neustadt later wrote that Macmillan had made it clear that he wanted Polaris. In any event, the conversation lightened the atmosphere and cleared the way for a more cooperative spirit at the talks themselves. It also cleared the way for a little light relief that evening. After an official reception at Government House in Nassau, the delegates repaired to the luxurious Emerald Beach Hotel for a press reception and beach barbecue, where a specially written calypso was sung for the guests. Patrick Wright, Ormsby-Gore's Private Secretary, who later in his career would become the Permanent Under-Secretary of the Foreign

Office, admits to an abiding memory of going for 'a very nice swim'. However nice the swim might have been, it could not have struck a greater contrast with the mass hedonism, even debauchery, that attended the Congress of Vienna (though, according to some sources, one of the President's girlfriends was smuggled into Nassau sitting on the floor of a car in the presidential cavalcade). But then, the diplomacy was wholly different too: just two teams, locked in intense bilateral negotiation over a few days, with the outlines of agreement possibly – probably – fixed in advance by the two leaders themselves.

Negotiations began at 9.45 a.m. the following morning at an unostentatious private house called Bali-Hai in the millionaires' playground of Lyford Cay, where Macmillan and some of his entourage were staying. From the very start, Macmillan delivered a bravura performance, employing all his skills, thespian and otherwise. He began with his age. He spoke as the voice of history, saying that his memory of government 'perhaps went back further than that of anyone else in the room'. Over the coming meetings he would repeatedly remind Kennedy of his status as a veteran of two world wars, invoking his personal memories of both Casablanca and Passchendaele. He recalled the wartime development of tube alloys, to underline how Britain and the US had worked together on the nuclear project since its earliest inception. He moved with seamless logic to the Skybolt agreement, struck with Eisenhower two years previously at Camp David. It was, said Macmillan, a 'gentlemen's agreement', on which Macmillan would never renege – implying clearly that Kennedy would have to be a cad to go back on Eisenhower's word. But, continued Macmillan, it went beyond a question of honour. By harbouring American missiles in Scotland, Britain was making itself a target. It was therefore only right that it should have greater protection. Macmillan combined sentimental appeals to the special relationship with references to the dire consequences if Britain did not get its way. Without American assistance, Britain would have to go it alone, and 'this would lead inevitably to a deep rift in United States–United Kingdom relations'. The missile system that Britain needed was Polaris, not Skybolt. The 50–50 offer would not do, as was generally known by now (though the President still went through the motions of making and justifying the offer; it may be that this had been previously rehearsed during the walk on the beach, to give Macmillan the opportunity to lay out British objections in detail for the benefit of Kennedy's delegation). As Macmillan recalled later, 'I observed that although the proposed British marriage with Skybolt was not exactly a shotgun wedding, the virginity of the lady must now be regarded as doubtful. We were being asked to spend hundreds of millions of dollars upon a weapon on which the President's own authorities were now casting doubts, both publicly and privately.' Macmillan knew that he could turn Kennedy's sense of humour to his advantage.

The invocation of the special relationship for once went beyond sentimentality; it served a specific diplomatic purpose. It met Kennedy's point that, if Britain got Polaris, everyone else would want it too. The President gave ground. He conceded that Polaris might be offered instead of Skybolt; but this would have to be as part of a multinational NATO force. The US could not afford to hand out missile systems to anyone who had developed a bomb. Many of his advisers shared Dean Acheson's view of Britain as a fading power that was unwilling and unable to come to terms with its diminished status in the world. They wanted to build stronger relationships with France and Germany, and were reluctant to upset these and other European governments by appearing to give the British favoured treatment.

Macmillan had a compelling answer for those who would spread American favours more equally in Europe. The French and Germans would, he said, understand perfectly well if there were a special relationship with Britain in nuclear matters. After all, it was so strong and well established. They would not expect the same treatment as the country which had been America's partner in nuclear development from the start. In allusion to Britain's attempts in 1962 to join what was then called the Common Market, which the French were threatening to block, Macmillan observed:

if France accepted, Britain would join the Common Market. It had been said that he was going against a thousand years of history by doing this. He would be going against it far more if he were to abandon Britain's independent power.

This was an argument not just for getting Polaris; but for having it as an independent nuclear deterrent. Independence was the heart of the matter for Macmillan. Without it, not only would Britain's standing in the world be at risk, but also its history as an independent island nation, with the strength, values and qualities which the British had shown in two world wars:

[Macmillan] sympathised with Americans who did not know what the Europeans were worrying about: the Americans were perfectly willing to defend Europe and had ample means of doing so. So why should the British want these new weapons? He would admit that part of the reason was to keep up with the Joneses. This was a universal and perfectly respectable feeling in the world. But there was another reason. The world was not yet organised politically or economically in a way that took cognisance of the disappearance of national independence. In this age of transition there were great nations like Britain, France and perhaps Germany, that felt they must have a means of defence which gave them the dignity and the authority of being participants in this strange new game. Previously in history there had been differences of degree between the defences of one country and the defences of another but now the difference was one of quality. Nuclear Powers lived in a different world and great nations felt that they ought to be represented in it.

Macmillan invoked his personal experience in the trenches: 'when in the 1914 war his battalion had been nearly wiped out, the officers and men had fought not because of the "entente cordiale" but because of their loyalty to their King and country.' Loyalty to the nation, said Macmillan, still took precedence over international alliances, a sentiment as true of America as of anywhere else in the world.

Macmillan had appealed to Kennedy's sense of fairness; and had tugged on every rope that had tied Britain and America together in the wartime alliance. There was much sentiment in his performance; and the fact that Macmillan had seen active service, and had the wounds to prove it, was compelling, as it always is, to an American audience that respects patriotic and martial virtues. But mixed with the sentiment was the true grit of *realpolitik*. It took the form of an unambiguous threat. Macmillan made it clear exactly what America stood to lose if he did not get his way on the matter of independence. Britain would be forced to abandon the negotiations. The whole future of Anglo-American cooperation would be in peril, and 'much as he would regret it if agreement was impossible, the British Government would then have to make a reappraisal of their defence policies throughout the world'.

The threat of the 'agonising reappraisal' seems to have hit home. The meeting was adjourned. When it reconvened, the Americans had redrafted the agreement with significant concessions on independence. There were further wranglings; but by the time the agreement was finalised on 21 December, the key paragraph read:

These forces, and at least equal United States forces, would be made available for inclusion in a NATO multilateral nuclear force. The Prime Minister made it clear that *except where Her Majesty's government may decide that supreme national interests are at stake*, these British forces will be used for the purposes of international defence of the Western Alliance in all circumstances. [My emphasis.]

It was a triumph for Macmillan and Ormsby-Gore. The reference to Polaris' being part of a multilateral force was no practical constraint on its sovereign use by Britain, since, by definition, it would only be unleashed in circumstances in which the government judged that 'supreme national interests' were at stake.

After Nassau, there were still details to be worked out, most of which were left to Ormsby-Gore. Sod's Law struck immediately after the Nassau meeting with a successful test firing of Skybolt. Kennedy was profoundly irritated. Macmillan took a more philosophical view, writing to Kennedy that 'it was rather provoking that Skybolt should go off so well the next day. It would have been better if it had been a failure. However, those are the chances of life.' The British press, focused on the cancellation of Skybolt, did not at first give the Polaris deal terribly good reviews. But Macmillan had the reassurance of a message from the Queen, who congratulated him on having shown that Britain's status and pride were not diminished.

There is no denying Macmillan's bravura performance at Nassau. It was in many ways a master class in negotiating technique. It was one from which Tony Blair – another political actor of the first order, who cherished a close relationship with the US – could have learned much, had he seen the need for negotiating the terms and conditions for Britain's participation in the second Iraq war. Macmillan described the proceedings thus:

three days hard negotiation – nearly four days in reality. The Americans pushed us very hard and may have 'out-smarted' us altogether. It is very hard to judge ... The discussions were protracted and fiercely contested. They turned almost entirely on 'independence' in national need. I had to pull out all the stops – adjourn, reconsider; refuse one draft and demand another, etc, etc.

He combined these adjournments and redraftings with a dogged insistence on 'closing the deal' before either he or Kennedy left Nassau. The President wanted time to consider the Polaris offer and hold consultations on the possible impact on relations with Europe, but Macmillan knew this could spell disaster. As Kennedy's National Security Advisor McGeorge Bundy put it, Macmillan could see that

if he didn't get a concrete offer at this juncture he would never get it later. If he went for a joint study, and another meeting, there would be no Polaris at the end of the road.

Ormsby-Gore wrote to Macmillan later that the Americans had all appreciated 'the intimate friendly atmosphere with the flavour of a close family gathering which has become a feature of your talks with Kennedy'. The influence of intangibles, like personal chemistry, on the course of a negotiation is always hard to gauge. A reliable rule of thumb is that a personal relationship, however intimate and trusting, will never trump a hard national interest, though it may soften the edges. At Nassau, without the Kennedy/Macmillan rapport, there might have been no agreement on Polaris. However, this is not the same thing as saying that Macmillan was able to use his personal relationship with Kennedy to prevail on him to act against the best interests of the United States.

Admittedly, George Ball, Under-Secretary of State, who was present at the talks, concluded afterwards that 'the emotional baggage of the "special relationship" got in the way of cooler judge-ment'. But, as a leading Europeanist in the State Department, he was one of the losers from the Nassau Agreement. There was an American sub-plot beneath the negotiations, which helped Macmillan's case. Inside the US administration of 1962 the State Department was a hawk in opposing independent national nuclear deterrents. Instead, it favoured a NATO Multilateral Force (MLF) under American command, which would comprise ships with mixed crews from all the NATO member-countries. Macmillan dismissed the MLF idea, commenting tartly on the difficulties for 'our fellows sharing grog with Turks aboard an MLF ship'. McNamara also doubted the military utility of the MLF; and, though no lover of small European nuclear weapon systems, was less hostile to the notion of Britain's getting Polaris. Kennedy was even more biddable. In reality, the deal fitted American interests pretty well. First, the deal placed the British nuclear submarine force at the service of the Western Alliance; second, in satisfying the British, the Americans had avoided a crisis with a major ally at a time when the Cold War put a premium on the cohesion of the Atlantic Alliance; and, third, though this is perhaps more a judge-ment of hindsight, the Polaris deal (and its Trident successor) in practice led to a substantial alignment of British foreign policy with that of the US.

There are some who argue that, for domestic political reasons, Macmillan exaggerated the scale of the crisis at Nassau, the more to boost his achievement in securing Polaris. But, there was no dissimulation in the many British expressions of anger and alarm before the meeting. There seems to have been much mutual mis-understanding; and an inability on either side to read and under-stand the signals sent by the other. But, in 1962, both governments had been distracted by the Cuban missile crisis, on top of which Macmillan had to cope with a shoal of domestic problems.

The Polaris Sales Agreement was signed in April 1963. It became the template for Britain's acquisition in 1982 of Trident II, the successor missile to Polaris. In 2007 Parliament voted to replace Trident, with the government expressing the judgement that it would be 'unwise and dangerous' to abandon the independent nuclear deterrent.[6]

If, indeed, Britain does purchase a successor to Trident, and decides that it can afford also the submarines to carry and launch it, the legacy of Harold Macmillan and David Ormsby-Gore will stretch far into the twenty-first century. So will the challenge to the British government of managing a relationship with a country on whom we will be crucially dependent for our security but with whom our interests will not always be aligned.

PART II

PROSPERITY

Ask any diplomat to describe in a sentence their job and you should get the answer: to safeguard the security and prosperity of the nation.

Trade and the quest for riches were the engines of Britain's maritime exploration of the world. At its Victorian height, the British Empire was the climax of a process started by the venture capitalists – the Merchant Venturers – of Elizabethan England. The English settlers, who went to America in the seventeenth century, were in search not only of freedom from religious persecution, but of freedom from penury. India was brought under Britain's control in the eighteenth century not by the government, but by the East India Company. We went to war with the Americans in 1812, and burnt down the White House, because of a row about trade. Commercial blockades were weapons used both by Britain and France in the Napoleonic Wars.

William Pitt the Younger, Prime Minister when Bonaparte was at the height of his conquests, said that 'British policy is British trade'. As the first European power to benefit from the Industrial Revolution, Britain had become the workshop to the world, with goods in profusion seeking markets abroad. In most of our history it was a case of the flag following the trade, and not the other way round.

From the earliest years of European maritime exploration, the East had exerted a powerful influence on the sea captains' imagination. It offered the lure of fabulous wealth. Many an expedition met its doom in the futile attempt to find a passage to China somewhere on the American continent. At the end of the eighteenth century, the British decided to crack the Chinese market. The following three chapters tell the story of how they did it: failing at the first attempt in the eighteenth century, succeeding at the second in the nineteenth, and living with the consequences in the twentieth.

4

HEAVEN IS HIGH, THE EMPEROR DISTANT:
Macartney's Mission to China

In late September 1792 Portsmouth Harbour witnessed extraordinary scenes. Three ships were being filled to the brim with the
finest British wares and an eclectic array of the latest gadgets. A
planetarium was dragged across the gangplanks. Ornate clocks,
telescopes, barometers and Wedgwood vases followed. Sword
blades, royal portraits, carriages, diving bells and air balloons were
hurriedly carried aboard. The feverish activity marked the start of
an enormously elaborate and ambitious diplomatic mission. Its
destination: China.

Behind the goods came the mission personnel, and a vast and
varied crew they were. Among their ranks were under-secretaries,
scholars, doctors, artists, interpreters, a watchmaker, a metal-
lurgist, a gardener botanist, a mathematical instrument maker, a
'natural philosopher', a military escort and five German musicians.
Together with servants and sailors, the party numbered nearly
seven hundred.

It was a convoy designed to impress, a seaborne exhibition of the
very best that Britain's Industrial Revolution could produce. At its
head was George, Viscount Macartney. And his mission: to persuade
the Emperor Qianlong to open the closed walls of China to British
trade.

The background to Macartney's expedition was not encouraging.
There had been occasional English overtures to China in the past,
but little had come of them. The first official approach had been
instigated by Elizabeth I some two hundred years before, when

the Age of Discovery was in full flood and England was emerging as an outward-looking, trading nation. As one of her seacaptains, Sir Walter Raleigh, put it: 'he who controls trade, controls the world's wealth, and therefore the world itself.' For Britain, Raleigh's axiom would hold good until well into Queen Victoria's reign.

With Protestant England embroiled in a struggle for survival against the hostile Catholic powers of Continental Europe, there was another dimension to the entrepreneurship of Elizabethan privateers. As they scoured the world for goods and treasure – some of them little better than licensed pirates – the depredations of the English privateers fell for the most part on treasure ships belonging to the Queen's greatest enemy, Philip of Spain. Getting rich quick may have been the big ambition of the English sea captains, their crews and the venture capitalists who bankrolled them in London – and plundering Spanish vessels laden with goods from the Americas was the surest means to achieve this goal – but religion and patriotism also played their part. Sir Francis Drake, the most famous of the privateers, was on hand in 1588 to help defeat the Spanish Armada and safeguard Elizabeth's throne.

Elizabeth's letter to the Chinese Emperor setting out the advantages of closer ties between the two countries received no reply. Either the letter, sent in 1596, failed to arrive or it was simply ignored by the imperial court. Two centuries later, Britain was ready to try again. In the intervening years the nation had grown vastly in power, wealth and self-confidence. Its aggressive mercantilism had created a global network of lucrative trading posts. Rivals, such as the Dutch and the Portuguese – similarly small countries with big naval and merchant fleets – had been seen off. At the end of the eighteenth century, as Macartney set sail for China, Britain was locked in the final stages of a prolonged struggle with its last and greatest rival, France. It would eventually emerge victorious on the battlefield of Waterloo in 1815. But as early as 1792, the French had already been soundly trounced in India, leaving the way clear for Britain's East India Company to dominate trade to and from the Indian subcontinent.

By the eighteenth century, trade had become the engine of Britain's economy and national prosperity. It was the natural consequence of our geographical position as a small island state. British ships carried more goods than any other European nation, and they traded across five continents. In its own way, it was an age of globalisation. At school I was taught that 'trade follows the flag'. But in reality it was usually the other way round. The flag, like war, followed the trade. Apart from occasional military interventions in Continental Europe to hold in check Bourbon ambitions,[1] the century-long struggle for supremacy over France was fought in a series of wars,[2] on land and sea, where trade, not territory, was the prize. Much flowed from this for Britain: a first-class navy that operated world-wide and protected the trade routes; the importation of raw materials and other goods for the factories that were the spawning ground of the Industrial Revolution; the acquisition of overseas markets to take the manufactures from the self-same factories; the importation of slave labour to work the sugar plantations in the British colonies of the Caribbean; and the development of a government bond market that raised money for wars more efficiently than the French. For most of the twenty-five-year struggle with Napoleon, such was confidence in the pound that the government was able to suspend the convertibility of paper money into coin. This was akin to a perfect virtuous economic circle, whose outward and visible sign was the British Empire – or, in Macartney's words 'this vast empire on which the sun never sets'.

As in the sixteenth century, Britain infused hard politics and material ambition abroad with high moral purpose. This was to reach its apogee in the Victorian era, when commerce, civilisation and Christianity were fused indivisibly in Britain's imperialist mission. The moral impulse was to mutate again in the twentieth and twenty-first centuries, taking the form of an attempt explicitly to insert human rights into the conduct of foreign affairs.

It was the Scottish moral philosopher, Adam Smith, who, through his publication in 1776 of *The Wealth of Nations*, had offered the first intellectual rationale for free trade and capitalism. Smith saw free markets, and the commercial self-interest that drove them, as working for the good of society. This was because of what he called the 'invisible hand'[3] that brought profitable order out of the chaos of unbridled competition. Smith not only described, but blessed, the greater purpose behind the everyday business of supply and demand: the liberating, innovating and civilising consequences of buying and selling. It applied in equal measure to the international exchange of goods, which, to Smith's way of thinking, worked to the benefit of mankind by spreading prosperity around the globe. It was no surprise that the government in London should hug Adam Smith to its bosom. In 1787 the Prime Minister, William Pitt the Younger, gave a banquet in honour of the grand old man of the Scottish Enlightenment, saying: 'after you, sir, for we are all your disciples.' Unfortunately for Macartney's mission, the Chinese were not among the disciples: 'Confucius never read Adam Smith', as the French historian, Alain Peyrefitte, drily puts it.

At the end of the eighteenth century, Britain had very specific commercial ambitions for India and China, which could be summarised in one word: tea. British and Dutch companies had first begun importing tea into Europe in the seventeenth century. Though it proved popular everywhere, there was something about tea that was particularly pleasing to the British palate. First popularised in England by the Portuguese princess, Catherine of Braganza, on the occasion of her marriage to Charles II in 1662, it soon spread from the drawing rooms of the aristocratic and wealthy, and by the eighteenth century, tea was pouring downwards into the cups and mugs of the lower echelons of society. The entire country was gripped by tea-mania, and its social impact was profound, akin to that of fast food in the twentieth century. The drinking of tea gave sustenance to those working the long hours of the Industrial Revolution's new factories. It provided a centrepiece for the social occasions of the more affluent. It was cheap, easy to prepare, and could be sweetened with the sugar imported from the slave plantations in the British West Indies. (The addition of milk was a peculiarity of Northern Europe. It was wholly alien to the millions of Chinese tea growers and consumers; yet another mark of the profound cultural gulf between China and Britain.)

In 1784 Pitt the Younger, acting on the advice of his friend Richard Twining, of the Twining Tea Company, passed the Commutation Act, slashing taxes on tea in Britain from 119 per cent to 12.5 per cent. Profits from the tea trade for Chinese and British merchants soared. As the incentive for smuggling disappeared, British government revenue went up. Tea boomed. By 1791 the British were buying 17.25 million pounds of tea at Canton; it was the most profitable product on the East India Company's books. The tea trade represented almost 5 per cent of Britain's GDP and helped make the East India Company the most important actor in Britain's international commerce. With the demand for tea came the demand for cups and saucers: that eponymous product of China ... china. Nestled within each tonne of tea would be six tonnes of porcelain. This had the added advantage of providing ballast that did not contaminate the tea leaves.

The tea trade may have been booming, but it was utterly unbalanced. In due course, in the nineteenth century, the British would diversify their sources of tea and put down vast plantations in India and Ceylon. In the 1790s, however, only China could slake the British thirst for tea – a thirst that was threatening to drain Britain's silver reserves just when every ounce was needed to pay for the war against Napoleon. The problem was that the Chinese appeared to want few of the goods that Britain or other European traders offered in return for their tea, porcelain and silks. What China wanted was hard cash. A director of the East India Company remarked in despair, 'I cannot recollect any new article that is likely to answer. Almost everything has been tried.' China built up huge reserves of Western European silver, becoming possibly the richest country in the eighteenth-century world.[4]

There was one commodity that the director of the East India Company failed to mention, the exception that proved the rule. This was opium, grown in India and imported into China through Canton. The market was growing fast to meet Chinese demand. In the nineteenth century the British would come to see Indian opium as the immensely profitable antidote to their trade deficit with China. The Opium Wars – in which Britain used force to oblige the Chinese to buy Indian opium and open Chinese ports to foreign trade – would transform the balance of the relationship between the two countries in Britain's favour. But, this was yet to come.

Prime Minister William Pitt the Elder had already rejected some thirty years earlier a plan to conquer China, proposed by Lord Clive – 'Clive of India' – flush with the military victories in Bengal and Southern India that entrenched the dominant position of the

East India Company. The administration of his son, Pitt the Younger, decided instead on peaceful negotiation to put trade with China on a more formal and balanced basis. High-powered diplomacy duly swung into action in 1787, but immediately got off to a bad start when the government sent Charles Cathcart to China as Britain's first official envoy. After a wretched journey, blighted by disease and appalling weather, Cathcart died within sight of his destination. In 1792 they tried again. The call went out to Lord Macartney.

Macartney was in his mid fifties, more or less the age at which I went as Ambassador to Washington. He had been born to landed gentry in Ireland and from an early age had shown ambition and resourcefulness in advancing his career. He had a particular gift for what nowadays is called 'networking'. While a young man on the Grand Tour of Europe, the eighteenth-century gap year, he became friends with two French stars of the Enlightenment, Voltaire and Jean-Jacques Rousseau. He had also got to know Stephen Fox, brother of Charles James Fox and heir to the aristocratic house of Holland. He must have impressed Lord Holland, who variously made him a large interest-free loan, tried to get him a parliamentary seat, and procured him an 'envoyship-extraordinary' (a kind of ambassador) to the court of Catherine the Great, Empress of Russia, where his task was to negotiate a new commercial treaty. With his diplomatic appointment came a knighthood and his portrait painted by Sir Joshua Reynolds. All this at the age of twenty-seven! At a similar age, I was near the bottom of the diplomatic food chain, a Second Secretary in our Embassy in Madrid, running errands for the Ambassador and his wife. As for interest-free loans, in those days I could not even get a mortgage.

This was the start of an extraordinary career as diplomat, politician, soldier, merchant venturer and administrator. It took him all over the world: Russia, Ireland, the West Indies, India, China, and South Africa. He wrote well and interestingly about many of these experiences. Contemporary accounts speak of his good looks, social graces and intelligence. Though very keen on money, and very short of it in early life, he does not appear, unlike many of his contemporaries, to have tried to enrich himself through corruption. When offered jobs, however, he argued hard for generous remuneration. Before agreeing to lead the mission to China, Macartney secured for himself a salary of £10,000, an allowance of £5,000, and a new title: Viscount Macartney, with the promise of an earldom later on.

The whiff of the adventurer and ladies' man drifts over the centuries. In 1779 he was briefly taken prisoner of war by the French after the capture of Grenada in the West Indies. Macartney's time in India as Governor of Madras was marked by a propensity to pick quarrels and fight duels, from which he emerged with wounds of varying gravity. This was of a piece with a certain abrasive pride and haughtiness first discerned in his behaviour in Russia. Macartney was prone to stand on his dignity and would kick up a fuss if denied a position he considered proper for an envoy of His Gracious Majesty. Yet it was in Russia that he managed to stain his early diplomatic career by seducing two women of the Empress Catherine's court (Macartney had married the well-connected, but physically unappealing Lady Jane Stuart of the Bute family). In my experience, ambassadors tend to be a tad frisky. But at least Macartney was a good deal more stylish than one British Ambassador to the Soviet Union, who shacked up with his Russian chambermaid, thoughtfully provided by the KGB. Or another, who had his wicked way on the table of the secure-speech room of an embassy in a communist country.

Arrogant and prickly he may have been, but Macartney was a heavyweight. He had the experience to lead a big mission. After his time with the East India Company in Madras, he was no stranger to Asia. And he was backed by the direct authority of his king, George III. As Foreign Secretary Lord Grenville wrote during the planning stages of the expedition:

the Great part of the hopes entertained of the success of this mission rests on the greater degree of attention which, it is supposed, the Government of China will show a person coming here, as authorised by the King, than if he came only in the name of a trading company.

Yet, Macartney, like his government, had unrealistically high hopes of what awaited him in the Middle Kingdom. The fundamental problems were two-fold: China had no interest in a deeper and broader relationship with Britain; and the British did not understand this. Britain may have seen herself as a great maritime and commercial power, leader of the Industrial Revolution; but to China she was nothing more than 'a handful of stones in the Western Ocean'. For the Chinese, their homeland lay at the centre of the world; the Middle Kingdom was the only civilisation under heaven, and beyond its borders lurked Barbarians. Even the highest officials had only the vaguest idea of the geography of the Western Ocean. Immured in its isolation, the Qing dynasty had risen to the zenith of its power and prosperity in the late eighteenth century. Nearly 390 million people bowed to the Emperor Qianlong. Never before in history had so many been ruled by a single authority. Behind this extraordinary power lay the idea that the Emperor was divinely appointed, that he ruled under the 'Mandate of Heaven', and that his powers were universal.

The recent arrival of European traders, nibbling at the Empire's periphery with their requests to set up trading posts, was seen as a threat to the established order of things. Trade was an inferior activity in the hierarchy of Confucian values. Foreigners were a disruptive force. So the Chinese put in place rigorous systems to keep the troublesome outsiders in check and eliminate the risk of the local population being contaminated by barbarian influences. A limited amount of trade was to be allowed on Chinese terms, with only the port of Canton, on the outer fringes of the Empire, open to the British. Even there, direct contact with Chinese merchants was forbidden. Foreigners were restricted to a small enclosed area of the port, where they were permitted to reside only in the trading season (between September and April). They were not allowed within the city walls, nor could they wander further afield. It was expressly forbidden to bring women ashore. All this made London, government and importers, highly anxious. In practice, Chinese restrictions placed the vital tea trade at the mercy of Cantonese officials, with foreigners obliged to deal with the Cohong, a group of local businessmen who acted as an arm of government by setting prices and the conditions of trade.

Against this background, Macartney's official objectives, which he himself helped to draft, look absurdly unrealistic. They included opening new ports in China to British trade; relaxing the restrictions on trade at Canton; securing a piece of territory where merchants could live under British jurisdiction; establishing a permanent mission in Peking; and above all, paving the way to friendly and mutually prosperous relations between the two empires.

This was already mission impossible. But, Macartney's vaulting ambition went beyond even tea and China. Then, as today, British industry saw China as a vast market waiting to be tapped. Pitt's government was under pressure from thrusting manufacturers like Wedgwood and Boulton to find new outlets for their growing catalogue of products. The hull of HMS *Lion* was crammed with the finest products to come out of Britain's bustling factories. And with the entire Orient at their fingertips, why stop at China? Along with his instructions, Macartney received accreditations to approach the Emperors of Japan and Annam (part of modern-day Vietnam) and the Kings of Manilla, Korea and the Moluccas (an archipelago in Indonesia), where he was to do what he could to open up trade by concluding treaties.

It was not as if Macartney had not made a serious attempt, like any good diplomat, to prepare himself thoroughly for his mission. With ten months at sea, he'd had plenty of time for reading. The problem was the paucity of material. Though he'd stocked *Lion*'s library with every book he could find on China, this did not amount to much. Western accounts of China tended to fall into two camps: the over-enthusiastic writings of Jesuit missionaries, who lived in fear of offending the Chinese; and the damning reports of visiting British sailors who had received a frosty reception. Admiral George Anson's account of his 1743 visit to Canton was typical. He concluded that 'in artifice, falsehood and an attachment to all kinds of lucre, many of the Chinese are difficult to be paralleled by any other people'.

As an envoy, it is essential to learn everything you can about a country, above all its language, before you start to do business. Before I took up my post as Ambassador to Germany, I spent months on intensive language training, living incognito in Hamburg and at a think-tank outside Munich. I would not have been able to do my job as Ambassador to Washington if I had not already been able to get under the skin of the US in a previous posting to the Embassy.

Again, as a young diplomat in Spain in the 1970s, I could never have hoped to have kept close to the political opposition to General Franco – one of my main jobs – without good Spanish and an ability to read Catalan.

Macartney did not get these kinds of opportunity. There was no reading matter available that could have prepared him adequately for his mission. In 1792 not a single person in Britain could speak Chinese. For once this was not down to the characteristic resistance of the British to foreign languages but a result of strenuous efforts by the Chinese authorities to insulate their country from foreign influence. Cantonese who had dealings with Western merchants were forbidden, on pain of death, to teach them the Chinese language. It was therefore no small feat to find interpreters to accompany Macartney's mission. There was, however, one breach in the wall of Chinese isolationism. It had been made by the Jesuit order, whose missionaries, remarkably enough, had been operating in China since the late sixteenth century. The ever-resourceful George Staunton, Macartney's deputy, tracked down in Naples two Chinese Jesuit priests, who were keen to return home. Neither Father Zhou nor Father Li spoke any English, but they did have passable Latin. This allowed Staunton's son, twelve-year-old Thomas Staunton, who acted as Macartney's page, to learn Chinese on the long voyage from Portsmouth – the very first Briton to do so.

Fathers Zhou and Li were returning to an uncertain fate, having first defied the Emperor by leaving China without authorisation and then by putting themselves in the service of a foreign power. On arrival at Macao, Father Zhou thought discretion the better part of valour and jumped ship. But Father Li stuck with Macartney's mission, suffering the nickname Mr Plum, which young Staunton had bestowed on him (Li means 'plum tree' in Chinese).

Macartney's diary conveys the sublime confidence that, whatever he may have lacked in experience and linguistic knowledge, he somehow knew China. He drank Chinese tea out of Chinese cups, and valued his lacquer writing case, filled with mother-of-pearl images of figures in Chinese dress. At the time, chinoiserie was all the rage in Europe. Chinese pagodas and arched bridges popped up in the gardens of English stately homes. Chinese-style

Chippendale furniture was the centrepiece of fashionable drawing rooms. Replica Ming vases sold faster than manufacturers in Bristol and Limoges could churn them out. But this newfangled consumerism was no substitute for a profound understanding of the intricacies of Chinese culture, which was essential to the success of his mission. Macartney was guilty, like many of his class and generation, of a condescension and superficiality towards an alien culture.

By late June 1793 the British convoy had been at sea for nine months. It had taken in Madeira, Cape Verde in West Africa and, thanks to powerful trade winds in the Atlantic, Rio de Janeiro in Brazil, before sailing east again to round the Cape of Good Hope and enter the southern Indian Ocean. Ten days in Batavia (Jakarta) came as a huge relief. But once the flotilla entered the China Seas, sailing towards China's south-eastern coast, Macartney was wary of making immediate landfall. Though his deputy, Staunton, went ashore, he decided not to disembark at the Portuguese island of Macao, for fear he would be forced up the Pearl River towards Canton, something he was eager at all costs to avoid. Instead the three vessels dropped anchor at Zhoushan in Zhejiang province, and Macartney sent Staunton ashore to reconnoitre.

Staunton's observations form one of the first real eye-witness accounts of China in the English language. He marvelled at the intricate construction of the rice paddies. He was disgusted that the local choice of fertiliser was not animal dung, but 'matters more offensive to the human senses'. (I discovered on a visit to a Chinese village at the end of 2008 that human waste was still being used to fertilise the fields.) Staunton was, however, impressed by the spirit of industry, for everyone seemed hard at work despite the heat and humidity. The local peasants were dumbfounded at the presence of such strange aliens among them. Staunton remarked that 'none asked alms', but Father Lamiot, a French missionary who had joined the party at Macao, cynically noted that 'if they saw no beggars it was because they were hidden from them'. This brings to mind the removal of migrant workers from Beijing's streets before the 2008 Olympics; China keen as ever to project the right image to the visiting aliens. As the diplomat and sinologist Percy Cradock, who knew China as well as any Westerner, remarked some two hundred years later: 'it remains China through the foreigners' distorting glass. The real China, whatever that may be, eludes us.'

It was in Zhoushan that the British first heard a sound that was to torment them throughout their stay in China: screams of laughter. To the locals, Macartney and his men were figures of ridicule. Crowds would gather to watch them wherever they went. They guffawed to see them sweating in their uncomfortable attire or fumbling with chopsticks. Their tight clothing earned them the nickname 'devils', as in Chinese theatre only devils wore close-fitting clothes. One member of the British party bemoaned the fact that 'they could not refrain from bursting into fits of laughter on examining the grease and powder with which our hair was disfigured'.

Macartney used his diary for his own observations. He was amused to recall the reaction of Chinese pilots, when they boarded his ship:

[They] examined everything with great curiosity, and observing the Emperor of China's picture in the ambassador's cabin, immediately fell flat on their faces, and kissed the ground several times with great devotion.

This was, of course, the kowtow, the submissive posture that was later to prove such a complication in the pursuit of Macartney's mission. He thought it preposterous to kowtow to a mere image. With hindsight, he should have taken this as a warning of how the Emperor expected those in his presence to behave. But, Macartney was wholly unprepared for the manner in which his mission would be regarded by the Chinese.

Macartney's misconceptions may have stemmed in part from his time in Russia as a British envoy. A Russian acquaintance had warned him that dealing with the Chinese was like 'sailing in fog'. What Macartney had perhaps not appreciated was that this judgement had been based on Russia's unique position as the only foreign state with whom China was prepared to negotiate. This was because the two countries shared a common frontier and were competitors for possession of vast swathes of Asia, particularly the plains inhabited by Tartar nomads. (I found in communist Russia a continuing disdain for the Chinese, exemplified by a remark from the

Soviet leader, Leonid Brezhnev, that nuclear war with China ran the risk of wiping out the 'white races'.) As for the rest of the world, China took a different approach. Negotiations were out of the question. Foreign envoys could approach the imperial court only through the ritual of paying tribute to the Emperor. To permit otherwise was unthinkable. To acknowledge that another nation was China's equal would be to deny the universal power of the Emperor. Macartney was nothing more than another barbarian envoy come to pay homage to the Emperor and the superior culture over which he ruled.

As the mission and its cargo of British wares were loaded on to junks for the journey upriver to Peking, banners in Chinese were attached to the masts that read: 'The English Ambassador bringing tribute to the Emperor of China.' Macartney tried hard to swallow his pride and irritation. He was not to be treated like some vassal. He was a representative of 'the most powerful nation on the globe', and envoy of King George III, 'sovereign of the seas'. He intended to negotiate with the Chinese on a basis of equality and to become the first British Ambassador to be accredited to the imperial court … He might as well have been on another planet.

On hearing of the approaching mission, Chinese Viceroy Liang Kentang wrote to the Emperor:

Your servant observes that Your Majesty's virtue and immense prestige have spread so far and wide that foreign Barbarians spare no effort in undertaking long voyages to manifest their loyalty and to bring tribute. [...] Your servant cannot contain his joy and it seems to him that in the circumstances it would be appropriate to reward the British for the sincerity they are demonstrating in their desire to contemplate Civilization.

Macartney and his party now found themselves face to face with one of the most ritualised societies on earth, where an ancient protocol served to reinforce the Emperor's relationship to heaven. Macartney was confronted with a perennial diplomatic dilemma. To ensure the success of his mission, how far could he go in submitting to local ritual without compromising his dignity and that of his sovereign?

This is not merely the dilemma of a bygone age. Even today, in the era of globalisation, every country clings to its protocol, its rites and rituals, which foreign diplomats ignore at their peril. Even at Buckingham Palace there is a fairly elaborate ritual when you go to meet the Queen. Get the protocol wrong – where to stand, when to speak, how to address the president or monarch – and you can scupper your mission before it has even started. I knew a British Ambassador who so upset the local foreign minister at their first encounter that he was sent to Coventry for the rest of his tour. It helps also to remember which country you are in. A new British Ambassador to a Latin American nation once managed, while presenting his credentials to the President, to express delight at his appointment to the country next door. That was the end of a promising career.

Macartney, having left the flotilla of junks at Tongzhou, completed the journey to Peking by land. The mission's baggage train comprised a vast and unwieldy caravan of 85 wagons and 39 handcarts alongside some three thousand porters carrying 600 packages, some so large that it took thirty-two men to lift them. The convoy must have been a sight to behold. But Macartney's men were themselves intrigued by what they saw:

the sides of the street were filled with an immense concourse of people, buying and selling and bartering their different commodities ... Pedlars with their packs, and jugglers, and conjurers, and fortune-tellers, mountebanks, and quack-doctor comedians and musicians, left no space unoccupied.

To Macartney's disappointment, Peking proved not to be their final destination. The Emperor had left the city to escape the summer heat. He was now at his summer hunting lodge in Jehol, some 140 miles north-east of Peking. The long journey, plus the time needed for loading and offloading the vast cargo of gifts, had given the British party ample time to observe the country, and the Chinese ample time to observe their visitors. The Emperor provided a warm welcome in the form of generous supplies and lavish banquets en route. But he was also watching their every move, with his officials sending regular updates on their progress and comportment. Of particular concern was the foreigners' ignorance of Chinese court etiquette. Alarm bells had been raised at a banquet in Tientsin, where the British had failed to kowtow to the spread laid on by the Emperor. Macartney and his men had simply removed their caps while everyone else had dropped to the floor. This was unacceptable behaviour, so much so that the legate Zhengrui pulled his punches in a report to the Emperor, to suggest that the British had acted more respectfully. The Chinese officials knew that their necks would be on the line if the British did not conform to protocol on meeting the Emperor. They therefore approached Macartney to give him a lesson in the finer points of the kowtow, as his diary explains:

They therefore apprehended much inconvenience to us from our knee buckles and garters, and hinted to us that it would be better to disencumber ourselves of them before we should go to Court. I told them they need not be uneasy about the circumstance, as I supposed, whatever ceremonies were usual for the Chinese to perform, the Emperor would prefer my paying him the same obeisance which I did for my own Sovereign. They said they supposed the ceremonies in both countries must be nearly alike, that in China the form was to kneel down on both knees, and make nine prostrations or inclinations of the head to the ground, and that it never had been, and never could be dispensed with. I told them that ours was somewhat different, and that though I had the most earnest desire to do everything that was agreeable to the Emperor, my first duty must be to do what might be agreeable to my own king.

Macartney's opening position was clear: kowtowing to the Emperor was out of the question, and not just because of his tight breeches. It would mean humiliating himself and his king. It would also, as he saw it, weaken his negotiating position.

. Macartney was not so unbending as to be unaware that the success of this mission might be at stake. So, like any professional diplomat, he began to search for a solution that would be amenable to both sides, deploying the principle of reciprocity, one of the most sacred in the diplomatic canon.[5] His first offer was to go down on one knee before the Emperor and kiss his hand, as he would with his own sovereign. This was rejected by the Chinese. Hand-kissing was not on, because no one was permitted to touch the Emperor. Instead, the Chinese courtiers suggested that Macartney go down on both knees. Macartney refused; he would go down on two knees only before God. He countered that he would kowtow if an official of the same rank as he were to reciprocate by kowtowing before a picture of King George III. This suggestion was considered so offensive that neither the Chinese officials, nor the French missionaries aiding the negotiations, were prepared to put it in writing. Eventually, it was young Thomas Staunton who put the proposal into an official note in Chinese, which was reluctantly sent on to Jehol. All the while, as Jehol grew closer, the Emperor was receiving false reports that the British had been practising their kowtow, but that they were not very good at it.

Macartney's original instructions from Home Secretary, Henry Dundas, offered no clear way out of the *impasse*:

conforming to all ceremonials of that Court which may not commit the honour of your Sovereign or lessen your own dignity, so far as to endanger the success of your negotiation . . . While I make this reserve I am satisfied you will be too prudent and considerate to let any trifling punctilio stand in the way of the important benefits which may be obtained by engaging the favourable disposition of the Emperor and his ministers.

Masterly ambiguity. This was simply a way of telling Macartney to use his own judgement. The problem was that the 'punctilio' was 'trifling' neither for the British nor the Chinese. Do not think that this kind of ambiguity has disappeared with the advent of instant communication. Ambassadors are still plagued by instructions where, behind a verbal smokescreen, the real message is that you are on your own – but woe betide if you get it wrong!

Meanwhile, in another neck of the protocol woods, things seemed to be going wrong on the delicate question of gifts. This too was a minefield for the untutored Barbarian. Macartney reckoned that the larger and more delicate presents would not survive the rough roads over the hilly terrain to Jehol. He decided to leave them in Peking for the Emperor's return. This was most unconventional. It caused much muttering among the mandarins, who made plain that the normal procedure would be to bring the gifts to the Emperor, wherever he was. Then, Macartney wrote out a list of the gifts in what he described as 'somewhat in the Oriental style', in other words with much hyperbole. He and his colleagues had gone to great trouble to select some of the finest examples of British ingenuity and he was keen that the Chinese should know it:

[it would not] be becoming to offer trifles of momentary curiosity but little use. His Britannic Majesty had been, therefore, careful to select only such articles as might denote the progress of science, and of the arts in Europe, and which might convey some kind of information to the exalted mind of His Imperial Majesty.

High-flown stuff; but, unfortunately, the custom in China is for the donor to understate the value of gifts so as not to embarrass the recipient. The list irritated the Emperor hugely, as did the translation of Macartney's title at the end: *qin chai* – legate of the sovereign. The Emperor felt impelled to issue an edict:

In an effort to honour the envoy, the English interpreter has imitated the titles of Our Court. To act in this way is to be ignorant of the weight of words. In conformity with the rites, Ma-ga-er-ni is entitled only to the appellation gong-shi [conveyer of tribute].

Gifts are one of the great diplomatic minefields, even where you are not dealing with protocol of arcane complexity. President Obama's advisers were generally judged, at least in the British press, to have got it wrong in 2008 in giving Gordon Brown a set of DVDs in return for the Prime Minister's carefully considered gift of a pen holder made from the timbers of HMS *Gannet*, a Victorian naval vessel that helped put a stop to the slave trade (though some naval historians dispute this). When I was responsible in the Foreign Office for the Soviet Union, we gave the Foreign Minister, Andrei Gromyko, a valuable antique barometer when he visited London. Gromyko looked at it in some puzzlement and then tried to play it like a balalaika. Most gifts to British Prime Ministers end up being sold at knock-down prices in government auctions.

The British caravan crawled from Peking to Jehol. The Chinese escorts were under orders from the Emperor on no account to arrive early; he was not looking forward to having to deal with Macartney. The party were forbidden from taking the well-maintained highway reserved for the use of the Emperor. They passed the Great Wall of China, which Macartney considered to be 'the most stupendous work of human hands', and many of the party collected bricks as souvenirs. His Chinese escorts looked on with suspicion as Macartney ordered his men to take thorough measurements of the wall together with notes on the soldiers stationed nearby. It seems that, even then, the British might have been preparing for a less friendly approach, if the diplomatic negotiations failed to prosper.

Macartney's mission finally arrived in Jehol in early September 1793, almost a year after their departure from Portsmouth. The city was something of a slum, and only the imperial trappings and tents lent it any kind of appeal (Chengde, as it is now called, is still a drab town today). Macartney's valet, Anderson, commented that without all the imperial pomp their destination would scarcely have been worth the 'tedious and tiresome journey'. Macartney was to present himself to Emperor Qianlong six days later during the latter's eighty-third birthday celebrations. In the meantime, the British were finally able to show to Qianlong's chief minister, Heshen, their letter from George III, which outlined the objectives of the mission. It was a letter that ruled out any aggressive intent but requested 'fair access to your markets' and the appointment of a British ambassador at the Emperor's court. It was signed 'Your good brother and friend, Georgius R'.

Heshen was in no mood for discussing trade when there was the issue of court protocol to be addressed. The kowtow dispute was to continue for several more days, with numerous fresh pleas from the Chinese for Macartney to respect the etiquette and to agree to kowtow before the Emperor. Macartney stood his ground, holding to the argument that it would be improper for him to show more respect to a foreign sovereign than to his own.

Eventually, and perhaps surprisingly, given the lack of pre-cedents, the Chinese gave ground and agreed that the British party could kneel while others kowtowed. For Macartney, it was a proud victory and something of a relief: 'and thus ended this anxious negotiation, which has given me a tolerable insight into the character of this Court, and that political address upon which they so much value themselves'. But for the Chinese, the matter was far from over.

On 14 September 1793, the day of the grand meeting finally arrived. The British had been told that an early start was essential and that, having dressed in their finery, they must set out no later than three in the morning to await the arrival of the Emperor. As their hosts had failed to provide them with torches, they were forced to stumble many miles in darkness. Much of the party struggled to keep pace with the swift-footed Chinese porters, who carried the Ambassador's palanquin. Anderson, the valet, recalled that 'we found ourselves intermingled with a cohort of pigs, asses and dogs, which broke our ranks, such as they were, and put us into irrecoverable confusion'. It was not the most dignified start to the day.

On reaching the imperial tent, the party joined a crowd several thousand strong, awaiting in the darkness the arrival of Emperor Qianlong and the dawn. The British were by no means the sole attraction, as they might have hoped, finding themselves in the company of Tartar princes, mandarins, musicians, soldiers, even, to their slight dismay, another foreign party (from Burma), there to pay tribute. The sun arrived first, followed half an hour later by the Emperor and his entourage. Qianlong was carried aloft in a chair by sixteen men dressed in gold, and as he passed, the crowd dropped to the ground in kowtow – all except the British, as Macartney recalled:

The music was a sort of birthday ode or state anthem, the burden of which was 'Bow down your heads, all ye dwellers upon earth, bow down your heads before the great Ch'ien-lung, the great Ch'ien-lung'. And then all the dwellers upon China earth there present, except ourselves, bowed down their heads, and prostrated themselves upon the ground at every renewal of the chorus. Indeed, in no religion either ancient or modern, has the Divinity ever been addressed, I believe, with stronger exterior marks of worship and adoration than were this morning paid to the phantom of his Chinese Majesty.

Shortly afterwards, Macartney, the two Stauntons, and Father Li were admitted to the vast yurt in which the Emperor was holding court. Again, the British party went down on one knee before Qianlong, and then delivered the King's letter in a diamond-encrusted, gold box, together with some small presents. The Emperor reciprocated with gifts; but no objects passed directly between sovereign and ambassador. Instead they were passed via a Chinese minister. Nor were any words directly exchanged, except between the Emperor and young Thomas Staunton, who was asked to speak in Chinese. It seems that the Emperor took something of a fancy to Thomas, who was accorded the singular favour of being given a yellow purse taken from Emperor's own waist.

Macartney felt that this was not the occasion to get straight down to business. Instead he saw this as the start of the relationship. He left the tent feeling buoyant. Qianlong had other ideas. In his view, the British had paid their tribute and their mission was over. For the next week the Chinese treated their British guests with great hospitality. Macartney was invited to lavish banquets and spectacles, and shown the Emperor's hunting grounds. But every time he attempted to broach the subject of his mission, he was brushed off by the Emperor or his ministers. Macartney did not realise that at the very moment when he was celebrating what he thought had been a kowtow triumph, the Emperor had issued a furious edict:

I am extremely displeased. I have already ordered their supplies reduced. [. . .] When Barbarians manifest sincerity and respect, I shall unfailingly treat them with kindness. When they are full of themselves, they do not merit the enjoyment of my favours. The ceremonial must therefore be curtailed, so as to make it clear to them what our system is. Such is the road to follow with the Barbarians.

It seems that the Emperor's acquiescence in the matter of the kowtow was no more than a tactical retreat, to avoid casting a shadow over his birthday celebrations and, perhaps, losing face. But, in reality, Macartney's refusal to kowtow was an insult that ran deep: so much so that official Chinese histories state that the British did in fact kowtow. Qianlong's son and successor, Jiaqing, issued an edict in 1816, confirming that he had witnessed Macartney kow-towing before his father. The official line on the matter became:

when the Ambassador entered His Majesty's presence he was so overcome with awe and nervousness that his legs gave way under him, so that he grovelled abjectly on the ground, thus to all intents and purposes performing an involuntary kowtow.

As for the mission itself, it failed utterly. The British party left Jehol, and then, having had no further success in Peking, set sail for home on 7 October. One member of the party later commented: 'We entered Peking like paupers, we remained in it like prisoners, we quitted it like vagrants.'

Awaiting them on board was a communication from the Emperor in reply to George III's list of requests. To each of them, the response was a firm 'no'. There were to be no new ports, no new trading privileges and no resident British ambassador. The Emperor's letter was bowdlerised in translation to spare British pride. But, only the original text can convey the chasm in culture, attitude and sense of place in the world between the two countries:

Although your country, O King, lies in the far oceans, yet inclining your heart towards civilisation, you have specially sent an envoy respectfully to present a state message, and sailing the seas he has come to our Court to kowtow and to present congratulations for the imperial birthday, and also to present local products, thereby showing your sincerity [...]

[...] As to what you have requested in your message, O King, namely to be allowed to send one of your subjects to reside in the Celestial Empire to look after your country's trade, this does not conform to the Celestial Empire's ceremonial system, and definitely cannot be done [...]

[...] If it is said that your object, O King, is to take care of trade, men from your country have been trading at Macao for some time, and have always been treated favourably [...] Why then do foreign countries need to send someone to remain at the capital? This is a request for which there is no precedent and it definitely cannot be granted [...] all kinds of precious things from over mountain and sea have been collected here, things which your chief envoy and others have seen for themselves. Nevertheless we have never valued ingenious articles, nor do we have the slightest need of your country's manufactures. Therefore, O King, as regards your request to send someone to remain at the capital, while it is not in harmony with the regulations of the Celestial Empire, we also feel very much that it is of no advantage to your country. Hence we have issued these detailed instructions and have commanded your tribute envoys to return safely home. You, O King, should simply act in conformity with our wishes by strengthening your loyalty and swearing perpetual obedience so as to ensure that your country may share the blessings of peace.

The irony of it all was that the Emperor's edict had been written some days before Macartney even arrived in China. So the debate – to kowtow or not to kowtow – was irrelevant to the fate of his mission. It had been sealed for the worse long before he reached Jehol. There were, in due course, to be several European envoys, who chose to kowtow, but all suffered nonetheless the same rejection as Macartney.

I have frequently asked myself whether I would have kowtowed. There is really only one question to be answered in diplomacy: how do you get from A to B? If I had thought I could secure my sovereign's list of requests by doing the kowtow, I would have prostrated myself with the best of them. Britain's prosperity mattered more than a single envoy's dignity.

This is not to blame Macartney. The problem was one which diplomacy alone could not resolve. The two empires simply did not understand each other. There were no common points on which a broader relationship could be built. The reports of each side at the time are littered with phrases like: 'the Chinese character seems at present inexplicable' and 'the barbarian nature is unfathomable'. But the Macartney mission, though it failed in its immediate objectives, was not without consequence. He and his men had boldly gone where no British expedition had been before. The accounts that they published on return created a public view of China: that it was a backward, harsh society of draconian punishments, where the Emperor ruled by fear. One of Macartney's crew had himself received a bamboo caning for drinking alcohol. This planted the idea in Britain that what the Chinese needed was the civilising hand of British influence.

It would be almost another fifty years before Britain finally got its way with China and began the dismemberment of the Canton Trade Laws. But, it would be diplomacy, backed by force, that did the job. The so-called Unequal Treaties that resulted were the Chinese Emperor's kowtow to the British Queen.

5

THE HOUR OF THE GUNBOAT:
Bowring in China

The Exeter wool trade into which John Bowring was born in 1792, the very year Macartney had set sail for China from Portsmouth, was never going to satisfy his vaunting ambition. The quintessential nineteenth-century gentleman, Bowring had big ideas, strongly held values and supreme self-confidence; in short, the world was his oyster. Introduced to foreign languages and enticing tales of far-flung lands by merchants on the Exeter quayside, young Bowring picked up a passion for trade and travel. By the time he reached middle age he had journeyed extensively throughout Europe and Russia and become an extraordinary polyglot – he once claimed he could understand two hundred languages and passably speak one hundred of them. He had served as a Member of Parliament, a journalist, a political economist and an anthologist of central European poetry. Yet somehow, he remained unfulfilled, and his gaze turned eastwards.

China, some sixty years after Macartney's mission, remained an elusive, exotic and irresistible prize. It was a stage on which great deeds might be performed. It was, above all, a market, which, once penetrated, would prove of incalculable benefit to Great Britain's growing Empire. When in 1848 Bowring was given the post of Consul at Canton, his every instinct told him that China was the last great frontier for diplomats and traders alike. For him personally, it had been something of a lifelong obsession:

When I was a little boy, I had a singular dream. It was that I was sent by the King of England as Ambassador to China. No doubt my head was filled with the gorgeous representations of Chinese life which are found in the narratives of the Macartney and Amherst Missions to Peking [...] But to China I went as the representative of the Queen, and was accredited, not to Peking alone, but to Japan, Siam, Cochin China [Southern Vietnam], and Corea, – I believe to a greater number of beings – indeed not less than a third of the race of man – than any individual had been accredited before.

For a small boy, it was a dream as singular as it was ambitious. Decades later, as he took up his post in Canton, Bowring stood on the verge of its realisation. He was under no illusions. He had a mighty challenge on his hands. But, his self-confidence was boundless. It was in China that Bowring would secure his legacy; though, perhaps, not in the way that he would have hoped.

The failed Macartney mission to China was followed not long after by the failed Amherst mission. Bowring had studied the reports of both, which amounted to little more than intelligent, well-observed travelogues. In 1817 William, Earl Amherst had managed a near carbon copy of Macartney's expedition, except that he had failed even to meet the Emperor. Amherst appeared to have learnt nothing from Macartney's experience. With the grand title of Ambassador Extraordinary to China, he had made the same long, gift-laden journey and had, like Macartney, refused to kowtow. The Emperor sent him packing; and Britain's relations with China soured a little more. A generation later, would Bowring fare any better? Things had changed a great deal since 1817. The vexed issue of the kowtow had lost its salience. The terms of trade had been transformed; and force had entered British calculations.

The dangerous trade deficit with China, which had motivated the Macartney and Amherst missions, had evaporated. This was thanks to opium, which was as much in demand in China as was tea in Britain. The British were by no means the first to export opium to the Middle Kingdom. From as early as the seventh century, small quantities had been brought into China by Turkish and Arab traders. Opium was enjoyed by the élite for its medicinal and aphrodisiac qualities. As with tea in Britain, the habit then drifted down the social scale. Demand for opium spread across the vast nation, first in the form of *madak*, tobacco blended with opium, that was imported through Taiwan. But it was only when the British East India Company began to import large quantities of pure, Indian-grown opium into Canton that China's habit really took hold. Supply and demand surged. In the late eighteenth century the East India Company had secured a monopoly on the export of opium from India. The best-quality crop was grown around Patna. It gave the British almost complete control over the supply to China. Trade flourished. In 1817, 3,210 chests, each containing 150 pounds of Indian opium, were imported into China.

In 1833 the East India Company's monopoly on trade in general expired. Independent merchants like Dent and Jardine Matheson took over. Influenced by hostile public opinion at home, the East India Company had exercised some restraint in the narcotic's supply. But the new companies had fewer scruples, and the trade exploded. The newcomers also had faster ships and more aggressive merchants. The scenes at Canton became chaotic. That year, the amount of opium carried in by British ships exceeded the amount of tea they carried out. By 1837, 34,000 chests were being brought into China to supply around 10 million users. China was no longer the 'silver graveyard' of the world; its accumulated wealth was flowing out to pay for its addiction. Over the first decade of the nineteenth century, China had enjoyed a trade surplus of 26 million Spanish dollars (Spanish dollars, or Pieces of Eight, being the international trading currency of the time). Between 1828 and 1836 this had turned into a deficit of 38 million. The poppy had vanquished the tealeaf.

The Chinese authorities were not happy. The opium craze was not only draining China's bank balance; it was also having a profound, and often damaging, impact on the population. Addicts, too poor to pay for their fix, would scale opium-house chimneys to inhale the vapours. Groups of people now came together, especially in opium houses, to enjoy the drug. The authorities saw this as a threat to the Emperor's rule, even a potential incitement to rebellion. Though many Chinese opium users had only a modest habit – and opium was not without its benefits (in the area surrounding Canton, malaria and dysentery were rife, and the drug could relieve pain, repel mosquitoes and stop diarrhoea) – the official view centred on the corrosive perils of addiction:

They have come to China, and brought us a disease which will dry up our bones, a worm that gnaws at our hearts, a ruin to our families and our persons. Since the Empire first existed it has run no such danger. It is worse than a world deluge, than an invasion of wild beasts.

Official edicts banning the trade in 'foreign mud' dated back to 1729. But, then as now, the threat of death neither deterred smokers in the grip of a powerful addiction, nor the traders and corrupt officials who profited from the lucrative trade. Prohibition only served to whet the appetite. A thriving contraband network had sprung up. Fearing that he was losing his grip on his subjects, the Emperor decided that enough was enough. On 3 June 1839, Lin Tse-Hsu, the Emperor's opium 'tsar', confiscated from foreign traders at Canton 20,283 chests of opium, worth over six million Spanish dollars (a Spanish dollar being worth around five shillings at the time), and burned them. To explain his actions, Lin wrote an open letter to Queen Victoria:

We find that your country is sixty or seventy thousand *li* from China. Yet there are barbarian ships that strive to come here for trade for the purpose of making a great profit. The wealth of China is used to profit the barbarians. That is to say, the great profit made by barbarians is all taken from the rightful share of China. By what right do they then in return use the poisonous drug to injure the Chinese people? Even though the barbarians may not necessarily intend to do us harm, yet in coveting profit to an extreme, they have no regard for injuring others. Let us ask, where is your conscience?

There is no evidence that Victoria received Lin's letter, still less replied. Instead, with the opium trade temporarily halted, British merchants returned home and demanded official action, plus compensation for their loss. The government decided that behaviour of this kind was intolerable; and swiftly declared war on China.

The Chinese had a large, well-trained army, but no concept of maritime defence and no navy. When the main British fleet arrived off the coast in 1840, the Chinese stood little chance; they had underestimated the despised Barbarians. By August 1842 the war was over. China was forced to sign the Treaty of Nanking on board HMS *Cornwallis*. The 'Unequal Treaty', as the Chinese came to call it, granted the British access to five ports: Canton, Shanghai, Foochow, Ningpo and Amoy, as well as compensation for the destroyed opium and naval expenses. Britain even gained a permanent base at the small island of Hong Kong. War had delivered what Macartney's diplomacy had failed to secure from the Emperor some fifty years earlier.

One of the Macartney requests that was still not met was that for the accreditation of an ambassador in Peking and full diplomatic relations between the two empires. There was also, quite remarkably given the causes of the First Opium War, no mention of the conditions for the future trade of opium. It was a step too far for China to accept the Western system of diplomacy, governed by rules based on the notion of equality between sovereign nations. China could not bring herself to deal with the British as equals and throw over the centuries-old belief in her superiority. Barbarian military might was one thing; the Emperor's divinity, another. China had been forced to sign a shameful treaty under duress and Britain had got her way; but China would not forget this humiliation in a hurry.

Into this picture stepped Sir John Bowring. His appointment as Her Majesty's Consul at Canton at the age of fifty-six was his first foray into diplomacy. He was something of an odd choice. A curious combination of Unitarian, intellectual, and businessman, with a string of failed commercial ventures behind him, Bowring was best known for his close friendship with Jeremy Bentham, the radical philosopher famous for his championing of liberal causes, from the Chartist movement to the anti-Corn Law League. For a decade Bowring had sat in Parliament as a radical. As a staunch nonconformist who lacked charm and was impatient of the opinions of others – hardly the best credentials for an aspiring diplomat – he tired of Westminster, and Westminster tired of him. Douglas Hurd, who has studied Bowring's life and legacy, is not alone in suggesting that the then Foreign Secretary, Lord Palmerston, accepted Bowring's application for the Canton consulate simply to get him as far away as possible. From Bowring's point of view the posting offered salvation from financial ruin after yet another business disaster, along with an opportunity to add more languages to his repertoire.

Bowring's manifest imperfections as a diplomat were to a degree compensated by his single-minded devotion to the development of Britain's trade. That was what our Man in Canton's job was all about. Bowring shared the views of Palmerston and the government that international trade brought material and moral progress to everyone, and that it was a natural part of the onward, upward march of civilisation. It was the gospel according to Adam Smith. Bowring, who had commerce in his veins, had once declared, 'Jesus Christ is Free Trade, and Free Trade is Jesus Christ.' It was trade not territory that Britain was after. When negotiations over the cession of Hong Kong began in 1841, Palmerston as Foreign Secretary did not approve, dismissing it as 'a barren island with hardly a house upon it! [It] will never be a mart for trade.'¹ Palmerston, of course, got it wrong. Hong Kong was to become the greatest entrepôt of the Eastern world. But that is not the point. Victorian governments were highly sensitive to the costs and headaches of running an empire. The plan was not to fly the British flag over China, but to secure access to its markets.

On his arrival at Canton in 1849 Bowring was horrified to discover the squalid conditions that fifty years earlier had deterred Macartney from visiting Canton. Foreigners were still forbidden to enter the walled city of Canton and were confined to the squalid factory areas. They remained objects of curiosity and ridicule to the locals, especially when the merchants emerged from their cramped quarters to take exercise in a small garden nearby. How could the cause of free trade be advanced when the traders were virtual prisoners? Worse, Bowring found that he could do little to improve the situation. In the absence of diplomatic relations, an approach to Peking was out of the question; to keep troublesome foreigners at arm's length, the Emperor had appointed an Imperial Commissioner for Canton. But the Commissioner kept to himself in his residence within the walled city and ignored requests from the consuls on the outside.

Bowring's predecessors, Sir John Davis and Sir George Bonham, had both attempted to open Canton to foreigners, but their requests had been firmly rebutted on the grounds that foreigners were excluded for their own safety, the Cantonese being so hostile towards them. It reminds me of the similarly xenophobic Soviet Union. It used to be impossible to travel without prior permission beyond a radius of forty-five kilometres from the centre of Moscow. Vast tracts of Soviet territory were permanently closed to foreigners for reasons of state security. When I was in the British Embassy in Moscow in the sixties and eighties, my requests to travel around the country were often turned down with the excuse that the local hotels were not up to scratch. When I was able to fly somewhere, I found myself invariably seated over a wing so that I could not see the ground.

The year that Bowring arrived in Canton, a new Imperial Commissioner was appointed in the formidable shape of Yeh Ming Chen. Yeh was soon to earn the appreciation of the Imperial court in Peking as a skilful handler of Barbarians. The court were happy to leave Yeh to his own devices, while he in turn rarely saw the need to bother the Emperor with issues concerning Canton's foreign traders. Among the local Chinese population he had a fearsome reputation as a scourge of rebels; he had been known to oversee the beheading of some two hundred people in a day. Foreign consuls, while safe from Yeh's executioners, were forced to endure his infuriating filibustering and procrastination. His excuses for declining meetings were many and varied, often involving astrological considerations. He used to claim that it was imperative to wait for an auspicious conjunction of the stars, which would rarely transpire. Bowring was driven to distraction. For him, Yeh symbolised everything that was wrong with trade relations between Britain and China.

In 1841 Palmerston had firmly and clearly stated, with words which might just as well serve today, that 'it is the business of government to open and to secure the roads for the merchant'.[2] But now, in spite of the Nanking Treaty, Britain found the roads in China blocked. Within a year of his arriving, Bowring was urging military force to open the city of Canton and to implement in full the terms of the Treaty. In 1850, Palmerston appeared to be moving in Bowring's direction:

the time is fast coming when we shall be obliged to strike another blow in China [...] These half civilised Governments such as those of China, Portugal, Spanish America, all require a dressing every eight or ten years to keep them in order. Their minds are too shallow to receive an impression that will last longer than some such period [...] they must not only see the Stick but actually feel it on their Shoulders.

Yeh's astrological charts should have told him that war with the Barbarians was in the stars.

Victorian attitudes, epitomised by Palmerston and Bowring, towards 'half civilised' peoples in need of a regular thrashing are horribly jarring today, especially when linked, as they so often are, to expressions of high moral purpose. But if we are to understand their motives and aims, the Victorians must be judged in the context of their times. It is neither a straightforward nor static picture. On the one hand, there was patronising disdain for the 'half civilised'. To many, the largely unknown or recently discovered peoples of Africa, Asia and Latin America were lower forms of life, to whom European humanitarian standards did not apply. On the other hand, the first half of the nineteenth century saw a religious revival in England, which spawned missionary societies and the campaign to abolish the slave trade. The British Empire became a curious, contradictory, and sometimes hypocritical mix, in which commerce, international power politics, the Anglican Church and 'civilisation' sat awkwardly together. Great decency and brute force grew entwined. This was not a unique historical phenomenon. The genius of great empires is to be able to fuse their interests with their values and to sell them to the world as universally applicable. That is what the *Pax Romana*, the *Pax Britannica* and the *Pax Americana* achieved when each was at the height of its power. All these strands would come together in the person of Bowring himself and the matter of opium.

As a young radical, Bowring had been a strong critic of the opium trade. But in the Far East he changed his views, asserting that only legalisation would control the traffic. 'It is idle to think of stopping the trade,' he wrote to Lord Clarendon, Palmerston's first Foreign Secretary after the latter had become Prime Minister in 1855. Bowring's intention was to 'minimise the evil which I cannot cure'.

His critics were quick to point out that he had a personal interest in promoting the opium trade, having become personally indebted to Jardine Matheson, the largest opium dealers in the Far East; moreover his son was a partner in the company. These conflicts of interest would not be allowed today; but nor would a diplomat have the freedom of action to start a war, as Bowring was about to do.

London shared Bowring's view that the current state of trade, with its smuggling, corruption and profiteering, was highly unsatisfactory to Britain and China alike. And like Bowring, they believed that free trade, 'the natural parent and ally of peace', was the way to improve this messy situation. Free trade lay at the heart of Palmerston's foreign policy at a time when a supreme pragmatism, allied to massive national self-confidence within a well understood system of values, rendered it superfluous for the government formally to define the national interest (contrast and compare with the recently published strategic objectives of the Foreign and Commonwealth Office for 2008–9–2010–11, negotiated with the Treasury through the medium of 'Public Service Agreements'). Palmerston declared in 1856:

When people ask me [...] for what is called a policy, the only answer is that we mean to do what may seem to be best, upon each occasion as it arises, making the Interests of Our Country one's guiding principle.

Dr Henry Kissinger, the grand master of diplomacy, put it this way:

Great Britain required no formal strategy because its leaders understood the British interest so well and so viscerally that they could act spontaneously on each situation as it arose, confident that their public would follow.

This applied not only to those in the halls of Westminster, but to the diplomats on the ground. To a headstrong man like Bowring this was a gift. He would, to use the jargon of EU diplomacy, take his responsibilities – that is, act without formal instructions – and run with them.

After several lonely and frustrating years in Canton, Bowring was rewarded with a promotion in 1854, with the impressive title of

Plenipotentiary and Chief Superintendent of Trade in the Far East and Governor, Commander-in-Chief and Vice Admiral of Hong Kong. This was despite doubts expressed in the Foreign Office about his suitability for the job. Edward Hammond, Chief Clerk, wittily warned Clarendon:

Of his talent and intellectual vivacity there can be no doubt but there might possibly be a question of his carrying sufficient ballast to countervail his superfluity of sail [...] He would probably be over the Great Wall before we had time to look around us.

In other words, for all his talent, Bowring was, to persist with the naval metaphor, a loose cannon.

To add further gravitas to his grand title, Bowring was knighted by Queen Victoria. Barbarian titles, unfortunately, meant little to the Chinese, who were liable to view Bowring as, at best, head of the local merchants. Shortly afterwards Bowring and his family became the first residents of Hong Kong's Government House, and Bowring set about his mission with a renewed vigour. He had, after all, recently inspired Manchester manufacturers by assuring them that if every man in China bought a single cotton nightcap, their mills would keep going indefinitely.

A few days after his arrival in Hong Kong, Bowring held discussions with his French and American counterparts about revising the Treaty of Nanking and pressing for more commercial access to China. After a rebuff from Commissioner Yeh at Canton, who once again refused to meet him within the walls of the forbidden city, Bowring went north to Shanghai. There, after a conference with the Governor of Kianseu, it looked for a moment as if peaceful diplomacy might win the day. The Governor offered to present Bowring's request to the Emperor himself in Peking. In a revealing insight in a letter to his son Edgar, Bowring expressed himself overjoyed as much at the prospect of personal glory as with the fulfilment of his nation's best interests:

If I go on making no serious blunder, my old age will be crowned with the glory of having rendered services more important in the field of peace than the conqueror can affect in war.

Unfortunately, the Governor soon retracted his offer. A dejected Bowring returned to Hong Kong; but only after his colleagues had had to persuade him against trying a direct approach to the Emperor in Peking. Bowring's mind began to move in another direction, as he vented his frustration in a letter to the Foreign Office: 'It is hard to get on with these stubborn Mandarins,' he complained. 'Before the end I am afraid we shall have to employ something harder than brain bullets.' Bowring wanted gunboats. But with the Crimean War still unfinished, his instructions were to sit tight and 'remain a quiet observer'.

Quiet observation was not Bowring's strong suit. His roving trader's eye soon had him looking for fresh markets to conquer. In March 1855 he set sail for Siam (modern-day Thailand) on board the aptly named HMS *Rattler*, to negotiate new trading rights with King Mongkut. This too would be a challenge. Many in Siam shared the Chinese mistrust of Western Barbarians; only five years earlier the remarkable James Brooke, first 'White Rajah' of Sarawak, had been turned away from Bangkok. But the Siamese had a healthy respect for British military power. They were aware of the damage it had inflicted in China, and were worried by the recent occupation of neighbouring Burma. Bowring had already flexed a little military muscle in a letter to the King before leaving Hong Kong: 'I have a large fleet at my disposal but I would rather visit you as a friend than as a bearer of a menacing message.'

Once in Siam, Bowring successfully negotiated the court protocol and had several friendly meetings with the King. It must have helped that Mongkut shared Bowring's passion for European literature, an unusual attribute in an Eastern potentate of the time. But a moment came when negotiations stalled and Bowring grew impatient. He threatened to bring the *Rattler* near to the Royal Palace. The effect was instantaneous; and Bowring soon after returned to Hong Kong with a 'Treaty of Friendship and Commerce'. This allowed free trade with all seaports in Siam, the duty-free import of opium, and the establishment of consular jurisdiction at Bangkok with wide extra-territorial powers. The treaty even featured a 'most favoured nation' clause for Britain – what is known today as MFN treatment. It means that a nation automatically benefits from the most favourable terms that any other nation may secure. This meant that, should other powers some time in the future negotiate even more favourable terms from the Siamese monarchy, Britain would get them too.

Bowring had got his way in Siam. He was elated, celebrating the signing of the treaty with a twenty-one gun salute that terrified the local population. He reported somewhat boastfully to Clarendon from the deck of the *Rattler*:

I feel myself one of the happiest of men. I most cordially anticipate immense benefits to my country and to mankind – and to the oppressed people of Siam especially – from the emancipation of so large, productive and promising a proportion of the oriental world. And I am really amazed at my won success which once or twice seemed almost hopeless.

In fact, many attributed the success of the mission more to the tact and determination of Bowring's young secretary, Harry Parkes. Who knows? Any good negotiation is a team effort; an ambassador cannot do it all on his own. Still, the other side's mind is wonderfully concentrated if there is a gunboat round the river bend, with a Commander-in-Chief and Vice Admiral willing to use it.

Bowring returned to Hong Kong in buoyant mood, and with a new zeal to prise open China. Before leaving Bangkok, he had asked London for permission to approach China in the same way: with the 'instruments of peace' in one hand and 'a co-operative naval force' in the other. But once again the orders from home were for him to do nothing. Bowring turned his energies instead to improving the infrastructure of Hong Kong – introducing building regulations and the first public water supply system. Finally, in March 1856, the Crimean War came to an end. Bowring had long been on the lookout for a *casus belli*, and he soon found one.

On 8 October 1856, Chinese officials boarded the lorcha *Arrow* in Canton harbour, and arrested her crew on suspicion of piracy and smuggling.[3] The *Arrow* was Chinese-built, Chinese-owned, and manned by a Chinese crew sailing in Chinese waters. But, she had an Irish captain and had been registered in Hong Kong. This granted the *Arrow* the right to fly the British flag and claim British protection. Harry Parkes, now the Acting Consul at Canton, hurried to the scene and demanded the release of the prisoners. There was a bit of a scuffle on board, and Parkes returned to shore to lodge a letter of protest with Commissioner Yeh.

On hearing of the incident, Bowring looked up the *Arrow*'s registration papers. He found that her registration had just expired and with it her claim to British protection. It seemed also that the Chinese had not lowered the British flag, as Parkes had claimed, because the *Arrow* was at anchor at the time, when flags are not flown. Bowring should probably have dropped the issue then and there, as he appeared not to have a leg to stand on. Or, as I might have said in a diplomatic report, he had no *locus* to intervene. But he chose to press on. Banking on the assumption that the Chinese could not have known about the expired register, he wrote to Commissioner Yeh claiming that 'there is no doubt that the lorcha *Arrow* lawfully bore the British flag under a register granted by me'. This was, of course, a bare-faced lie. But Bowring had his eye on the bigger picture. He sent some carefully worded despatches to London, heavily economical with the truth; and a private communication to Parkes, which revealed his motives:

Cannot we use this opportunity and carry the City question? If so, I will come up with the whole fleet. I think we have now a stepping-stone from which with good management we may move on to important sequences.

Here at last was Bowring's chance to force the trade issue with the Chinese, and more besides. It was soon to emerge that the *Arrow* had indeed been involved in piratical activities; and her Irish skipper confessed that he was captain in name alone, hired to give the vessel a veneer of respectability. But Bowring and Parkes decided to stick to their accusation that a gross insult to the British flag had been committed. They continued to press Yeh for an apology. When, unsurprisingly, one was not forthcoming, Bowring ordered a Royal Navy bombardment of Canton.

Nowadays, when it is the hour of the generals or admirals, the diplomats tend to leave the stage. It is beyond imagining that a modern ambassador could find himself in a position to start a war, still less to plan and direct one. In Bowring's time, as instructions from London took some two months to arrive, diplomats had to use their initiative in ways unknown to their modern counterparts.

But even by Victorian standards, to start a war was no light matter. Bowring must have known that, if things failed to go to plan, he would find himself in hot water at home.

Bowring's critics would later question his motives. They would accuse him of becoming obsessed with the idea of breaking open Canton and settling scores with Yeh, who had snubbed him on so many occasions. There may well be much to that. We have already seen evidence of Bowring's difficulty in separating his personal interests from his official duties. But this does not alter the fact that it was a clear, well-established British policy to establish free trade with China. It was equally clear that diplomacy alone could not achieve this. Fifty years of trying had got almost nowhere. There had again to be a show of force and a whiff of cordite; it had become a case of simply choosing the right moment to act. Whatever charges might be levelled against Bowring, he never lost sight of the big picture. As he explained in a letter to the Foreign Secretary:

The gate of China is Canton, and unless we can subdue the resistance and force an entry there, I believe the difficulties of obtaining an improved position in China will be almost invincible. But success at Canton will, I am assured, be followed by a general and satisfactory change in the state of our relations with the entire Empire.

It did not take long to force the gate of China by blasting a hole in Canton's walls. Bowring, who was in Hong Kong at the time, was bitterly disappointed to have been beaten by Parkes as first British official to enter the city. By this time, all mention of the *Arrow* incident had disappeared from Bowring's correspondence. Canton was now the openly avowed prize.

Commissioner Yeh's response was to close down all trade and to burn the European settlement. It soon became apparent that, in the face of strengthening Chinese resistance, the British would not be able to hold the city. As British forces bombarded Yeh's residence, he issued an order for retaliation:

The British have attacked our city, killing our soldiers and people; their crimes are extreme. I now command you, inhabitants of the whole province, to unite and spare no effort in assisting the troops to fight any Briton, on land or water. $30 will be rewarded to anyone who succeeds in killing one Briton and brings his head to my office.

The violence continued to escalate. On 29 December eleven Europeans travelling to Hong Kong on a postal steamer were beheaded by Yeh's militia. Bowring was not to be deterred. He wrote to his son:

I still think this mode of action more worthy of a Great Nation than the stoppage of duties and the disturbance of trade – out of these troubled waters I expect to extract some healing food.

By December news of the *Arrow* incident and of the escalating violence had reached Westminster. It was clear that Bowring – and Britain – had a war on their hands. Not all of Palmerston's Cabinet felt that Bowring had acted wisely, but they agreed that he was right to press for entry into Canton and for revision of the Nanking Treaty. In fact, when the government heard about the *Arrow*, it had already been preparing to use force to extract treaty revisions from China; Bowring had merely jumped the gun. In any event, the government had little choice but to support him. Matters had gone too far. To repudiate him now would be hugely damaging to British standing throughout the Far East.

The *Arrow* was something not everyone in London was prepared to overlook. Since the eighteenth century there had been a vigorous, undeferential press; and Parliament had been a turbulent force since the late sixteenth century. By the mid nineteenth century the male franchise for the House of Commons had been increased in the Great Reform Act of 1832 and was about to be enlarged further in 1867. There were two distinct political parties in the Conservatives and Liberals with clear ideological differences; and there was a mass public opinion capable of both being manipulated, and exerting pressure, through the press and Parliament.

Richard Cobden, a leading manufacturer and liberal politician, led the attack on his former friend, Bowring, from the Commons backbenches. A vigorous debate was joined in both Houses of Parliament and the *Arrow* dossier carefully scrutinised. As the layers of confusion and embellishment were stripped away, some hard truths emerged. The *Arrow* was not a British vessel flying a British flag. Commissioner Yeh had been right. Lord Lyndhurst, an eminent jurist specialising in international law, was incensed over Bowring's reason for going to war:

It is extraordinary that Sir John Bowring should think he had the power of declaring war [and] to carry on offensive operations on such a ground, such a pretence, is one of the most extraordinary proceedings to be found in the history of the world.

When Palmerston heard that the Opposition were planning to accuse Bowring of violating international law, he took the then unprecedented step of inviting the Attorney-General to address the Cabinet. International law was in the early stages of its modern development. But the Attorney-General's opinion – unlike, apparently, Lord Goldsmith's in 2003 on the legality of invading Iraq – confirmed Palmerston's fears that the Opposition had a strong case against Bowring. In the fierce debates that followed, William Gladstone, leader of the Liberal Party, gave a barnstorming speech, in which he invoked morality as well as law, proclaiming that 'power could not be well founded on injustice'. There were accusations of double standards: one for the East, and one for the West, and that Britain would hardly behave in such a cavalier fashion in Europe. In the end, this was the argument that the government co-opted, claiming that international law could not realistically apply to 'barbarous states', especially when British trade was at stake. The Foreign Secretary, Lord Clarendon, argued:

I fear that we must come to the conclusion that in dealing with a nation like the Chinese, if we intend to preserve any amicable or useful relations with them, we must make them sensible of the law of force, and must appeal to them in the manner which alone they can appreciate.

The case against the Chinese was set out in a Blue Book of documents, entitled 'Correspondence Respecting Insults in China', and laid before the House of Commons. Its 225 sexed-up pages were replete with accounts of Chinese misbehaviour, but omitted to mention the provocative acts of violence and disorder committed by British merchants. The Blue Book was dismissed by critics as an attempt to mislead Parliament and the British public, a dodgy dossier indeed.

When the issue was put to the vote in the House of Commons, the Government was defeated by sixteen votes. Palmerston responded by dissolving Parliament and fighting a general election, dominated by the Chinese question. If patriotic feeling had not triumphed over legal and moral scruple inside Parliament, he hoped that it would do so with the public at large.

Bowring, meanwhile, was far from the long knives of Westminster in the relative security of Hong Kong. Then, suddenly, he found himself under attack from a wholly unexpected quarter. A mysterious outbreak of vomiting swept through the European population of Hong Kong. It was soon discovered that arsenic had been added to their bread. This was a premeditated attempt at mass poisoning. The cry of 'poisoned loaves!' rang through the streets. Relations between the British and Chinese communities plumbed new depths. Fortunately for the bread-eaters of Hong Kong, the poisoners had botched their work. The three to four hundred victims suffered only severe bouts of sickness. In the panic that followed, many in Hong Kong called for the strongest measures against the Chinese suspects. But Bowring, once he had recovered from his own bout of vomiting, insisted that they be given a proper trial. A baker and other suspects were all acquitted for lack of evidence.

The British press was not prepared to be so lenient. It unleashed the hounds of xenophobia and railed against the 'yellow peril'. The *Morning Post* was typical:

Talk of international law with sanguinary savages such as these! There is but one law for such demons in human shape, and that is the law of severe, summary and inexorable justice.

Today's tabloid press is by contrast a model of sober restraint. This was a gift from heaven for Palmerston, who played the China card to the hilt. His general election address began thus:

An insolent barbarian wielding authority at Canton has violated the British flag, broken the engagements of treaties, offered rewards for the heads of British subjects in that part of China, and planned their destruction by murder, assassinations, and poisons.

Thousands of copies of his address were distributed around the country. It was a first for British political history. Never before had the Prime Minister addressed the nation as a whole in this way. It worked, carrying Palmerston to a resounding election victory, though there were still voices of dissent who claimed that he had misled the country. But the tough men of British trade knew which side their bread was buttered. It went beyond mindless xenophobia and getting even with that 'insolent barbarian' Yeh for insulting the British flag. It was not the flag, but free trade with China that was at stake. Bowring and Harry Parkes could be rightly criticised for the disingenuous and dishonourable way in which they had provoked hostilities with the Emperor, but even many of Palmerston's critics accepted that an aggressive approach was the only way to further British trading interests.

The conflict in China was to last another three years, and grew into the full-scale war that Bowring had hoped it would become. British troops, aided by French, American and Russian contingents, forced a surrender at Tientsin in 1858, where a 'Treaty of Peace, Friendship and Commerce' was signed. The Chinese, unsurprisingly, called it again an 'Unequal Treaty'. When, two years later, the treaty had still not been ratified by the Chinese, Britain and France burned down the Old Summer Palace in Peking, and seized the opportunity to add a few more clauses. The improved treaty opened eleven more ports to Western commerce, legalised the opium trade, and ceded foreigners the right to travel in the interior of China. Most significant of all, the Chinese begrudgingly agreed to allow Britain, France, the United States and Russia to establish diplomatic residences in Peking. This was not only everything that Bowring had hoped for, it was, finally, the realisation of Macartney's ambitions of some sixty years before.

Bowring was not in China to see the conclusion of the war that he had started. Even before the general election, Palmerston was taking measures to cut him down to size. He had become too controversial. When a diplomat becomes the story, he gets in the way of his own mission. Bowring was allowed to retain the governorship of Hong Kong for the time being. But he could only watch from the sidelines as Lord Elgin, who had been made High Commissioner to China in 1857, led the troops against the Emperor and conducted the negotiation of the new treaties. It was a bitter blow, leaving him hurt and disappointed. Further embarrassment was to strike on his journey home, when he was shipwrecked, nearly drowned, and left on a reef in the Red Sea for three days in nothing but a nightgown. Commissioner Yeh, meanwhile, was captured and taken to Calcutta, where he died in exile.

Later, in his autobiography, Bowring wrote:

I have been severely blamed for the policy I pursued, yet that policy has been most beneficial to my country and to mankind at large [...] I had during my tenure of office the pleasure of seeing the population nearly trebled, and the shipping trade increased nearly cent per cent. I not only made the revenue, in which there had been a large deficit, equal the expenditure, but I left a large balance in the treasury chest. I carried out the principles of Free Trade to their fullest possible extent.

There is no arguing with Bowring's statistics. British exports had risen from £0.54 million in 1854, when Bowring was appointed, to £5.09 million by 1866, an almost ten-fold increase. The opening of further ports after the war brought a great increase in trade, and access to the interior of China allowed the export of cheaper tea.

On one level Bowring had reason, therefore, to feel aggrieved at the way his government and critics had, as he saw it, failed to appreciate his achievements in China. But, on other levels, he made every mistake in the book. It did not help that his charmless arrogance cost him colleagues and friends who might otherwise have rallied to his side when the going got tough. The harsh truth is that he was a rotten diplomat and envoy, who committed the ultimate crime of bringing his own country into disrepute. The *Arrow* incident was at the root of it all. The great French diplomat, Talleyrand, had instructed his staff: '*Surtout, pas trop de zèle.*' ('Above all, don't be too zealous.') That was Bowring's problem: he was dangerously and self-destructively zealous. He allowed vanity and ambition to get the better of his judgement. This opened the door to another cardinal diplomatic sin: he exceeded his instructions, and then went on to lie to his government, to his colleagues and, of course, to the Chinese. Palmerston's administration found themselves trapped in Bowring's web of deceit, and were only able to escape it by appealing to the nation's baser instincts. Bowring lost the confidence of the government and paid with his career and reputation. As the Foreign Office Chief Clerk had spotted from the beginning, Bowring should never have been given a job with such heavy responsibilities at such distance from London.

'To understand all is to forgive all.' The old French proverb can almost be made to work for John Bowring. There is something in him of genuine bewilderment that standing up for 'the principles of Free Trade' was not answer enough to his critics. Bowring, like Palmerston, was of a generation that believed free trade to be intrinsically virtuous. It was the classic demonstration of a great power fusing its national interest with high moral purpose. During Bowring's lifetime, however, Britain's political, intellectual and social landscape had begun to shift markedly. The spread of democracy and literacy introduced to a wide audience the radical reformist ideas of writers and thinkers like Jeremy Bentham, John Stuart Mill, Robert Owen, et al. Some of these ideas found expression in Liberal Party opposition to Palmerston's administration. Bowring, himself once a radical MP allied to the reformer Richard Cobden, should have known this. But, one way or another, he committed the ultimate diplomatic sin; he lost touch with his own country and found himself representing an idea of Britain and its national interest that was on the edge of obsolescence.

Free trade to this day preserves an aura of virtue – the natural partner of peace and prosperity. It is a measure of its potency as an idea that few argue openly for protectionism. The opponents of free trade prefer the euphemism 'fair' trade, as in the attacks by Democrats in the US Congress against the North American Free Trade Agreement. But, to say, as you could in the late eighteenth and early nineteenth centuries, that free trade is good – end of argument – does not wash today; and was washing less and less well when Bowring was in China. Something wholly new was entering attitudes to the ends and means of British foreign policy, and the content of the national interest was itself changing. The vexed issue of ethics and foreign policy had arrived: whether there could be an autonomous ethical benchmark against which the justice and wisdom of Britain's conduct overseas should be measured. Bowring was out of touch with it all.

Britain had got her way, and further reinforced the foundations of her wealth and status. It was in the end a hugely popular policy in Britain. Nevertheless, the Second Opium War left a bad taste. Bowring's successor, Elgin, referred to it as 'a scandal to us', and even Clarendon, who had supported Bowring throughout, called it 'a miserable case'. As for the Chinese, it would store up a legacy of trouble in their long memory of foreign humiliation. The 'burden of history' would return to haunt Sino-British relations and the negotiations at the end of the twentieth century to give back Hong Kong to the People's Republic.

6

HONG KONG:
A Tale of Two Systems

On 30 June 1997 the sun set on the last significant colony of the British Empire. On the border with China, four thousand troops of the People's Liberation Army awaited the order to cross into Hong Kong. In the presence of the Prince of Wales, the Union Jack was lowered. The rain came sheeting down. Chris Patten, Hong Kong's twenty-eighth and last Governor, wept openly. Later, the British government in London received the following communication:

I have relinquished the administration of this government. God save the Queen. Patten.

The handover or, as the Chinese preferred it, the reversion of Hong Kong to China, had been accomplished.

The handover marked the end of over one hundred and fifty years of colonial rule. It was also the conclusion of a fifteen-year diplomatic engagement between Britain and China that had seen many twists and turns, successes and near-breakdowns. It had been a negotiation shot through with complexity and the burden of history: Chinese resentment at the humiliation of the Opium Wars and the Unequal Treaties of the nineteenth century; the capacity of each side for miscalculation, mistrust and mutual misunderstanding; the complicating entry of human rights into the negotiations; the conflict on the British side between politicians and professional diplomats over negotiating objectives; the conflict in Hong Kong between pro-Beijing and pro-democracy parties about the nature of their future autonomy inside China; Communism versus Capitalism. If this were not enough, the premise of the negotiations was unique in Britain's post-imperial history. We were trying, from a position of substantial and obvious weakness, to set the terms of Hong Kong's internal governance after its incorporation into China. There was an irony too. In the very year that Prime Minister Margaret Thatcher drove the Argentines out of the Falkland Islands by force of arms, she acquiesced in a negotiation, the result of which would mean the cession to China of territory that Britain had the right to hold in perpetuity.

The ceremony of 30 June 1997 was also the climax of a conflict between two highly personal visions of Hong Kong's destiny: that of the greatest of the Foreign Office China experts, Sir Percy Cradock; and that of the smart Tory politician-become-Governor, Chris Patten. Each antagonist is today alive to give his version of events.[1]

I had a tiny walk-on part. I was never a sinologist. I belonged to the rival Foreign Office clan of Kremlinologists. But in 1984, I returned from a posting to our embassy in Moscow to become the Foreign Office spokesman and press secretary to the Foreign Secretary, Sir Geoffrey, now Lord, Howe. Anything I knew about China had been strained through a Russian filter. In communist days there was an abiding Soviet fear of China; Russians would talk quite openly about the 'yellow peril'. It was a complex relationship: there was a long-standing border dispute between the two countries; they were competitors for influence in Asia and within the international communist movement; but there was also a fair bit of cooperation and trade between them. In Moscow, in the difficult quest for reliable information about what was going on inside the Soviet Politburo, I found that diplomats from communist and non-aligned[2] countries could be useful. I had a contact in the Chinese Embassy with whom I would exchange nuggets of information in a typical diplomatic barter. He would sometimes give me lunch, embellished with produce from the Chinese Embassy's excellent vegetable garden.

My first trip abroad as Foreign Office spokesman was to Beijing in December 1984 with Margaret Thatcher and Geoffrey Howe. They were to sign with Chinese leaders the Joint Declaration that established the framework and principles for the return of Hong Kong to China. It was an occasion of grandiose ceremony. On a cold and misty morning, Thatcher reviewed troops on Tiananmen Square. There was a banquet in the Great Hall of the People, at which solemn speeches were made. A great signing ceremony was organised, at which the two premiers, Thatcher and Zhao Ziyang, put their names to the Joint Declaration. There was also a carefully choreographed encounter between Margaret Thatcher and Deng Xiao Ping, at which the two faced each other in overstuffed armchairs. Deng, though never president nor prime minister, was China's most important politician. He had survived the Cultural Revolution and begun the process of economic reform. There would have been no Joint Declaration without his approval or his pragmatism. He once said: 'I don't care if it's a white cat or a black cat. It's a good cat so long as it catches mice.' Even with its guarantee to preserve Hong Kong's capitalist way of life for fifty years, the Joint Declaration was evidently for Deng a very good cat indeed.

I was allowed to take photos of the diminutive, chain-smoking Deng at his meeting with Thatcher. There is an unwritten rule at high-level diplomatic encounters that the more ceremonial the occasion, the larger the delegations in attendance on each side. The fact that a relatively junior official like me was admitted to the meeting showed that it was of little substantive importance. Had Thatcher and Deng met to thrash out some final and sensitive point in the Joint Declaration, the respective delegations would have been small, expert and intensely focused.

The British delegation returned to London, well satisfied. The Joint Declaration on the Question of Hong Kong had been a significant diplomatic achievement. But, as Ronald Reagan once said in another context, 'You ain't seen nothing yet.' In the thirteen years that followed, before the Union Jack was lowered forever over Hong Kong, there were moments when it looked as if disagreement between Britain and China would leave the Joint Declaration stillborn.

The gunboat diplomacy of the First Opium War had gained for Britain the thirty-one square miles of Hong Kong Island, which passed formally into British possession on the signing of the Treaty of Nanking in 1842. At the time, few in Britain had seen the little island as a worthy addition to the British Empire. Queen Victoria commented that: 'Albert is much amused at my having got the island of Hong Kong.' Thirty-eight years later, the spoils of the Second Opium War, which Bowring had so deviously engineered, had included a chunk of the Kowloon peninsula. In 1860, this too had been ceded in perpetuity to Britain. In the years that followed, trade between Britain and China had rocketed. So had Hong Kong's population, with many Chinese and Western fortune-seekers arriving in the late nineteenth century. By 1898, the rapidly expanding population had threatened to overwhelm the tiny territory. Britain had, therefore, struck a deal with China to lease a large tract of land to the north of Kowloon, together with some two hundred outlying islands. The term on the lease was ninety-nine years. The New Territories, as they became known, increased Hong Kong's area twelve-fold.

Hong Kong had been quick to demonstrate that the early disdain of Victoria and Palmerston was ill-judged. It had developed rapidly into a busy commercial centre and entrepôt with a unique character, intimately close to, yet separate from, China. It had become a safe haven for refugees from various Chinese revolutions and upheavals, from the creation of the Republic of China in 1912 to the Cultural Revolution of the 1960s. As a gateway between China and the outside world, Hong Kong had grown to become a source of wealth and investment for the mainland. The Chinese had always claimed that the Unequal Treaties were, by their very injustice, not binding. For fear of killing the goose that was laying golden eggs in such profusion, China had made no move to oust the British.

However, neither side could ignore the clock that was ticking on the New Territories. By the 1970s it was starting to concentrate minds. In 1979, the Hong Kong Governor, Sir Murray MacLehose, received an official invitation to visit Beijing. MacLehose, Hong Kong's longest serving governor at over ten years, was an enlightened reformer who wrought many changes of long-term benefit to Hong Kong's people. In the impressive surroundings of the Great Hall of the People, Deng Xiaoping told MacLehose in unambiguous terms that Hong Kong would have to return to Chinese sovereignty in 1997, but he also promised that steps would be taken to protect its special characteristics.

On his return to Hong Kong, MacLehose assured its citizens that no agreement had been reached and that the colony's unique status was safe. In reality, Britain's future role in Hong Kong was anything but certain, but China had at least agreed to talks. The head of the British team was Percy Cradock, British Ambassador in Beijing since 1978. As a seasoned, Mandarin-speaking sinologist who had weathered the hostilities of the Cultural Revolution, including the burning of the British Chancery in 1967, Cradock was well placed to lead Britain through the delicate negotiations.

Cradock was sharply aware of the weaknesses in the British negotiating hand, which came down to geography apart from anything else. The lease, which would expire at midnight on 30 June 1997, applied to 92 per cent of the territory of Hong Kong. Thanks to the Unequal Treaties, the remaining 8 per cent had been ceded to Britain in perpetuity, but that territory was unviable on its own. There would be nothing to stop the People's Liberation Army going to Boundary Street in built-up, congested Kowloon, crossing the road, and taking over Hong Kong. Apart from the street name, there was nothing to show that this was the dividing line between leasehold and freehold Hong Kong. (In reality, even this minor military manoeuvre would be unnecessary: the freehold territory was wholly reliant on China for food, water and electricity. The Chinese could turn out the lights of Hong Kong at the flick of a switch.)

Cradock was faced with a formidably difficult double challenge. He would have to enter talks with China as the underdog, something that must have smacked of sweet revenge for the Chinese side of the table. But, first, he had to persuade his Prime Minister, Margaret Thatcher, that the only realistic basis for negotiation would be an acceptance that, if push came to shove, Hong Kong could not be defended against China. It was not obvious which of the two challenges was the more daunting.

In 1982, Thatcher was at the top of her game. Her victory over Argentina in the Falklands War had vindicated a brave, but risky, decision not to let stand the Galtieri regime's occupation of the islands. She was a fierce nationalist and visceral anti-communist.

I first met her in 1969 when she visited Moscow where I was a Third Secretary, deputed by the Ambassador to look after her. She was at the time in Edward Heath's Shadow Cabinet, but I knew next to nothing of her and asked a journalist friend how I would recognise her in a crowded hotel lobby. He told me to look for a woman dressed as if she were about to open a Conservative village fête. I picked her out instantly. We went to call on some high Soviet official who began to boast about the Revolution of 1917; Thatcher dismissed him with an impatient wave of the hand. The astonished Russian was told that he had nothing to brag about: Russia had had only one revolution, while in Britain we had a revolution every time government passed from one party to another after a general election. That, said Thatcher, was real democracy. I mentioned this later, with some pride, to a contact in the Soviet foreign ministry. His sour comment was that all British politicians, from whatever party, were 'jackals from the same lair'.

To give ground to a communist regime stuck in Thatcher's craw. She was already less than impressed by the Foreign Office and the strength of its backbone (though she came to respect and rely on certain Foreign Office individuals, notably John Coles and Charles Powell, both now lords, who were long-serving foreign policy advisers). Any Foreign Office recommendation to retreat was, therefore, automatically suspect. As Percy Cradock put it to me in an interview earlier this year, he had always followed 'Cradock's First Law of Diplomacy', which was: 'it's not the other side you need to worry about but your own.' This is an excellent diplomatic precept. One of the biggest challenges for an official is to tell a politician what he or she does not want to hear. Thatcher once took strong exception to a senior Foreign Office diplomat who criticised in her earshot President Reagan's unworkable Star Wars project to shoot down incoming Soviet missiles. I was accused by some in Tony Blair's Al Gore-loving entourage of Republican bias when the Embassy in Washington started to report in 2000 that George W. Bush could win the presidential election.

In the autumn of 1982 Thatcher went to Beijing and Hong Kong to find out for herself. She was in combative mood at her meetings with Deng Xaoping and Zhao Ziyang. Her exchanges with Deng, with his cigarettes and spittoon, were especially abrasive and diffi-cult. Deng was unaccustomed to being challenged so bluntly by a woman, and he repaid Thatcher in the same coin. She pressed for continued British sovereignty and administration, on the grounds that Britain had this far run Hong Kong successfully and would continue to do so. Deng countered in the plainest terms that China would resume sovereignty over all Hong Kong in 1997. The People's Liberation Army could march in and take over the colony that very afternoon, if they chose. But Deng and Zhao sugared the pill by vague references to assuring Hong Kong's stability and prosperity, which Zhao then repeated in public. The phrase was picked up in the brief joint communiqué, recording agreement to enter talks 'through diplomatic channels ... with the common aim of main-taining the stability and prosperity of Hong Kong'. The com-muniqué was a modest British triumph since it omitted any mention of a return to Chinese sovereignty. This was belatedly corrected in a unilateral Chinese statement. Meanwhile, Deng had given the diplomats a two-year deadline to complete the negotiations – or else.

The Deng–Thatcher meeting enabled each side to get a lot off their chests. In Deng's case, this included a fair amount of mucus. Two years later, just before the signing of the Joint Declaration, I mentioned to some of the accompanying journalists Deng's spit-toon habit. I learnt an early lesson in press handling when, to my horror, the next day's British newspapers were full of spittoon stories.

Sometimes in diplomacy a row leads to stalemate; sometimes, as in this case, it is cathartic. It cleared the way for a negotiation which, well within Deng's deadline, would lead to agreement. Two pennies dropped on the British side. The first was that there could be no comparison with the Falklands. There was no military option avail-able to Britain. The second was that, for the Chinese, though the economic argument was important, it did not trump the restoration of their sovereignty. There was a strong emotional element in this, which owed not a little to the humiliations visited on them in the nineteenth century by Britain and others. When, on her 1982 visit, Thatcher had insisted on the legitimacy of the so-called Unequal Treaties, for the Chinese leadership this was simply to rub their noses in the humiliation of the Qing dynasty. By the end of her visit, Thatcher seemed to hint that she had taken the point:

Our conversations have enabled me to attain a clearer insight into China's affairs, and a close personal understanding of the Chinese government's point of view. This complies with an old Chinese saying, which goes: 'Seeing for one's self is a hundred times better than hearing from others.'

In an interview fifteen years later, Cradock put it thus:

You were dealing with a very proud people who wished to recover national territory which had been lost under humiliating circumstances, as they saw it, and they had no doubt which came first: it was recovering the territory. Naturally they would like to recover it in prosperous circumstances and to get the economic benefits as well. Like everyone they would like to have their cake and eat it. But they made it very plain that if it came to the crunch they were prepared to recover the place as a wasteland if need be.

Paradoxically, far from dispossessing the British of what they considered to be their trump card – that they alone could guarantee Hong Kong's continuing prosperity – it gave them new cards for the negotiation. China attached such importance to formal sovereignty that it was willing to concede a great deal to get it by peaceful means. There was also a broader calculation in Beijing. The Chinese had in their sights not just Hong Kong; but also the nearby Portuguese colony of Macao and, above all, Taiwan. Deng Xiaoping had conceived the philosophy of 'One country, two systems' for all three territories. It would have two fundamental components: the reversion of sovereignty to the People's Republic of China; and a guarantee in treaty form that for fifty years the customs and practices of the territory would remain unchanged.

The big prize for Deng was Taiwan; or, to call it by its official name, the Republic of China, a large, prosperous, capitalist island of almost 20 million Chinese inhabitants lying off the mainland. It had come into being as a result of the 1949 civil war when, after his defeat by Mao Zedong and the communists, General Chiang Kai-shek and his nationalists had found refuge in Taiwan. Ever since, the two states had coexisted in open hostility. But by the 1980s, something was starting to move. At the beginning of the decade I found myself in a hotel in the southern Chinese city of Guangzhou. The dining room had been taken over by a large wedding party. They were being entertained by a woman singer, who was performing a Chinese pastiche of Western pop music. My interpreter commented that most Chinese pop stars were from Taiwan. On the same visit I was taken as part of an European Community delegation to the New Economic Zone of Shenzhen, just north of Hong Kong. Thirty years ago, it was little more than a building site. Our Chinese hosts, keen to attract foreign investment as part of Deng's economic reforms, reeled off a list of foreigners who had put their money into Shenzhen. Most were Taiwanese and Hong Kong businessmen.

In other words, Hong Kong was the sprat to catch Taiwan's mackerel. If the negotiations and handover went well, this would be an encouragement to the Taiwanese to acquiesce one day in Beijing's sovereignty. This significantly strengthened the British negotiating hand.

By the same token, the Chinese received reinforcement for their hand from British domestic concerns, though it is not clear to what extent they understood this. It was not just a question of the unavoidable *force majeure* of the 1997 deadline. There was a fear in London that a collapse in negotiations, leading to a collapse in confidence among the Hong Kong population, could provoke an exodus from the colony that would put irresistible pressure on Britain's highly restrictive immigration policy. Because of its exiguous population, Thatcher had felt able to allow any Falkland Islanders, who so desired after the Argentine invasion, to settle in the UK. To give a similar commitment to several million Hong Kong Chinese was just not on.

After the Deng–Thatcher meeting, Britain in effect dropped continuing sovereignty as a negotiating objective and instead went for the best terms possible for the return of Hong Kong to China. The talks followed a classic negotiating path: the British team made an orderly and necessary retreat from one negotiating point to another, sacrificing expendable positions, but getting ever nearer to London's bottom line. For a while, Cradock and his men tried to make a stand on British administration. This was a Foreign Office wheeze, agreed to by Thatcher, whereby Britain would abandon sovereignty's form in return for keeping its substance. The British argued that Hong Kong's prosperity was inextricably linked to British law and British freedoms. It was a bit too clever by half. It caused enormous heartburn on the Chinese side. They saw administration as a function of sovereignty. How could the two be separated? What were the British up to? Old stereotypes haunted the negotiating table; mistrust was thick in the air. Each side attributed to the other extraordinary powers of deviousness and cunning. The gulf in mutual misunderstanding sometimes appeared no less than in the days of Lord Macartney. Even the language of negotiation proved a problem. The British diplomats sought to tie things down in tight legal language. The Chinese had a preference for the style of the old imperial decree – more general and declaratory.

The Chinese began to smell a very large rat at the British mention of safeguarding Hong Kong's legal system or, worse, introducing democracy. From time immemorial Britain had seemed interested only in making money out of the colony. What did they care about its institutions or the freedom of its citizens? This new concern, they felt, was a trick to preserve British control. The administration of Hong Kong was none of Britain's business. If democracy was so important to Britain, why had the issue surfaced only now?

For Britain, however, there was now more to Hong Kong than just money. The negotiations had crystallised the issue of exactly what Hong Kong was, and what it represented. Public, press and parliamentary opinion in Britain was aroused. It was not possible to negotiate wholly over the heads of the Hong Kong people themselves. There was a highly vocal public opinion in the colony. I visited Hong Kong a couple of times with my old boss, Geoffrey Howe, just after the signing of the Joint Declaration. The toughest press conferences, bar none, were in Hong Kong, where a vibrant, aggressive press corps waited to devour you like a shoal of piranhas.

Hong Kong opinion became a complicating factor for both China and Britain. Britain began belatedly to view Hong Kong as a political entity in its own right, something the Chinese angrily contested. The British wanted representatives from Hong Kong to be involved in the negotiations. Again, the Chinese were having none of it. To them, the talks were strictly bilateral. Furthermore, they believed that they understood the Hong Kong people better than the British. Before and after the signing of the Joint Declaration, British negotiators found themselves under constant pressure from different Hong Kong constituencies that did not always agree on the way ahead. Cradock worried that some of the locals overrated British power. They put pressure on him to be tough: to issue ultimatums and walk out of the talks, if need be. The Chinese were bluffing, these Hong Kongers argued; they would do nothing that might jeopardise Hong Kong's prosperity. But, Cradock feared that a breakdown in the talks would result in untold damage to Hong Kong. He saw himself clinging to the coat-tails of the Chinese as they perched on the window ledge of negotiations, ready to leap off at any moment. Britain, thought Cradock, had done well to get the negotiations started at all. If we walked out, we would never get back in.

The fluctuations of the Hong Kong Stock Exchange – the Hang Seng Index – appeared to justify Cradock's fears. Confidence went up and down in lockstep with the progress of negotiations. In the autumn of 1983, when Britain was insisting on the continuation of British administration, it looked as if the talks might collapse. The Hang Seng and the Hong Kong dollar plummeted. There was panic in the streets. Britain considered using Treasury reserves to support the dollar. Then evidence emerged that the Bank of China itself was speculating against Hong Kong's currency. It was proof that, to get its way, China was quite prepared to pursue a scorched-earth policy with Hong Kong's prosperity. Britain backed down; negotiations resumed, and the Joint Declaration was quickly agreed.

The heart of the Declaration was Deng's 'One Country, Two Systems'. Hong Kong would revert to China in 1997. It would then become a Special Administrative Region (SAR) of China, enjoying a large degree of autonomy, except in matters of security and foreign policy. Its special status was guaranteed for fifty years, during which it could retain its capitalist economy and many other home-grown features, such as a free port, its own currency, and its legal system based on English common law. The Declaration provided a framework and a statement of principles. The detail would be filled in after discussion and debate by a joint committee of Chinese and Hong Kong representatives. The whole package, once agreed, would then be enshrined in a Basic Law enacted by Beijing.

The joint committee would have much to do. The references to democracy in particular were vague. The legislature would be elected and the executive accountable to the legislature. But the nature of the franchise was not specified. There were those who felt that the Joint Declaration could have secured more autonomy and a clearer commitment to democracy, but, overall, it was widely acclaimed. There was general agreement that the British diplomatic team had achieved the best possible result. The *Sunday Times* described it as 'a triumph of realism over woolly hopes'. Douglas Hurd called it 'one of the classical achievements of modern diplomacy'.

Diplomatic success brought early commercial reward. Just four days after the signing of the Joint Declaration, China announced a £120 million contract to buy ten British airliners. There were new agreements on nuclear and economic cooperation. The volume of Sino-British trade had been less than £400m in 1983. By 1988 it was more than £1.5 billion. Hong Kong's GDP went up 30 per cent in three years. And a new high was reached in 1986, when the Queen became the first British monarch ever to visit China.

Behind the scenes, however, the democracy issue would not go away. It was from the start a grumbling appendix. Hong Kong was a curious animal. The argument was frequently put forward that it was not a political city, and its single-minded focus on making money lent the argument some substance. Chinese peasants and Vietnamese boat people came to the colony, not in quest of democracy, but to find a safe haven and a standard of living that took them above simple subsistence. British rule took its cue accordingly, concentrating – especially under the Labour governments of the 1970s – on social issues and the building of affordable rented housing. But, paradoxically, Hong Kong had many of the attributes of a free and sophisticated society: an undeferential and exuberant press, well-established professional bodies, good education and extensive social services. All that was lacking was the citizens' right to elect those responsible for the running of the territory.

It was an unstable paradox that could not last. There had been a nascent democracy movement in the colony from at least the 1970s.

The negotiations with China over Hong Kong's future brought it to the fore. Even before the crisis provoked by the massacre in Tiananmen Square in 1989, controversy over democracy's place in Hong Kong's future had begun to rub off some of the gloss on the Joint Declaration. The Foreign Office found itself caught between a vocal pro-democracy movement in Hong Kong and a much more authoritarian view in Beijing. The schism exists to this day between the pro-Beijing and the pro-democracy groups in Hong Kong.

I worked for Geoffrey Howe as Foreign Office spokesman from 1984 to 1988, and Hong Kong was a continuing preoccupation throughout this period. The Joint Declaration had established a Sino-British joint liaison group, which was to oversee the implementation of the Joint Declaration. This meant regular meetings with the Chinese. Howe used them to hold China to its undertaking to grant Hong Kong a large degree of autonomy after 1997 – the so-called 'through train', which would convey the colony's special attributes through 1997 and beyond. The challenge was to persuade a highly suspicious China that the train should be carrying a degree of democracy unknown in China itself. I recall a very private meeting with the Chinese Foreign Minister in the modest suburban residence of his Ambassador in Brussels. To make the point, Howe suddenly rose from his armchair, seized a nearby vase, and, clutching it to his bosom, trotted across the room and handed it to a somewhat surprised Chinese Foreign Minister. It was Howe's way of conveying the notion of something precious, but fragile, that had to be protected in the transfer of power from Britain to China.

The problem for the Foreign Office was that Beijing could not be brought to agree to a system of suffrage broad enough to satisfy the democracy movement in Hong Kong. Worse, the movement had influential sympathisers in the British Parliament and press. One of its leaders, a highly articulate Hong Kong lawyer, Martin Lee, was a regular visitor to London, where he was able to drum up support. His ambition for Hong Kong's suffrage went way beyond what Beijing could bear, but his arguments convinced a number of British journalists who began to take against the way the Foreign Office was implementing the Joint Declaration. The dreaded word 'kowtow' resurfaced. I found, as Foreign Office spokesman, that I could make almost no headway against critics in the press. In effect I was arguing against democracy, an impossible wicket on which to bat.

The Foreign Office position was too complicated and difficult to summarise in a few sound-bites. The argument revolved around how many representatives to the Legislative Council would be directly elected by universal suffrage from geographical constituencies; how many by limited suffrage from 'Functional Constituencies', such as business and professional bodies; and the provisions for increasing progressively universal suffrage and direct elections. I may not at times have pressed the FO case with all the conviction that the job demanded. Functional Constituencies sounded very much to me like the 'organic democracy' of the Spanish dictator, General Franco, which had prevailed in Spain when I had been in the Madrid Embassy a decade previously. In any event, the Foreign Office sinologues grew impatient with the bad press we were getting and one even volunteered to brief the journalists himself; the clear inference being that he could do a better job than the Foreign Office News Department. He was put to the sword by a sceptical press.

The June 1989 killings in and around Tiananmen Square changed everything. The iconic video of one man in a white shirt and dark trousers, carrying a plastic shopping bag, barring the way to a column of tanks, seized the world's imagination. Hopes of a more open and democratic China were crushed. Nowhere was the shock more acutely felt than in Hong Kong. Over a million people took to the streets in an immense, silent march of solidarity with the Beijing students and their democratic aspirations. Events across the border prompted many to leave Hong Kong for good. In the period immediately following the massacre, over a thousand people were leaving each week. Confidence in Hong Kong's future dropped to a new low. The Hong Kong dollar fell like a stone. What price the survival of its autonomy now? Would the Joint Declaration be enough to protect its freedoms? How far would departing Britain be willing to stand up for Hong Kong's way of life?

Tiananmen shook the foundations of the Joint Declaration and the process of negotiation to which it had given rise. There were some who wanted Britain to walk away in protest. It provoked also a difficult passage in relations between Britain and Hong Kong itself.

The Tiananmen crisis threw up the tough question of Britain's responsibility to the residents of Hong Kong in an emergency. The Governor, Sir David Wilson, flew to London to request the right of residence in Britain for Hong Kong's 3.25 million British passport holders. Margaret Thatcher turned him down flat. Geoffrey Howe was booed by angry crowds on a 1989 visit to the colony. Thatcher later agreed to a more modest proposal that would give full British passports to 50,000 Hong Kong households, carefully selected from the business and economic sectors. This, of course, had nothing to do with any moral obligation and everything to do with limiting immigration into Britain and encouraging the top business talent not to desert Hong Kong. The security of a British passport helped restore confidence somewhat, but many left Hong Kong for Canada, Australia and the US, never to return. It was a warning to London – and Beijing – of what could happen if the Joint Declaration were terminally derailed.

Percy Cradock reflected coolly on the implications of the Tiananmen Square killings:

We could have kicked over the table and walked out and it would no doubt have made us feel very good at the time and the British press would no doubt have applauded loudly. But it would have been quite indefensible conduct given our responsibilities for Hong Kong. We were negotiating not for ourselves but for Hong Kong. And to them we stood in a position of trust. If we broke off negotiations [. . .] then the Chinese would have had a free hand. We would not have had to pay in Britain but the six million inhabitants of Hong Kong would have had to pay for our posturing.

Diplomacy so often looks like, and is, a choice of evils; of having to create a sliding moral scale. As a former foreign secretary, Douglas Hurd, recently said in an interview for the *Getting Our Way* television series:

The events in Tiananmen Square ... illustrate one of the problems of diplomacy. You're constantly having to talk to, make deals with, make concessions to, people, who in other ways are doing things which you thoroughly dislike and disapprove of.

In this instance, it is hard to discern the moral dilemma. If Britain were to take its responsibilities seriously to the Hong Kong people, then it was incumbent on the government to put in place safeguards against the Chinese doing in Hong Kong what they had done in Tiananmen Square. In other words, the worse the Chinese behaviour, the more imperative it was to stay in the negotiations and keep the 'through train' on track. This year's massive, peaceful and undisturbed demonstration in Hong Kong to mark the twentieth anniversary of the Tiananmen Square massacre was surely a vindication of Cradock's approach.

The Joint Declaration weathered the storm, though the turbulence caused difficulty over building a new, and much needed, airport. Governor Wilson sought to push the project; the Chinese authorities stalled. They were upset by both British and Hong Kong reactions to Tiananmen. According to the Hong Kong entrepreneur, Sir David Tang, whom I interviewed earlier this year for *Getting Our Way*, it took a meeting in 1991 between the new British Prime Minister, John Major, and his Chinese opposite number, Li Peng, to get the project back on track. Major had the doubtful accolade of being the first Western leader to meet Li Peng after Tiananmen. According to Tang, it took a 'secret' mission by Percy Cradock to Beijing beforehand to ensure that Major's visit would unblock the airport project. In his memoirs, Major is understandably defensive about his meeting with Li Peng, for which he took some criticism. Many felt that this was far too early for 'business as usual' with a regime that had blood on its hands. However, it was the price to be paid for a project that would be of inestimable benefit to Hong Kong. Successful diplomacy sometimes requires holding your nose.

The 'through train' gathered speed. There was agreement to a process of convergence by which China should have some control over running Hong Kong before 1997. Many objected, but Cradock thought that this would smooth the transition to the benefit of Hong Kong. In 1990 there was a breakthrough, with agreement on an increase in the number of directly elected representatives to the Legislative Council. In 1991 a modest 18 out of 60 seats would be directly elected, rising at each election to 30 seats – half of the legislature – by 2003. To ease passage through the 1997 watershed, it was agreed also that the legislature elected in 1995 would sit through the handover to form the first legislature of the new system.

John Major, who had replaced Margaret Thatcher as Prime Minister after her removal by an internal Conservative Party coup in 1990, decided to send an old political friend, Chris Patten, to replace David Wilson. Patten would be Hong Kong's last governor. He had masterminded Major's unexpected election victory over Neil Kinnock in 1992, but in the process had lost his own seat in Bath to the Liberal candidate. Patten was a Tory heavyweight who could have aspired to the leadership of the Conservative Party. According to Major's memoirs, he offered Patten various jobs including the governorship of Hong Kong. Patten took the governorship. In 1994, when I was John Major's press secretary and his government was in serious political difficulty, there was much talk in No. 10 of bringing back Chris Patten to help Major in London. I do not know whether the offer was ever made and subsequently refused.

Major tells us in his memoirs that he chose Patten,

knowing him well enough to realise he would want to entrench the maximum amount of democracy in the territory before it returned to Chinese sovereignty.

That is exactly what Patten sought to do. Major acknowledges that he was well aware of warnings from 'old China hands' and others that he should be careful not to alienate China.

Chris Patten was one of the very few Hong Kong governors not to have come from the civil service or Foreign Office. The last political appointee had been in the nineteenth century. Unsurprisingly, the leader of the great Foreign Office clan of sinologues, Percy Cradock, advised against Patten's appointment. A politician would, he said, have less understanding of the situation. He would be keen to make his own mark and 'strike out in new ways'. Cradock feared that years of careful and delicate negotiation would go for nothing, and that a complex, sophisticated, yet fragile relationship of near-trust with China would be smashed.

There is a perennial debate about the respective merits of politicians and professional diplomats as ambassadors and envoys. One argument can be dismissed straight away: that diplomacy is an arcane craft, requiring rare skills, accessible only to the few who have steeped themselves for years in its mysteries. It is nothing of the kind. Diplomacy may not be everyone's natural habitat; and that includes a fair number of professional diplomats. In the Washington Embassy, I had staff from all over Whitehall. Those from the Foreign Office were a small minority. The latter were not intrinsically superior in engaging and negotiating with the Americans. (One of the best diplomats on my staff was a civil servant from the old Ministry of Aviation.) What should distinguish a professional diplomat from other civil servants and politicians is an insatiable curiosity about abroad; an abiding interest in foreign policy; a willingness to serve at least half a working life outside the UK; and a profound knowledge and understanding of certain foreign countries. Domestic politicians, by definition, do not fit all those categories, but this need not disqualify them from top diplomatic posts. Provided they are able to learn fast, and are backed by a good and expert staff, there is no reason, all other things being equal, for them not to do a good job. Most American ambassadors are political appointees, because the US has a different political spoils system from us. Many prove mediocre or even disastrous; but many succeed, bringing a fresh approach to the job and a keen awareness of the domestic political consequences of a course of action abroad. You might, of course, say the same thing about professional ambassadors. The real problem with the American system is that, if you make political appointments a near-universal practice and block off the top jobs to the career diplomats, you risk a demoralised professional service, which is unable to attract recruits of the highest calibre. For this reason alone, it is not to be recommended for Britain. Used sparingly, however, there can be a time and a place for political appointments.

The governorship of Hong Kong in 1992 transcended by far the conventional run of diplomatic posts. It always had. The old Colonial Service had been as much, if not more, about administration as diplomacy, but the distinction had evaporated when it was absorbed into the Foreign and Commonwealth Office in the 1960s. With only five years remaining before the handover, the Hong Kong governorship still demanded a talent for administration and diplomacy – and much more besides. The job had become highly sensitive politically, with its tentacles reaching far back into Westminster and the British media. The government had a choice: either a professional diplomat with sensitive political antennae; or a politician, who could administer and do the diplomacy. In principle, it was six of one and half a dozen of the other. John Major went for a politician whom he knew and trusted. But, though I have no evidence to support the contention, I suspect that Chris Patten gave him a wilder ride than he had expected or wanted.

For most in Britain and many in Hong Kong, Patten was the perfect post-Tiananmen governor. The events of 1989 had wrought a sea-change in attitudes. The careful, successful diplomacy of Percy and the sinologues, strongly backed by Geoffrey Howe, now began to look a little tawdry – too deferential to Beijing by half. Once again, the rank odour of kowtow was in the air and Lord Macartney was fidgeting in his grave. The time had come to stand up for the people of Hong Kong against the mainland communists. Democracy would be the weapon of choice. Too bad if this meant confrontation with China, opined large swathes of British parliamentary and press opinion. Meanwhile, the professionals of King Charles Street, aghast, feared that a more confrontational policy, far from being a guarantee of democratic freedoms after 1997, would simply derail the 'through train'.

Patten wasted no time. In his inaugural speech to the Legislative Council (Legco) he set out his stall for democratic reform:

I owe it to the community to make my own position plain. I have spent my entire career engaged in the political system based on representative democracy. It would be surprising if that had not marked me. It has! My goal is simply this: to safeguard Hong Kong's way of life. [...] So the pace of democratisation in Hong Kong is, we all know, necessarily constrained. But it is constrained, not stopped dead in its tracks. [...] Standing still is not an available option.

Patten called for reforms tantamount to universal adult suffrage for the so-called functional constituencies.

This put the cat among the pigeons. Many in Hong Kong were overjoyed. At last they had a governor who would stand up for their democratic rights. Others, mindful of, or sympathetic to, Beijing's concerns and likely reaction, were alarmed. They were right to be. The response in Beijing was one of vituperative fury. The Chinese were enraged as much by the manner of Patten's proposals as by their content. In a single speech he had overturned the custom and practice of a decade's negotiation. It had come without warning. Patten had put his proposals to Hong Kong before consulting China first. The Chinese were accustomed to confidential discussion in advance of any initiative; and, if need be, a veto. They saw Patten's speech as a plain breach of the Joint Declaration. The old demons returned like Dracula emerging from the coffin. It was the devious British up to their treacherous tricks again. Caricature confronted caricature. It was kowtow versus the gunboat.

Patten was unrepentant. He was, he said, working entirely within the terms of the Joint Declaration. It was unthinkable to debate Hong Kong's democratic future behind the backs of its citizens. The Chinese responded with an astonishingly low level of personal abuse, calling Patten variously a 'strutting prostitute', 'serpent', 'tango dancer' and 'whore of the East'. More seriously, they made plain that any reforms introduced unilaterally by Patten would be scrapped after 1997. The 'through train' looked to be in trouble. At worst it was about to come flying off the rails; at best it would be shunted into the sidings.

The philosophical and political gulf was vast, not only between Patten and the Chinese, but between Patten and Cradock. Patten thought convergence – an agreed, negotiated way of doing things – to be a fallacy. Since China was always going to do what it liked after 1997, it was not Britain's job to second-guess it and make concessions accordingly. As Patten put it:

Once China had a foot in the door, there was to be no closing it. Britain lost authority, moral and political; it lost the initiative; it placed itself in the position in which it was subsequently obliged to give a sort of tacit blessing to the plans for the post-1997 arrangements produced by China (the so-called Basic Law) even when they had a distinctly questionable relationship to the premises given in the Joint Declaration. From that moment on, Britain was on a slippery slope. For the next dozen years, all one could hear diplomatically was the squeak and squelch of British boots trying to find a footing in the mud.

The idea behind Patten's reforms was to give resilience and vitality to Hong Kong's democratic system, the better to withstand Chinese pressure after 1997. A smooth transition was desirable; but not at the expense of maximising democracy for the final years of British rule. After his first, fruitless visit to Beijing as Governor, he put it like this:

What is the sense in me making accommodations – dishonourable accommodations – now on the assumption that the establishment in Peking is going to remain exactly the same until 1997? What would I look like then? I'd be an ornament – not a very attractive ornament – for most of my time here. And it would all look like a very dishonourable way for Britain to end an important story.

There were plenty who disagreed with this approach, among them Percy Cradock, Patten's most trenchant critic. Cradock declared that he was not prepared to 'watch in respectful silence while the Governor takes Hong Kong over the edge'. Cradock even flew to the territory to voice his criticisms of Patten in public. Their disagreement developed into a feud, which endures to this day.

In Cradock's view, Patten was reckless. Reform was illusory without Chinese support. A row with China would inflict lasting damage on Hong Kong. He saw Patten as a vain politician, searching for personal glory at the expense of the people of Hong Kong. They, not he, would be the ones to suffer if things went wrong after the last Governor's departure. Cradock saw also in Patten's approach a new version of an old arrogance towards China:

The gunboat diplomacy was very present in the Chinese minds. On the British side I suppose you could say also that some ghosts walked. Mr Patten's approach of pressing on with what he wanted and disregarding what the Chinese wanted, had a whiff of the old style, unfortunately it was tried at a time when we were no longer the stronger party.

Patten, in response, accused Cradock of the worst diplomatic sin of all: going native. He would sacrifice democracy in Hong Kong for the sake of good relations with China:

I did feel perhaps more strongly than Sir Percy thought was seemly that I had responsibilities to do what Parliament told would be done, and that I had responsibilities to behave as well for the people of Hong Kong as I could. My principal responsibilities weren't to go on having a good relationship with my distinguished Chinese opposite numbers to whom I could speak Mandarin.

Patten enjoyed wide support and popularity in Hong Kong for his stand. But the acclaim was not universal. There was a strong pro-Beijing constituency, just as there is today. A group of Hong Kong's most powerful business leaders attacked Patten's reforms. A row with China, they said, would be bad for business; and they understood China far better than he did. The notion of Hong Kong as the golden goose was out of date now that Napoleon's prediction for China had come true: 'When China wakes, she will shake the world.' China was no longer reliant on Hong Kong's economy; Hong Kong needed China more than the latter needed Hong Kong.

These concerns were shared by many British businessmen, who feared that Patten's row with the Chinese would damage trade. In 1994 the Chinese threatened to discriminate against British imports, which led to a stern warning from the European Commission. But I got a different take from Sir David Tang. He argued that, during Patten's governorship, Hong Kong had enjoyed five years of uninterrupted economic growth:

Can anybody with a modicum of common sense believe that China, wishing to trade with Britain over things that they wanted, or to sell things to Britain, that they would actually not do so because of the inconsequential governorship of a lowly minister – and that was the rank that Governor Patten held in the Chinese eyes – in a faraway dot in the Chinese empire, that gave no trouble to China whatsoever? I don't think so.

Or as Patten himself put it:

There were those who thought that the only way you could do business with China was by doing whatever China wanted politically. It's drivel. It isn't true, it never has been true. You can't blame the Chinese for not gainsaying the proposition because it's done them quite a lot of good down the years! But if you actually take the trouble to look at patterns of investment and exports and set them against whether or not you're agreeing with China on everything, there's no relationship between the two. The Chinese do business on the same basis as everybody else. They buy what they need at the best price they can get.

After the 1997 handover, China duly abolished Patten's reforms and disbanded the Legislative Council for a year. But, in 1998, the Chinese took the 'through train' out of its siding and let it resume its slow journey to a democratic destination. In the 2008 elections for the sixty seats of the Legislative Council, half were contested in geographical constituencies by universal suffrage, half in functional constituencies by a more limited suffrage. The pro-democracy parties won a clear majority of the popular vote; but, because of the peculiarities of the voting system, they won fewer seats than the pro-Beijing parties. In Beijing, the Standing Committee of the People's National Congress promised universal suffrage by 2017.

Today, Percy Cradock is in retirement; Chris Patten has gone to the House of Lords and is Chancellor of Oxford University; and Martin Lee has left front-line Hong Kong politics to a new generation. Much of the heat has gone out of the democracy debate in Hong Kong. Yet, it is still too soon for history to render a final verdict on the matter of Hong Kong's return to Chinese sovereignty, though there are a number of conclusions to be drawn in the interim. The Joint Declaration was a significant achievement for British diplomacy. The supreme challenge for a diplomat is to have to negotiate from a position of weakness. Cradock and his team rose admirably to the challenge, showing how, like a shanty town tapping illicitly into the power supply, a clever diplomat can syphon off some of the other side's strength and turn it to the benefit of his own position. It is hard to conceive of the possibility that he could have got more out of the Chinese from 1982 to 1984.

The charge of 'going native' does not really stick. The point at which profound and expert knowledge of a country tips into undue sympathy to the detriment of the British interest is not always easy to identify. But, Cradock, whom I barely knew until I interviewed him earlier this year, was by reputation hardly a sentimentalist. He came from that dry, rigorous, old school of public service that looks askance at emotion and would not have wept in public under any circumstances. He is, I think, outraged by the notion that he had anything but the British interest at the forefront of his concerns.

But after the signing of the Joint Declaration, in the period 1984–88, when I was Geoffrey Howe's press secretary, I could never shake off the feeling that we were being too cautious in our dealings with Beijing in the Sino-British Liaison Group – that we could have pushed harder and got a little more on the democracy issue, that Howe's china vase would have been strong enough to take the pressure. Whether we could have ever bridged the gap between Beijing and Martin Lee and his pro-democracy companions is another matter.

By the time Chris Patten became Governor in 1992 I had moved on to the embassy in Washington. Hong Kong never loomed large again in my professional life, even when I was John Major's press secretary in 1994–96. Despite the turbulence of the Patten governorship, Hong Kong had, compared with the 1980s, slipped down the order of things. Observing from afar, I had a lot of sympathy for Patten. I recalled how uncomfortable it had been to argue against democracy with journalists. But, diplomacy, like politics, is the art of the possible. What Chris Patten wanted was not possible because the Chinese did not want it – and there was nothing we could do about it. His outspokenness for democratic values was in many ways admirable, but it forfeited China's trust. His epitaph must be, to paraphrase the French general's comment on the Charge of the Light Brigade: *C'est magnifique, mais ce n'est pas la diplomatie.*

Nevertheless, Chris Patten's governorship cannot be written off as a noble, but futile, gesture. More than any of his predecessors, he tapped into a rich, indigenous seam of yearning for democracy in Hong Kong that became plain for all to see. The Chinese heaped obloquy and insults on Patten's head, but he did them a service. He showed that all the talk of democracy in Hong Kong was not some devilish plot cooked up by the treacherous British. It was the real thing.

Kowtow versus gunboat politics: Cradock and Patten, in their exchange of polite, very British, stiletto thrusts, also caricatured each other. Cradock was no obsequious groveller to the Chinese; Patten no rash adventurer, ready to sacrifice the people of Hong Kong on the altar of a politician's vanity.

Trade and investment boom between Britain and China. A vast crowd holds a peaceful vigil on the twentieth anniversary of the Tiananmen Square massacre. It is a legacy to be proud of; and on the British side it is shared by Percy and Chris.

PART III
VALUES

Values + interests = foreign policy. The simplicity of the equation is matched by the difficulty of putting it into practice. It begs a thousand questions. Whose values, which interests? What is the link between values and interests? Should values drive national interest? Or is it the other way round, with values rationalising a nation's *realpolitik*? Is it enough for us to say that, because Britain is a mature democracy, with the government answerable to Parliament and the people, our foreign policy is automatically imbued by democratic principles of universal value? Or, as has been the vogue over the last generation, do we need an extra ingredient: an explicit ethical or human rights policy, against which the justice of our actions abroad can be measured?

These questions have tied Britain's politicians and diplomats in knots. In 1977, when I was working in the Planning Staff of the Foreign Office, we had a unit that wrote speeches for the Foreign Secretary. That unit was me. I had started writing for 'Sunny' Jim Callaghan. When he became Prime Minister after Harold Wilson's sudden resignation, I was inherited by Anthony Crosland, a grand figure in the Labour Party. Just as I was getting used to his oratorical style, he died unexpectedly. Callaghan replaced him with David Owen, now Lord Owen, who at thirty-eight became one of Britain's youngest Foreign Secretaries. Owen brought a brisk, abrasive, restless energy to the Foreign Office, allied to a sharp intelligence. Senior mandarins' feathers went flying. Owen was determined to put his stamp on the FO. He looked across the Atlantic and saw how President Jimmy Carter was trying to make human rights an integral part of American foreign policy. Owen decided to do the same.

The Planning Staff was entrusted with the task of devising a formula for systematically integrating human rights into Britain's foreign policy. We created a grid. Every independent nation in the world was on it. Against a series of benchmarks like freedom of the press and an independent judiciary, each nation was given a mark.

Then, add up the numbers and you could give each country a numerical value. This in turn would set an objective standard against which decisions on, say, arms sales or aid could be taken. We used Britain as the gold standard, putting ourselves at the top of the human rights league. We took some pleasure at marking the French relatively low. Uganda under Idi Amin and the then Kampuchea under Pol Pot were at the bottom.

From day one the grid did not work. Marking governments out of 10 or whatever might tell you something useful about their human rights record. What it could not tell you was the relative weight to give the mark against competing strategic, political and economic interests. Arms sales to a Third World despot? Looks like an open-and-shut case. But what if the contract will guarantee several thousand jobs in a politically sensitive constituency? To whom does the government owe the higher duty – to the suffering peasants of wherever or to an important chunk of the British electorate? Nine times out of ten the domestic argument will prevail. And who is to say this is wrong? Isn't the government's first duty to those who put them in power?

The case in 2009 of the release from gaol on compassionate grounds of the Libyan Al-Megrahi, sentenced to a lengthy prison term for blowing up an American airliner over Scotland, gave rise to even greater complexity. It pitted one morality against another: whether the quality of Scottish mercy should be strained by the enormity of the crime. It also set *realpolitik* against *realpolitik*: whether the benefits of a closer relationship with Libya outweighed the first public rebuke from an American president to a British prime minister since the Suez crisis of 1956. There was a case to be made for repatriating Al-Megrahi. But the manner in which his release was executed and explained made the British government look dishonest and dishonourable. The result was to damage Britain's reputation and interests.

These dilemmas have been with us in sharp relief ever since the irruption of public opinion and the press into the political arena of the nineteenth century. In the three stories that follow, British diplomats find themselves caught in the crossfire between *realpolitik* and values, the latter articulated by increasingly vocal sections of the public and the media. In the first two, *realpolitik* prevails; but in the process Sir Henry Elliott in nineteenth century Istanbul and Sir Robert Vansittart in London between the two World Wars are destroyed professionally. In the third, in the Balkan crisis of the 1990s, diplomacy flails uselessly until values and interests come into alignment; and a foreign policy worthy of the name kicks into action.

7

THE GRAND TURK AND THE RUSSIAN BEAR:
Disraeli, Gladstone and the Eastern Question

Mosques are plenty, churches are plenty, graveyards are plenty, but morals and whiskey are scarce. The Koran does not permit Mohammedans to drink. Their natural instincts do not permit them to be moral.

This was how Mark Twain, with acid-tinged irony, described the city of Constantinople after his visit in 1867. The Ottoman capital offered a cornucopia of delights for the Victorian traveller: exotic sights, sounds, and smells lay in wait around every corner, from sultans, harems, eunuchs, whirling dervishes, to throngs of men in outlandish headgear and costume, and slave girls sold from dark corners . . . There was no shortage of exquisite detail to fill the diaries of those kept awake at night by the howling of feral dog packs and the call to prayer from countless minarets.

As the once great Ottoman Empire fell into decay, an indelible caricature of 'the Turk' had taken hold of the British imagination. He was seen as corrupt, lazy, despotic and debauched: an offence to Victorian sensibilities. The Ottoman court had come to symbolise, not an ancient and sophisticated culture, but the exotic vice of the harem: '. . . in the European mind the *seraglio* of the Grand Turk in Istanbul became a locus of near mythic license and promiscuity.'[1] In his 1862 painting of the *Turkish Bath*, Ingres' voluptuous nudes were Victorian fantasy made flesh.

But, tied to the fate of the 'Grand Turk' were vital British interests in the Mediterranean, in the Levant, and even in India. For some ambitious nineteenth-century diplomats, 'Ambassador to the Sublime Porte'[2] was a more desirable destination than the Paris

Embassy; and certainly preferable to that barbarian outpost, Washington.

This Turkish delight of a posting fell to Sir Henry Elliot in 1867. It was a role that would require him not only to get to grips with a culture quite different from his own, but to keep the most watchful eye on his fellow diplomats. The European quarter of Pera in Istanbul was crowded with ornate embassies. Here, ambassadors of empires and nations engaged in ruthless competition for influence, advantage and prestige, as the Concert of Europe, established at the Congress of Vienna a half-century before, gave way to a new and brutal power politics.

Elliot conducted business from Pera House, an impressive Italianate structure, which is today Britain's Consulate-General. It was a place already accustomed to being at the centre of things. One of Elliot's predecessors, Stratford Canning, had been an ambassador of unusual influence in the Constantinople of the 1840s and 50s. It was said that the Crimean War, in which Britain and France allied to thwart Russian designs on Turkey, was fought from the parlour of Pera House.

Elliot was to be involved in a drama of a different type. It would not be diplomatic machination that was to give him the greatest grief, but an explosion of hostility among the British public towards the Turks. This would not only engulf Elliot personally, it would confront his masters in London with a wholly new kind of diplomatic puzzle: how to reconcile the conflicting demands of a strident public opinion with the unsentimental needs of British foreign policy. It is a puzzle unresolved to this day.

Constantinople – or Istanbul, as it is now known – has always been at the junction of things. For a thousand years it was the Christian capital of the East Roman, or Byzantine, Empire, until in 1453 it fell to the armies of the Ottoman Turks. The symbolic meeting place of Islam and Christianity, it is the only city in the world to sit athwart two continents, Europe and Asia. The Turks themselves have deep roots both in Asia Minor and Europe (at one time Turkish rule extended as far as Vienna, and the Balkans today still bear a distinct Islamic and Turkish footprint from the long years when large tracts of southern Europe lay under Ottoman rule).

The Asian and European dualism in Turkey's outlook persists to this day. When I was a teenager, my parents lived in Ankara, modern Turkey's capital, where my step-father, an officer in the Royal Air Force, had been posted to something called CENTO, the Central Treaty Organisation. This defunct and long-forgotten organisation was intended as the Asian equivalent of NATO, the North Atlantic Treaty Organisation, still alive today. Turkey was a leading member of both CENTO and NATO. Today, Turkey competes in UEFA's European Football Championship and in the Eurovision Song Contest, competitions which may at times be considered the extension of war by other means.

Turkey's application for membership of the European Union has proved controversial among many EU members, precisely because of the ambivalence of the Turkish pedigree. In 1997, the then German Chancellor, Helmut Kohl, made a speech to a convention of Christian Democrat parties in which he insisted that the EU must remain a Christian organisation. This was a none-too-subtle plea for Turkish membership to be rejected, for fear of an influx into Europe of millions more Turks than the two million or so who had already settled in Germany. I was Ambassador in Bonn at the time. The British government's policy, then as now, was to support Turkish membership of the EU (without, it has to be said, having thought through properly the consequences for immigration policy). I went to see one of Kohl's senior colleagues, Wolfgang Schäuble, to establish more clearly Germany's policy towards Turkey. This provoked, from a normally calm and measured man, a tirade about German schools being swamped by the children of Turkish immigrants.

It is this Euro-Asian dichotomy which, over history, has made Turkey variously important, influential and vulnerable. In the latter half of the nineteenth century it was simultaneously important and vulnerable. Constantinople itself was a city of self-evident strategic importance, commanding the Bosphorus Straits, the only passage connecting the Black Sea and the Mediterranean, and intersected by the Golden Horn, a natural and easily fortified harbour. No wonder the city had been long the envy of predatory neighbours. Over the centuries, it had withstood wave after wave of attack and siege from the likes of Germanic barbarians, Arabs, Crusaders, Russians and Turks. The first responsibility of Byzantine emperors had long been to keep the city's massive defensive walls in good repair.

When Constantinople fell finally in 1453 to a Turkish dynasty from the Anatolian plateau, it was the culmination of decades of encroachment on the territory and authority of the old Eastern Empire. Under Turkish, or Ottoman, control, Constantinople grew rapidly in wealth and influence. It became again not only one of the great trading cities of the world but a military and political capital of the first order. From this strategic seat, the Islamic Ottoman Empire reached out to control great swathes of territory. At its peak, in the reign of Süleyman the Magnificent in the middle of the sixteenth century, the Empire stretched from Baghdad in the east to Algiers in the west; along the entire southern littoral of the Mediterranean, to include today's modern Egypt; north through the Balkans to the southern borders of Russia, Poland and Austria – where Ottoman ambitions finally met their match. Like all imperial expansions and later retreats, the Ottomans left behind territorial and ethnic landmines which would detonate centuries later. The Turkish occupation of the Balkans, including in particular the defeat of the Serbs at the battle of Kosovo in 1389, complicated still further what was already a complex pattern of shifting ethnic and religious rivalries that plague the region to this day.

By the time that Henry Elliot presented his credentials at the Sublime Porte, the once great Empire had long been in decline. The high tide had reached as far as the gates of Vienna, where the Sultan's 1683 defeat at the hands of John Sobieski, King of Poland and Grand Duke of Lithuania, marked the start of a slow, uneven, but inexorable decline. By the mid-nineteenth century, Tsar Nicholas I could justifiably characterise the Empire as the 'Sick Old Man of Europe', a title which remains in common currency to this day to describe the continent's economic invalids. Britain itself was the unhappy holder of the title in the 1970s; and there are those who fear that we will hold it again before too long.

The Ottoman sickness was of a different nature. The Empire was rife with corruption and incompetence. The once feared army was now technologically inferior to those of the West. The janissary system – an elite formation of infantry owing personal allegiance to the Sultan – which had once brought such discipline and martial skill to the Ottoman armies, had collapsed in corruption and mutiny until, in the curiously named 'Auspicious Incident' of 1826, Sultan Mahmud II had been forced to move against the janissaries and have them bloodily disbanded.

Turkey's control over its multi-ethnic and multi-religious domain was crumbling. In 1821, the Greeks rose in rebellion against the Ottomans. Many in Britain were attracted to the Greek cause. The poet Byron gave his life for it; he is to be found today in the Greek pantheon of national heroes. Ottoman decay was such that it acquired a title: the Eastern Question. It came to dominate European foreign policy in the later nineteenth century. There were fears that, were the Ottoman Empire to disintegrate, Europe would succumb to a general war over the division of the Turkish spoils. As Metternich put it: 'The complications which may ensue in the East defy all calculation.' Among the predators circling the moribund 'Sick Man', none was greater nor more menacing than the Russian Bear, licking its chops as it looked southwards towards Constantinople.

The Turks and the Russians were old enemies, much like the British and the French. After Constantinople's fall, they had become rivals for the title of successor to the Eastern Roman Empire. They had gone to war four times in the eighteenth century, and would do so four times more in the nineteenth. The spoils of war had turned the Russians into a Black Sea power. Now the old Russo-Turkish rivalry had been given a new twist by Russia's evolution in the nineteenth century into an aggressive, expanding empire. In the twenty-five years preceding Elliot's arrival in Constantinople, Russia's borders had pushed forward 700 miles to the south, towards Turkey, and 900 miles to the south-east, into Central Asia. By the 1870s, Russian armies were close to the Afghan frontier. The Foreign Office was alarmed.

For much of the nineteenth century Russia was the bogeyman for Britain. (Germany, as a threat to national security, was a late arrival on the scene.) When Elliot took up post in Constantinople, Britain's over-riding strategic interest was to keep the Russian Black Sea fleet out of the Mediterranean; and to counter any Russian threat to India, the famous jewel in Britain's imperial crown. Throughout the nineteenth century, Britain and Russia engaged in a struggle for influence and advantage over what is today Iran,

Afghanistan and Central Asia. This became known, thanks to Rudyard Kipling's hugely popular novel, *Kim*, as the 'Great Game'. In Britain, we were shocked and bemused in June 2009 to have been picked out by the Iranian regime for having engineered popular protests against President Ahmedinejad's re-election. Set in its historical context, it is easier to understand why the Iranians should resort to this mendacious, and apparently daft, accusation. In the eyes of many Iranians, Britain had meddled in their affairs for the better part of two centuries, as we made our moves in the Great Game.[3]

Today there is debate among historians as to whether the Russians ever entertained serious designs on India. But there can be no question that the Russian empire was expanding into Central Asia and that Russian explorers, adventurers and agents turned up fairly regularly in Afghanistan and the northern approaches to British India. Twice we sent armies into Afghanistan to try to prop up regimes friendly to us. Twice we had to retire with a bloody nose. When in 1876, two years before the second military intervention in Afghanistan, Britain's Prime Minister, Benjamin Disraeli, conferred on a delighted Queen Victoria the title Empress of India, this was in part a blocking move against the Russian Tsar. It was not until the 1880s that agreement was reached on the demarcation of the Russo-Afghan border; and Afghanistan became in effect a buffer state between Russia and British India.

At one extreme, the British fear was to see a Russian army marching down the Khyber Pass into India; at the other, it was the prospect of Russian warships sailing through the Bosphorus into the Mediterranean and beyond. As Disraeli put it, Constantinople was the 'Key to India'. And sea power was *the* strategic weapon. The opening of the Suez Canal through Egypt in 1869 had vastly increased the strategic significance of the Eastern Mediterranean, creating not only the most important trade route in the world but also a shortcut to India. By 1875, Britain had bought Egypt's share in the Suez Canal, while Egypt itself, despite being formally under Ottoman suzerainty, was fast becoming a British protectorate in all but name. Britain, the world's greatest naval power and trading nation, would do whatever it took to protect its vital interests from encroachment by other powers, above all Russia.

To counter Russian ambitions, it had become a governing principle of British foreign policy to support the ailing Ottoman Empire. The national interest at stake was judged so important that, only forty years after the Napoleonic Wars, Britain had taken up arms with its ancient French enemy against Russia in the Crimean War of 1853–56. The British, meanwhile, set out to establish a special relationship with the Sublime Porte. Stratford Canning, Britain's Ambassador, made the point very publicly at Pera House when, at a grand reception shortly after the war in the Crimea, he descended the stairs to the ballroom, arm in arm with the Sultan.[4] The reality matched the symbolism. Britain became commercially dominant in the Ottoman Empire. British exports rose in value from £1.4 million in 1829 to £12 million in 1848, and continued to rise.

This was the bubbling diplomatic pot into which Elliot was pitched on his arrival. The international tensions arising from the Eastern Question gripped Constantinople's diplomatic community in claustrophobic microcosm. In particular, Elliot found himself confronted by a redoubtable opponent in Count Nikolai Pavlovich Ignatyev, the Russian Ambassador to the Sublime Porte. Ignatyev was cunning, agile and bold. He had had adventures aplenty and narrow escapes in Central Asia, where he had sought to build Russian influence. A particularly nimble piece of diplomacy had led to his acquiring Outer Manchuria from the Chinese Emperor. His *forte* as ambassador was to gain influence at the Sultan's court, while at the same time encouraging Christian Slav insurgencies against Ottoman rule, especially in Bulgaria. Ignatyev was to bequeath an unusual legacy: he became something of a Bulgarian national hero; he is the great-grandfather of today's leader of the Canadian Liberal Party (Michael Ignatieff, better known in Britain as intellectual, journalist, and television presenter); and he features as the villain in a couple of George Macdonald Fraser's *Flashman* novels about the Great Game.[5]

Elliot, for his part, seems to have been a thoroughly competent and conventional British diplomat, who had not, as the French say about those who plod a little, invented gunpowder. He was praised, perhaps faintly, by Lord Granville, the Foreign Secretary, for his 'quiet firmness' in dealing with the formidable double challenge of Ignatyev's intrigues and the capricious behaviour of the Ottoman court. As was the norm with senior diplomats in the nineteenth century, Elliot was well connected: his father was the Earl of Minto, and the former prime minister Lord Russell was his brother-in-law. He had enjoyed a varied and interesting career, serving on Palmerston's staff, and undertaking sensitive diplomatic assignments in Greece and Italy as each struggled towards independence. But all that was a mere prelude to representing Britain to the Ottoman Empire.

Elliot in Constantinople was to become trapped in an intolerable conundrum. In its support for the Turks, Britain was obeying the first law of diplomacy: that the nation's security must at all costs be safeguarded. Russia was a threat to our security; Russia must be thwarted. But in shoring up the Ottomans, Britain was placing itself on the wrong side of history. Nationalism and liberalism were on the march. Even in autocratic Russia, hardly a model of enlightenment, Tsar Alexander II had abolished serfdom and gone on to make a number of significant reforms. Meanwhile, in Britain, a politically conscious public opinion was on the rise. The great Reform Acts of 1832 and 1867 (the year of Elliot's arrival in Constantinople) had enormously enlarged the franchise. Newspapers proliferated to feed the appetites of the newly literate and enfranchised: *The Times, Telegraph* and (*Manchester*) *Guardian* were all in existence in Elliot's time. The invention of the electric telegraph was revolutionising international communications. Newspapers started to appoint foreign correspondents. It had never been easier to arouse the passions of the public at events abroad.

It was not, in this new world, an obvious vote-winner to be the strategic ally of a despotic, Islamic empire that was increasingly engaged in trying to suppress revolts by its Christian subjects. Elliot had, for instance, arrived in Constantinople when Crete was in revolt for the umpteenth time against the Ottomans. Unlike previous such rebellions, this was the first to be reported widely by telegraph. European opinion had been shocked to learn of the death of hundreds of Cretan women and children under siege by the Turks at the Arkadi monastery. A great collision was in the making between the harsh realities of international power politics and a public opinion that took a different view of how Britain should be getting its way. Poor Elliot was to be consumed in the conflagration that followed.

Those who were neither Turkish nor Muslim had long lived under Ottoman rule in reasonable harmony with their Turkish neighbours. They enjoyed freedom of worship and relative autonomy over ecclesiastical and community affairs. But, they did not live as equals. Christians and Jews paid extra, sometimes punitive, taxes. After the Napoleonic Wars, a turbulent restlessness against Turkish rule began to spread. When Greece gained independence in 1829, it set an example to other Christian communities, such as Crete. As so often happens, a period of reform and modernisation under Sultan Mahmud II in the middle of the century – which promised equality before the law for all – only stimulated the appetite to break free. From the Danube down through the Balkans, unrest spread through the 1860s and 70s. By 1875, the turmoil had infected what is now Serbia, Romania, Montenegro, Bosnia, Herzegovina – and Bulgaria.

The Austro-Hungarian and Russian Empires fished competitively in these troubled waters. The Russians did so in the name of Slav and Christian Orthodox solidarity; or as Dostoevsky put it in 1877: '... to serve Christ and to liberate the oppressed brethren ...' Yet, their motives were anything but altruistic. This was a Russian power-play to secure advantage over the Turks and Austrians. In the eye of Moscow, the southern Slavs were Russia's *chasse gardée*. Not much has changed in Russian attitudes today. In the 1860s and 70s, this perversely put the autocratic Russian Empire on the side of history, forcing the Foreign Office and Elliot himself on the defensive. When Elliot accused Ignatyev of posting Russian agents around the Ottoman Empire, the latter replied that this was hardly necessary: 'wherever there is a Christian, he is ready to bring his complaint to our notice. They are all spies for Russia.'

In 1876, a threat emerged in Continental Europe to Britain's strategic interest in Turkey. Russia, Germany and Austria, in a coalition called the *Dreikaiserbund* or Three Emperors' League, met to discuss the Balkan crisis. The League was a contrivance of the German Chancellor, Count Bismarck, to contain the dangerous rivalry of the Austro-Hungarian and Russian Empires in a manner which did not force Germany to have to choose between them. In

May they drew up the Berlin Memorandum, which issued a stern warning to Turkey against further repression. Disraeli, the British Prime Minister, reacted in alarm. The Three Emperors had not deigned to consult Britain on a matter of vital national interest. Disraeli complained to the Russian Ambassador that 'England has been treated as though we were Montenegro or Bosnia'. The Memorandum could be read as a manifesto for the dismantling of the Ottoman Empire. It fanned Disraeli's Russophobia. Only the year before a Russian army had appeared close to the Afghan frontier. In his view, the *Dreikaiserbund* was itself a threat to the balance of power in Europe, for all that Bismarck had put it together to balance rivalries that might otherwise tip into war.

With Britain's encouragement, Turkey rejected the Memorandum. In a classic show of strength and support for the Sultan, Disraeli sent a fleet to Beshika Bay, near the Dardanelles, assuring a somewhat alarmed Queen Victoria:

Your Majesty's fleet has not been ordered to the Mediterranean to protect Christians or Turks, but to uphold Your Majesty's Empire. Had Your Majesty sanctioned the Berlin Memorandum, Constantinople would at this moment have been garrisoned by Russia.

While the Great Powers argued, the Ottomans took action in Bulgaria. The most downtrodden of all of Turkey's European provinces, Bulgaria was poorly equipped and poorly situated for a successful rebellion. But, inspired by the actions of their Balkan brethren, and suffering from the depredations of Turkish irregulars and Ottoman tax collectors, the Bulgarians rose up, first in a failed attempt in September 1875, and then in fresh outbreaks at the end of April 1876 in the Rhodope mountains.

Tormented by these rebellions in the way that a bull is driven to fury by the matador's *banderillas*, the Ottoman government responded with exemplary brutality against the Bulgarians. Regular troops from Constantinople were joined by a massive force made up of irregular militia known as the *bashi-bozouks*, a nineteenth-century equivalent of the *janjaweed* irregulars used today by the Sudanese government to sow terror in Darfur. The *bashi-bozouks* had acquired their name from the Turkish for 'headless' or 'disorderly'. Notorious for their ferocity and lack of discipline, these militiamen were let loose on the general Bulgarian population, of whom only a tiny fraction had taken part in the insurrection. The result was a hideous atrocity. A precise figure for the dead was hard to establish, but the consensus is that around fifteen thousand men, women and children perished, with over 70 villages, 200 schools and 10 monasteries destroyed. Within a few days the rebellion had been crushed.

News of the massacres trickled back to Constantinople, with Robert College, an American school with a large proportion of Bulgarian students, first to get word. Members of the college called on Elliot, whom they regarded as a 'warm personal friend', asking him to use his close relations with the Ottoman government to rein in the violence.

Having established that the information was reliable (and having heard allegations from the Ottoman authorities of Bulgarian violence against Muslims), Elliot played the atrocities with a conventionally straight diplomatic bat. Though he would, of course, have been appalled at the news from Bulgaria, which was all too typical of south-eastern Europe's bloodstained history, his main concern was to see order restored as quickly as possible. He impressed on the Turks that 'no exertion should be spared' for assuring the 'immediate suppression' of the uprising. Elliot would have known better than most the reputation of the *bashi-bozouks*; and he later claimed to have advised the Porte against their deployment, but it seems his advice held little sway. Elliot then did what any ambassador of the day would have done: he lodged a strong protest with the Ottoman Grand Vizier and reported to headquarters in London. After that, so far as Elliot was concerned, and until London told him otherwise, it was business as usual. Nothing could have prepared him for the reaction back home.

Robert College had passed the news of the atrocities not only to Elliot, but to local correspondents of the London *Daily News* and *The Times*. At the same time as the British government was getting Elliot's report, the British people were reading the news from Bulgaria in the press. In some respects, the British public was getting more detail from the newspapers than the Foreign Office from their ambassador. Elliot claimed that his Vice-Consul in Adrianople had maliciously given information to a journalist which he had failed to pass to the embassy. A nightmare for an ambassador is to find that he is less well informed than a reporter. I remember hearing the damning words from a senior Foreign Office official about one ambassador: 'I don't bother to read his telegrams, because the *Economist* is so much better.'

In one of the earliest press reports, *The Times* described the predicament of Bulgarian women and children driven from their homes and caught in the fighting:

The Insurgents are supposed to muster about 20,000; but only about half of them may be reckoned as fighting men, the remainder merely consisting of women and children, whom either the fury of the Turks or the orders of the Insurgents have driven from their habitations. Of the scores of hundreds of killed or wounded in encounters, of which official bulletins give us frequent accounts, not a few belong to this helpless non-combatant class, falling in a quarrel in which they can take no part, falling both during and after the action. The Bashi-Bozouks are indiscriminating robbers, as well as cold-blooded murderers and their Christian adversaries are hardly any better.[5]

As time passed, the reports became more detailed and vivid, revealing the harrowing scale of the atrocities. Moral outrage swept the British public. People were not used to reading stories of atrocity in almost 'real time', still less when the crimes were committed by a regime that enjoyed British support. The cry went up: Not in my name!

In Constantinople, Elliot was shocked at the reaction. Years later he would express surprise that 'nothing occurring in a foreign country within my recollection ever caused in England a sensation at all to be compared with that produced by the Turkish excesses in Bulgaria'. As a professional diplomat, it was a phenomenon for which he was wholly unprepared. The interaction of the five 'P's – press, public, policy, politics and Parliament – was a novelty in the Victorian world. In domestic matters, politicians had quickly mastered the lesson that public opinion must now be considered an objective factor in political calculation. In foreign policy, where the public was usually less engaged, the lesson was learnt more slowly. Over a century later, when I ran the Foreign Office press operation in the 1980s, there was a sense that international affairs were too important to be swayed by the whims of public opinion, mediated through the press. My staff and I found ourselves inhabiting a no-man's land between the upper levels of Foreign Office hierarchy and the media, regarded with perhaps more suspicion by our own colleagues than by journalists.

At the end of June, Disraeli faced his first questions in the House of Commons over the reports from Bulgaria. At first he denied the reports' accuracy, dismissing them as 'coffee house babble'. Eventually, however, he was forced to admit that there had been 'proceedings of an atrocious character in Bulgaria'. For one so instinctively skilful in his conduct of foreign policy, Disraeli found it difficult to tune in to the mood of an outraged public. With a mordant, tasteless wit, which today would have forced his resignation from office, he dismissed claims that 10,000 Bulgarians had been thrown in prison:

In fact, I doubt whether there is prison accommodation for so many, or that torture has been practised on a great scale among an oriental people who seldom, I believe, resort to torture, but generally terminate their connection with culprits in a more expeditious manner.

It did not take the politically supple Disraeli long to realise that he had badly misjudged the situation. He bowed to pressure; and took refuge in the politician's favourite strategem when in a tight spot – he commissioned an Official Report, no doubt hoping that this would be an end to the matter.

For the fact-finding in Bulgaria, Elliot appointed on instructions a junior diplomat, Walter Baring, the Embassy's Second Secretary. Baring knew no Bulgarian and had no interpreter. He would have to rely on the Turkish authorities for information. This did not have the look of a thorough and impartial investigation. Robert College sought to redress the balance by persuading the American Consul, Eugene Schuyler, to go to Bulgaria, accompanied by a number of interpreters. In the event, the two men arrived in the small Bulgarian town of Batak on the same day. No amount of official Turcophilia could disguise what Baring was forced to confront: thousands of terrified citizens had barricaded themselves in the church only to be slaughtered indiscriminately. The church where the slain had been shot, beheaded or burned alive was still standing. The bullet holes and scorched wood remain to this day.

Baring's report stated:

I visited this valley of the shadow of death on 31 July, more than two and a half months after the massacre, but still the stench was so overpowering that one could hardly force one's way into the churchyard.

In a private letter to Elliot, he went further:

The whole of the main street was a mass of human remains, but the most fearful spectacle was the church and its enceinte: here the corpses lay so thick that one could hardly avoid treading on them . . . Altogether I can hardly describe the horror of the scene.

Baring's and Schuyler's reports were in the end very similar, differing only in their respective estimate of the number killed: Baring reckoned 12,000 Bulgarians (and 163 Muslims) and Schuyler, 15,000.

Baring's report was published in September 1876, Schuyler's a couple of months later. Well before then, vivid accounts of the scenes in Batak had appeared in the press. Schuyler had been accompanied by an American journalist, Januarius MacGahan, whose reporting lit the fuse of public outrage in Britain, America and elsewhere. In Britain, a national movement began to build. Town-hall meetings filled with ordinary people expressing abhorrence at the atrocities and protesting vehemently against the government's pro-Turkish policy. Over the summer of 1876 there were some five hundred demonstrations around the country. Even staunch supporters of Turcophile policy began to express concern. Queen Victoria wrote to Disraeli: 'I cannot rest quiet without urging the prevention of further atrocities which Sir Henry Elliot apprehends possible henceforth.' The ardent Turcophile, Stratford Canning, now ennobled as Viscount Stratford de Redcliffe, was said to have exclaimed: 'Good God! I would rather see Russia in Constantinople than the subjugation of the Principalities by such means.'

Despite the furore, Disraeli held stubbornly to the belief that it was in Britain's interest to prevent the disintegration of Turkey. He was motivated not only by fear for Britain's position in the eastern Mediterranean, but the prospect that any division of Turkey's European empire between Russia and Austria would lead to a general European war over the League's third emperor, Wilhelm I of Germany, demanding territorial compensation at the expense of France. First, however, Disraeli needed to ride out the domestic storm of anti-Ottoman feeling. In September of 1876 this became immeasurably more difficult with the entry into the fray of his long-time political enemy, the Grand Old Man himself, William Ewart Gladstone. The twenty-year rivalry between the two men culminated in a head-to-head battle over the Bulgarian Atrocities in one of the great set-piece dramas of Victorian politics.

Benjamin Disraeli had led the Conservative administration since 1874, when the Liberal Party under Gladstone had been defeated in the general election. The two dominant political figures of the mid to late Victorian period, Disraeli and Gladstone were polar opposites in character and political beliefs. In the words of Henry Kissinger, 'Disraeli – meretricious, brilliant and mercurial; Gladstone – learned, pious and grave'.

Disraeli was one of the Queen's favourites. She could not abide Gladstone, who, she complained, addressed her like 'a public meeting'. Though he had gone into retirement after his general election defeat (announcing that he wished to have a break between politics and the grave), Gladstone was still active in public life. He had, for example, published a thunderous pamphlet, the nineteenth-century equivalent of a press release, against the Vatican decree promulgating Papal infallibility. The events in Bulgaria prompted Gladstone to issue – from his sickbed (where he'd been driven by a bout of lumbago) – a lengthy pamphlet entitled 'The Bulgarian Horrors and the Question of the East', in which he described the Turks as an 'anti-human specimen of humanity'. The pamphlet flew off the shelves, selling 40,000 copies in a week and 200,000 by the end of the month. It put Gladstone at the head of what he considered a national moral crusade against the government's policy. Once out of his sickbed, he was soon to be found on London's Blackheath, where for an hour in pouring rain he addressed a crowd of ten thousand on the iniquities of the Ottoman Empire.

Gladstone's argument was that, through an amoral and coldly calculating foreign policy, Britain had been left with Bulgarian blood on its hands. The national aspirations of the Bulgarians were, said Gladstone, entirely legitimate. Britain owed support to fellow Christians. The British public was right to be appalled. Now, it was the nation's moral duty to prevent further atrocities in the Balkans, and 'to redeem the honour of the British name'. The answer, he suggested, lay in European cooperation through the Concert of Europe. Gladstone was highly critical of Disraeli's rejection of the Berlin Memorandum. Britain could no longer remain in 'splendid isolation'. It should join the *Dreikaiserbund* in putting pressure on the Ottomans, even if that meant the subordination of Britain's strategic interests.

I entreat my countrymen, upon whom far more than perhaps any other people of Europe it depends, to require, and to insist, that our Government, which has been working in one direction, shall work in the other, and shall apply all its vigour to concur with the other States of Europe in obtaining the extinction of the Turkish executive power in Bulgaria. Let the Turks now carry away their abuses in the only possible manner, namely by carrying off themselves. Their Zaptiehs and their Mudirs, their Bimbashis and their Yuzbachis, their Kaimakams and their Pashas, one and all, bag and baggage, shall, I hope, clear out from the province they have desolated and profaned. This thorough riddance, this most blessed deliverance, is the only reparation we can make to the memory of those heaps on heaps of dead; to the violated purity alike of matron, of maiden, and of child; to the civilization which has been affronted and shamed; to the laws of God or, if you like, of Allah; to the moral sense of mankind at large. There is not a criminal in an European jail, there is not a cannibal in the South Sea Islands, whose indignation would not rise and overboil at the recital of that which has been done, which has too late been examined, but which remains unavenged; which has left behind all the foul and all the fierce passions that produced it, and which may again spring up, in another murderous harvest, from the soil soaked and reeking with blood, and in the air tainted with every imaginable deed of crime and shame. That such things should be done once, is a damning disgrace to the portion of our race which did them; that a door should be left open for their ever-so-barely possible repetition would spread that shame over the whole.

This was stirring stuff that would have no truck with *realpolitik* and notions of the balance of power. In Gladstone's view, foreign policy should be infused and transformed by Christian decency and the values that it embodied. On one level, Gladstone was advocating a high-minded, altruistic foreign policy that tore up the entrenched wisdom of nineteenth-century British diplomacy and repudiated national interest as the foundation of foreign policy. Britain's destiny was, with other Christian nations, not just to rule the world, but to redeem it as well.

On another level, this was British imperialism by any other name. It is the conceit of great empires – *Pax Romana, Pax Britannica, Pax Americana* – to see their values and ideology as universally applicable. It was Gladstone's conceit too; his disdain for the Turks and Islam was ill concealed. But it was also his delusion. Britain may still have been the world's most powerful nation – though we would soon be feeling the hot breath of Germany and the United States on our neck – but Gladstone's ethical imperialism was confronted by several rival European imperialisms. Each of these – German, Austro-Hungarian, Russian – was imbued with its own ideology, interests and sense of destiny; and none had any desire to bend the knee to Britain. More to the point, none showed the least desire to abandon cold, pragmatic calculation in deciding where their interests lay. How else could that be in a Continental Europe dominated by the German arch-realist, Count Otto von Bismarck? He would have laughed at the notion of the League of Three Emperors embarking on an altruistic Christian crusade against the heathen Turk. Even Gladstone had to admit: 'I am not such a dreamer as to suppose that Russia more than other countries is exempt from selfish ambitions.'

Disraeli and Gladstone spent 1876 taking position at the opposite extremes of a fierce polemic. Disraeli did not mince his words. Gladstone was a madman, and the atrocities movement a 'Hudibrastic crew of High Ritualists'. 'Our duty at this critical moment', declared Disraeli, 'is to maintain the Empire of England.' Disraeli's problem was that the whole nation seemed to be in Gladstone's corner. He expressed his concerns in a letter to Elliot just before Gladstone's Blackheath speech:

Any sympathy previously felt in England towards Turkey has been completely destroyed by the lamentable occurrences in Bulgaria ... and to such a pitch has indignation in all classes of English society risen ... that in the extreme case of Russia declaring war against Turkey, H.M.G. would find it practically impossible to interfere in defence of the Ottoman Empire.

Elliot, to his horror, found himself ensnared in the controversy. He was accused in the House of Commons of suppressing reports, downplaying the atrocities, and being biased to the Turks – of 'going native'. Elliot was indignant at being criticised, as he saw it, for doing his duty in carrying out the policy of the government. That was what ambassadors did. He defended himself to London in a spirited despatch, which I could not have bettered myself:

To the accusation of being a blind partisan of the Turks, I will only answer that my conduct here has never been guided by any sentimental affection for them, but by a firm determination to uphold the interests of Great Britain to the utmost of my power; and that these interests are deeply engaged in preventing the destruction of the Turkish Empire is a conviction which I have in common with the most eminent statesmen who have directed our Foreign policy, but which appears now to be abandoned by shallow politicians or persons who have allowed their feelings of revolted humanity to make them forget the capital interests involved in the question.

We may and must feel indignant at the needless and monstrous severity with which the Bulgarian insurrection was put down, but the necessity which exists for England to prevent changes from occurring here which would be most detrimental to ourselves is not affected by the question whether it was ten thousand or twenty thousand person who perished in the suppression.

We have been upholding what we know to be a semi-civilised nation, liable under certain circumstances to be carried into fearful excesses, but the fact of this having just now been strikingly brought home to us all cannot be a sufficient reason for abandoning a policy which is the only one that can be followed with a due regard to our own interests.[7]

'Revolted humanity' versus 'capital interests': Elliot set out with admirable clarity, in his very Victorian way, the permanent tension in foreign policy between the 'idealists' and the 'realists', between human rights and *realpolitik*. He also made plain where his sympathies lay. The despatch became public and stirred a hornets' nest around Elliot's hapless head.

Without attacking Elliot by name, Gladstone retorted:

What is to be the consequence to civilisation and humanity, to public order, if British interests are to be the rule for British agents all over the world, and are to be for them the measure of right or wrong?

This displayed a profound misunderstanding of the role and duties of a diplomat (not even Gladstone's greatest admirers would claim for the Grand Old Man a place in history for his achievements in foreign affairs). There can and should be regular debate in Parliament about the nature and content of British interests abroad: the degree to which, for example, they should be defined by humanitarian, as opposed to commercial or strategic, considerations. But, once there is a settled policy, it is the diplomat's duty to carry it out, accompanied by analysis and advice to London as necessary. It is, of course, open to any ambassador, if he or she objects to their instructions, to resign; and some do. But an ambassador without instructions informed by a clear vision of the national interest is no better than a navigator without a compass. It is not enough to say, as Gladstone's supporters did, that they were just people 'who believe in right and wrong'. If only it were that simple! And it never is.

It is unusual for an ambassador to find himself under severe criticism back home for doing what he has been told to do by the government. But for a while, such was the strength of feeling against Disraeli's pro-Turkey policy, that Elliot became a lightning rod for the protesters. It was not long before the politicians began to discuss the need to sacrifice him. Encouraged by Queen Victoria, Disraeli had resisted Elliot's recall. The Cabinet, however, were not all members of the Elliot fan club; even the Foreign Secretary himself,

Lord Salisbury, was wobbly on the Eastern Question. Just at the moment when it looked as if the government might be in peril, Elliot did the decent thing and requested a transfer. He had been ill; and he had had quite enough stress and strain. His wish was granted. Honour was satisfied all round by sending him as Ambassador to Vienna, a prestigious, but less taxing, post. On arrival, Elliot point-edly expressed the hope that London would place more confidence in him in his new position than had been the case in Istanbul. In Austria, Elliot would conduct much of his business on the hunting field, where his horsemanship won him the respect of Emperor Franz Joseph and the leading Hungarian statesmen. Nowadays, I would not particularly commend riding as a useful attribute for the ambitious diplomat, although, in Washington at least, it helps to play tennis and golf and to shoot a little.

Elliot had been thrown overboard, not to signal a change of policy, but to make it easier to stick to the present one of supporting Turkey. Disraeli showed this straight away in his search for Elliot's replacement:

What we want is a man of necessary experience and commanding mind at this moment in Constantinople – and one not too scrupulous. But such men are rare everywhere.

Disraeli found his man in Sir Austen Henry Layard, an ardent pro-Turk. The Sultan read in his appointment a clear signal of support, as well as encouragement to resist demands for reform, which is what he did. Russia responded by declaring war on Turkey in 1877. This marked the turning of the tide for Disraeli, though it was not immediately obvious.

Between 1876 and 1878 Disraeli was obliged to play a canny game. He found himself both encouraging the Turks to resist the Berlin Memorandum of the Three Emperors and negotiating quietly with the Russians on the side. He had always feared that the Russians might attack Turkey, and that, because of the uproar in Britain over the Bulgarian atrocities, it would not be possible to come to Turkey's aid. If this were a tightrope, he appeared to have fallen off in 1877. Early that year, a possible resolution to the crisis appeared in the unlikely figure of Ignatyev, the Russian Ambassador to Istanbul, who was touting around European capitals a draft protocol to resolve the Eastern Question. Disraeli signed up to what became known as the London Protocol. It called, in a fairly innocuous way, for Turkish reform and an end to slaughter in the Balkans. More importantly, it included a confidential deal between Britain and Russia, by which London agreed to stay neutral in any war between Russia and Turkey, on condition that the Russians did not try to create a client state in the Balkans. Unfortunately for Disraeli, the Sultan, encouraged by what he saw as continuing British government support, rejected the very Protocol that Disraeli had signed. As a result, Russia declared war on Turkey; and, as Disraeli had feared, Britain felt unable to come in on the Turkish side.

It was a diplomatic debacle for Disraeli, but he was saved by Russian excess. After the Tsar's troops made short work of the Sultan's army, a defeated Ottoman Empire was forced to make humiliating terms with Russia in the 1878 Treaty of San Stefano. This provided for the creation of a greater Christian Bulgaria under Russian protection, which gave the Tsar a dominant position in the Balkans; effectively opened the Bosphorus Straits to the Russian navy; and made a number of other territorial adjustments in Russia's favour. The reaction in Europe was swift and hostile. The Austrians, taking violent objection to Russia's trampling on their own Balkan ambitions, threatened war. Disraeli, having withdrawn from the London Protocol, sent the British Mediterranean fleet to the Dardanelles to counter the Russian threat to Constantinople. An alarmed Bismarck summoned all parties to a Congress in Berlin, and the Russians duly backed down before the threat of war. In the Treaty of Berlin a few months later, the Tsar was forced to abandon several of his gains under the Treaty of San Stefano, sacrificing his ambition for a huge Bulgarian client state. The threat to Constantinople evaporated. Once again, lurking inside the Treaty, was a secret deal between Britain and Russia on certain territorial adjustments. A slimmer, autonomous Bulgaria emerged, though still formally under Ottoman suzerainty.

War had been avoided; and the Three Emperor's League, which Britain had never liked, collapsed under the strain of Russia's bitter anger with Germany and Austria (Ignatyev's career never recovered from the setback). It was game, set and match to Disraeli, though for a while he had had to live dangerously. He emerged from the Congress of Berlin proclaiming 'peace with honour'. Asked who had been at the 'centre of gravity' in the negotiations, Bismarck pointed to Disraeli, saying: 'The old Jew, he is the man.'

Meanwhile, back in Britain, the pendulum of public opinion had swung again behind the government. Already, at the end of 1876, as is the way with these things, some of the air was starting to go out of Gladstone's moral crusade. His second pamphlet on the Bulgarian Atrocities sold only 7,000 copies. When, in the following year, Russia declared war on Turkey, menacing once again Constantinople and the Straits, fear of the Russian Bear swept aside the anti-Ottoman movement. Crowds crammed into the London Pavilion to hear the popular singer, 'The Great MacDermott', perform a new patriotic song, composed for the moment:

> The 'Dogs of War' are loose and the rugged Russian Bear,
> All bent on blood and robbery has crawled out of his lair.
> It seems a thrashing now and then, will never help to tame
> That brute, and so he's out upon the 'same old game'.
> The Lion did his best to find him some excuse
> To crawl back to his den again. All efforts were no use
> He hunger'd for his victim. He's pleased when blood is shed
> But let us hope his crimes may all recoil on his own head.
>
> Chorus:
> We don't want to fight but by jingo if we do
> We've got the ships, we've got the men, and got the money too!
> We've fought the Bear before and while we're Britons true,
> The Russians shall not have Constantinople.
>
> The misdeeds of the Turks have been 'spouted' through all lands,
> But how about the Russians, can they show spotless hands?
> They slaughtered well at Khiva, in Siberia icy cold.
> How many subjects done to death we'll ne'er perhaps be told.
> They butchered the Circassians, man, woman yes and child.
> With cruelties their Generals their murderous hours beguiled,
> And poor unhappy Poland their cruel yoke must bear,
> While prayers for 'Freedom and Revenge' go up into the air.

(Chorus)

May he who 'gan the quarrel soon have to bite the dust.
The Turk should be thrice armed for 'he hath his quarrel just'.
'Tis said that countless thousands should die through cruel war,
But let us hope most fervently ere long it shall be o'er.
Let them be warned: Old England is brave Old England still.
We've proved our might, we've claimed our right, and ever, ever will.
Should we have to draw the sword our way to victory we'll forge,
With the Battle cry of Britons, 'Old England and St George!'

From this huge hit, the word 'jingoism' entered the English language to describe belligerent patriotism. Gladstone, meanwhile, was unwilling to match the fickleness of the public. He paid the price of being denounced as a Russian agent and having his windows broken by a jingo mob.

In the general election of 1880, the political tables turned once more, as Gladstone swept to victory. The election had been fought more than usually on matters of foreign policy as, around the Empire, British rule had encountered a number of setbacks, many of them laid at the door of the sick and elderly Disraeli. During the campaign, Gladstone enunciated six principles of 'international behaviour'. These included reconciliation through the Concert of Europe; no secret alliances; equal rights for all nations; 'love of freedom'; and so on. Gladstone made clear that these precepts, based on Christian moral values, were directed at Christian nations. He would strive 'to keep the Powers of Europe in union together. And why? Because by keeping all in union together you neutralise and fetter and bind up the selfish aims of each ... Common action is fatal to selfish aims.' In words more redolent of a sermon than a campaign speech, he went on:

remember that the sanctity of life in the hill villages of Afghanistan is as inviolable in the eye of Almighty God as can be your own. Remember that He who has united you as human beings in the same flesh and blood has bound you by the law of mutual love.

Again, this was stirring stuff. It was also revolutionary stuff. The

Concert of Europe, which Gladstone repeatedly invoked, had been the creation of the Congress of Vienna sixty-five years previously. It had been seen then as the embodiment of a carefully calibrated European balance of power, in which conservative stability was the greatest virtue. For Gladstone, the high-minded liberal, it would be the instrument of a new approach to international relations: the moral rearmament of foreign policy.

Gladstone's victory gave him the opportunity to put his moral precepts into action. Over the next five years, they would time and again collide with reality and fracture under the stress. For all his criticism of Disraeli's handling of the Eastern Question, Gladstone found it intensely difficult to practise what he preached. Having recalled Layard from Constantinople he was unable to force the Ottoman Sultan to reform his governance, as had been stipulated in the Berlin Treaty. Unlike Disraeli, Gladstone was not a fervent imperialist. He would have preferred to limit the Empire to the frontiers that had been in place when he took office. Instead, he was repeatedly drawn into ever-wider imperial responsibilities. In 1882, he felt obliged to invade and occupy Egypt to protect British interests in the Suez Canal. This in turn led him to occupy neighbouring Sudan. War ensued with the Mahdi, a militant Islamic leader and prophet; and, in 1885, at British headquarters in Khartoum, General Gordon died at the hands of the insurgents. Gladstone was blamed for the General's death on the grounds that he had failed to send reinforcements. To his mortification, the GOM (Grand Old Man) became known as the MOG (Murderer of Gordon). Under Gladstone, Britain became embroiled in the First Boer War in South Africa, suffering an embarrassing defeat at Majuba Hill. In 1885, he almost went to war with Russia over Afghanistan.

By the standards he had set in the election campaign of 1879–80, Gladstone's foreign policy failed dismally. To rub salt into the wound, the other members of the Concert of Europe failed to lift a finger in Christian solidarity with Gladstone's Britain when it ran into difficulty abroad. He had to learn the hard way that to seek the moral rearmament of foreign policy can lead all too quickly to unilateral diplomatic disarmament. Reciprocity in all things is a golden rule of diplomatic negotiation.

In domestic affairs, Gladstone may have been a great political and social reformer, but in foreign policy he was too much the sermoniser and naïve idealist. Yet his legacy has endured nonetheless. It is to be found in those places where importance is given to values and human rights in foreign policy: for example, in the covenant of the League of Nations and in the speeches of Tony Blair. In May 1999, when he was advocating intervention in Kosovo to stop Serbian atrocities, Blair said this in Bulgaria's capital, Sofia:

Today we face the same questions that confronted Gladstone over 120 years ago. Does one nation or people have the right to impose its will on another? Is there ever a justification for a policy based on the supremacy of one ethnic group? Can the outside world simply stand by when a rogue state brutally abuses the basic rights of those it governs? Gladstone's answer in 1876 was clear. And so is mine today. Then, as now, it would have been easy to look the other way; easy to argue that bigger strategic issues were at stake than the fare of a few hundred thousand people in the Balkans. Some people made exactly that argument. Some do today. They were wrong in 1876 over Bulgaria; and they are wrong in 1999 over Kosovo.[8]

Though the common Balkan context gave it a surface plausibility, Blair's historical analogy was far from exact. The Ottoman Empire, despite its unsavoury aspects, was hardly a 'rogue state'. But his speech was testimony to the power of an idea which will not go away: namely, that, without an overt ethical dimension, foreign policy is incomplete. This leads to a practical problem. Diplomats must today decide how much weight to attach to humanitarian considerations in deciding a course of action abroad. The decisions required are never easy, especially where a vociferous public opinion and strong, competing strategic and economic interests are also in play.

Henry Kissinger, who had to make these decisions as US Secretary of State and National Security Adviser, and who is widely regarded as the *doyen* of the Realist school of diplomacy, had this to say, when interviewed for the companion BBC television series to this book:

the real decisions ... are not what they teach in the academy, which is good versus evil, black versus white, they are 50.5 against, 49.5 for. They are very narrow decisions. Otherwise they would already have been made at a lower level. So when they come to the statesman, he must have some convictions that guide him through this maze. And so values are a crucial element.

The question ... is this: in America there is a standard debate between idealists and realists, and idealists are good and realists are bad, although I have never understood why the perceptive understanding of reality should be a sinful thing to do. And then it translates itself that idealists stand only by their values and are not deflected by these practical considerations. The difficulty with that is that you then have to shape the world into universal truths and that you become more ruthless in pursuit of universal truths than let's say relative truths. And my reading of history, which may reflect my predilections, is that a lot more people have been killed by prophets than by statesmen and so the assertion of values and ideals as the only criterion is not such a comforting lesson.

To which I would add from my own experience that, in matters of human rights, nations will move from declaratory posturing to action only when this does not cut across other national interests. It suited Britain to press aggressively the cause of dissidents in the old Soviet Union because we were engaged in a global war of ideas against Russian Communism. There is not the slightest chance of our acting similarly on behalf of Chinese campaigners for democracy, because China is in other respects too important for us to antagonise. The price of values in foreign policy was, is and always will be their inconsistent application.

In the end, the case of the Balkan Atrocities was less a manichean struggle between Realists and Idealists, more the simple fact that Disraeli's reading of the international situation in the 1870s was better than Gladstone's. Disraeli took the world as he found it, not as he might have wished it to be; Gladstone did the opposite. Disraeli was proved right, as the pragmatists usually are; and Britain got its way. But, the two great statesmen must have been aware, from their very different positions, that the tectonic plates were shifting under late Victorian certainties. The new force of a turbulent press and public opinion, and the replacement of the old Concert of Europe by an increasingly undisciplined competition between the Great Powers, were but two signs of things to come. Disraeli, for one, knew that support for the Turk was a holding operation against

Hong Kong in 1857. Palmerston's 'barren island' is beginning
to flourish. (Mary Evans Picture Library)

Deng Xiaoping and Margaret Thatcher meet in Beijing on 19 December
1984, the day the Joint Declaration was signed. The famous spittoon is
on the floor by Deng's feet. (Getty Images)

Chris Patten, the last Governor of Hong Kong, receives the Union Jack flag at Government House as 156 years of British colonial rule comes to an end. (Getty Images)

Thousands gather in a peaceful candlelit vigil in Hong Kong's Victoria Park to mark the 20th anniversary of the Tiananmen Square massacre, 4 June 2009. (Getty Images)

With Geoffrey Howe and his aides Tony Galsworthy and Robert Culshaw in Japan, wearing Yukata at a natural spa. Protocol in diplomacy sometimes requires dressing up ...

THE BULGARIAN ATROCITIES — MR. W. E. GLADSTONE ADDRESSING HIS CONSTITUENTS AT GREENWICH
A SKETCH FROM THE HUSTINGS

Gladstone in full flow, addressing a crowd of 10,000 in the pouring rain at Blackheath. (Mary Evans Picture Library)

The notorious bashi-bozouks lay waste to a village. (Mary Evans Picture Library)

A Spy cartoon from *Vanity Fair* of Sir Henry Elliot, British Ambassador to the Sublime Porte.

A satirical cartoon taps into the public outrage over Disraeli's perceived indifference to the plight of the Bulgarians. (Mary Evans Picture Library)

NEUTRALITY UNDER DIFFICULTIES.

Dizzy. *"Bulgarian Atrocities! I can't find them in the 'Official Reports'!!!"*

'The Flower', a cartoon by David Low showing the hopeful prospect of the League of Nations rising out of the horrors of the First World War. (Solo Syndication/Associated Newspapers Ltd)

'Reforming Our Diplomatic Service' by W. K. Haselden: a glimpse of the dressed-down New Diplomacy, *Daily Mirror*, 6 August 1918. (British Cartoon Archive, University of Kent, www.cartoons.ac.uk)

THE OLD DIPLOMACY —

— AND THE NEW (?)

HULLO, OLD BEAN! TAKE A PEW AND HELP YOURSELF TO A 'BINE!

W.K. HASELDEN.

International leaders meet in the Foreign Office in London to sign the Locarno Treaties in December 1925. (Getty Images)

Sir Samuel Hoare, Foreign Secretary, who was forced to resign after just six months in office over the Hoare-Laval Pact. (Getty Images)

Sir Robert Vansittart, Permanent Under-Secretary at the Foreign Office, the arch-realist who was the brains behind the Hoare-Laval Pact. (Corbis)

UN soldiers patrol the streets of Srebrenica, 25 April 1993. The buildings that remain standing bear the scars of Serb shelling. (Getty Images)

Bosnian refugees fleeing Srebrenica in July 1995 after the massacre of some 7700 Muslim men and boys. (Getty Images)

The Balkans Bulldozer Richard Holbrooke greets Slobodan Milošević as he arrives for peace talks in Dayton in October 1995. (Getty Images)

Presidents Milošević, Tudjman and Izetbegović sign the peace agreement on Bosnia in Paris, 14 December 1995. Prime Minister Gonzales, President Clinton, President Chirac, Chancellor Kohl, Prime Minister Major and Premier Chernomyrdin look on. (Getty Images)

Ottoman disintegration that could not go on for much longer.

In little more than a generation, the world in which he and Gladstone had operated would be turned upside down. In the early twentieth century all the strategic verities that had governed Victorian foreign policy would be jettisoned. Splendid Isolation would vanish. In 1904 an *Entente Cordiale* would be signed with France, the ancient enemy. In 1907 a lesser known, but equally important, *entente* would be concluded with Russia, yesterday's bogeyman. The Ottoman Empire would switch from long-standing friend to enemy, allying with Imperial Germany in the First World War. It would be the clearest illustration of Lord Palmerston's dictum that Britain had no permanent allies or enemies, only permanent interests.

Meanwhile, back in the Balkans, the Eastern Question never really went away. It was a Balkan assassin who triggered the First World War. It was a Balkan crisis in the 1990s that presented the UN, the EU and NATO with an unprecedented moral and military challenge. It is with us to this day in the fragile stability of Kosovo and Bosnia. It only goes to show that, as ever, diplomacy is more about managing problems than solving them.

8

HOBBES RULES, OK:
Vansittart and the Fall of the New Diplomacy

At 11 a.m. on 1 December 1925, eighteen men entered a large room in the Foreign Office in London. A series of inkstands were set out on a table. Large royal portraits had been hung on the walls to disguise the neglected décor. Later, this room would be refurbished in the grand style, to re-emerge as part of the Locarno Suite in honour of the occasion. It is today the largest and most resplendent room in the Foreign Office (available for hire at £3,500 for the day).

The sober-suited men had gathered for the formal signing of various treaties, which had recently been agreed at Locarno in Switzerland. The ceremony was taking place in London in recognition of the central role played in the negotiations by Sir Austen Chamberlain, the British Secretary of State for Foreign Affairs. Unusually for the signing of treaties, the occasion had seized the world's attention. A dense crowd of journalists was in attendance. Press photographers were perched at dangerous heights around the room. Even that staid organ of the Establishment, *The Times*, was moved to write, under the headline 'A Milestone', an almost euphoric editorial recalling the terrible devastation of the Great War and expressing the universal feeling of 'never again'. 'The Locarno Treaty', *The Times* went on, 'eliminates the risk of international war in a historical area of conflict for a long time to come.'[1] After the 'war to end all wars', there was a buoyant confidence in the air that touched all levels of society. A powerful idealism had clambered from the wreckage and blood-letting of the First World War.

It certainly looked to be the often invoked New Dawn. Representatives of Germany, France, Britain, Belgium, Italy, Poland and

Czechoslovakia had come together to sign agreements which would guarantee peace after a war of devastation without precedent. Like the Congress of Vienna in 1815 following twenty-five years of Napoleonic Wars, Locarno set out to create structures on which a durable peace could rest. But, in its essentials, Locarno was nothing like Vienna; and its signatories rejected the 'Old Diplomacy' that Vienna had represented. The prevailing view was not that Vienna had saved Europe from a general war for a century but that it had sowed the seeds of the 1914–18 conflict. Balance of power, so the argument went, was amoral and inherently unstable, the more so when constructed on the suppression of national ambitions. The Concert of Europe had been little less than a pressure cooker, doomed to blow sooner or later; and blow it did in 1914, sweeping away empires, creating new nations, and fundamentally transforming European societies.

A 'New Diplomacy' was announced with great fanfare. Europeans would no longer resort to war to settle grievances. Europe's leaders (for the first time) would henceforth behave like civilised human beings: they would work together and reach peaceful solutions to their problems. The optimism was remarkable. The German Foreign Minister, Gustav Stresemann, who received the Nobel Peace Prize for his contribution to Franco-German reconciliation, said soon afterwards that 'Locarno is the end of the policy of opposition and conflicting aims ... the powers are cooperating'.[2] It was to be a feature of the New Diplomacy that each nation would play an equal part in preventing war. Europe would no longer be divided between Great Powers, with the interests of the small fry cast to one side; instead there would be an open, sincere, and shared commitment to work for peace. This was the 'spirit of Locarno'. In the revolutionary, grandiose scale of its ambition, it embodied a yearning for peace to match the horror of the Great War. The message to the chancelleries of Europe was clear: foreign policy would be driven by universal values. The future lay in liberal internationalism.

It was all pie in the sky, of course. The Europeans were at each other's throats again within fifteen years of Locarno's signing. The air was thick with irony, when, in July 1997, Britain's new Foreign Secretary, Robin Cook, chose to launch New Labour's much-vaunted 'ethical foreign policy' from the Locarno Suite. Had New

Labour shown less disdain for history, Cook might have chosen a different venue. As it was, his ethical foreign policy went up in smoke as fast as the spirit of Locarno.

Even before the end of the Great War, there had been calls for a dramatic change in the way international relations were conducted. Europeans looked around at the needless waste, the millions of young lives cut short, and were disgusted. The British, in particular, had been unprepared in 1914 for a war of mass slaughter. The century of relative peace delivered by the Congress of Vienna had been punctuated by only the Crimean War and colonial campaigns; casualties had been met with a stoic Victorian acceptance, because they were relatively light and there was a strong patriotic confidence in Queen and Country. There was also a venerable British aversion to the notion of a large standing army. Partly this was on grounds of cost; partly it reflected a high confidence in the ability of the Royal Navy to keep enemies at bay. It was embodied in the small regular army of 'Old Contemptibles', who crossed the Channel in 1914 to come to the aid of the French.

Though it may have taken Britain by surprise, the rest of Europe had been introduced to mass conscription, citizen armies and savage casualties many years earlier, courtesy of Bonaparte. At the battle of Leipzig, half a million men were engaged, with over one hundred thousand casualties. Prussia's wars with Austria and France in the 1860s and 70s may have been short, but they were bloody. European military attachés, observing the American Civil War of the 1860s, saw slaughter on a scale that anticipated the Great War.

Having lost two and a half million men, killed or wounded in action, the British public's view of war in 1918 was vastly different from what it had been four years previously. More to the point, the casualties were drawn from a population that voted (though full female suffrage did not arrive until 1928), read newspapers, and could be mobilised into mass movements both within and outside mainstream political parties. These people had acquired an abhorrence of war. They were none too keen either on the politicians and diplomats who, in their view, had caused the war in the first place.

There had always been an indissoluble link between war and diplomacy. States had strategic goals abroad. They were achieved by war or diplomacy; or a combination of the two. So, if war was to be abolished, and disarmament pursued, diplomacy itself would have to change. There would have to be a new way of pursuing foreign policy goals and reconciling the clash of national interests that did not involve the mass mobilisation of armies. There would be no place for the kind of arms race that had led Britain and Germany before the Great War to compete furiously in the construction of capital ships. The 1920s and 30s would see attempts to limit navies in much the same way as America and Russia have negotiated agreements to regulate and reduce their holdings of nuclear missiles.

So, out with the Old Diplomacy and in with the New. What did this mean? Something had to be done about the practitioners and their practice. When they were not dancing the light fantastic in the chandelier's blaze, diplomats were seen – the image has not changed much, it has to be said – as upper-class denizens of an exclusive, shadow world, where unprincipled deals were cunningly constructed. Diplomats had always been players of a game in which resort to war was a regular gambit. The New Diplomacy would change all that. International relations would be conducted openly, according to agreed moral principles. Transparency would make foreign policy accountable to the people and prevent remote diplomatic élites from dragging the world into war. Conference – multilateral in the modern parlance – diplomacy would replace the secrecy of bilateral diplomacy. There was a widespread view that wars were caused by failures of communication; and that, if only statesmen could get together round a table and talk like civilised human beings, they would sort out the misunderstandings that in the past had led to war.

Not only the practice, but the principles, of diplomacy would have to change. Balance of Power, the Holy Grail of nineteenth-century diplomacy, never delivered the stability claimed for it, since, argued the New Diplomatists, states were always seeking to shift the balance in their favour. Bismarck, for example, had supported a European balance of power only after defeating Austria and France in battle and turning the Prussian King into a German Emperor. So, out with the Balance of Power and in with the new thing: Collective Security. In 1916, in a speech to the League to Enforce

Peace, the US President, Woodrow Wilson, suggested a way to ensure world security. What was required was a 'universal association of all the nations . . . to prevent any war begun either contrary to treaty covenants or without warning and full submission of the causes to the opinion of the world'. Four years later, in the Treaty of Versailles, which brought the Great War to a formal conclusion, the 'universal association' had become a brand new body, the League of Nations. The League would be the embodiment and instrument of the New Diplomacy. Its first task would be to make collective security a living reality.

According to the principle of collective security, a state should try every possible peaceful avenue of negotiation before going to war. Economic sanctions, enforced by the full membership of the League, were to be used against would-be aggressors. If push came to shove, an aggressor would be dealt with by the overwhelming military force of all the member states, standing together. The purpose of the Locarno treaties was to add detail and structure to the broad strokes of the League's Covenant. Germany's western border was set, healing, so it was hoped, the dangerous running sore in Franco-German relations. Germany itself had been accepted on equal terms during the negotiations. The following year it was to be taken into the League as a partner in peace, not a defeated rogue-state to be punished. France, Germany, and Belgium promised not to attack each other, with Britain and Italy as guarantors of the agreement; and all promised to come to the aid of the victim, if aggression took place. By the end of 1925, it looked as if the great dream of the League of Nations might be realised; and that, at last, world peace was just around the corner. King George V wrote in his diary 'this morning the Locarno Pact was signed at the Foreign Office. I pray this may mean peace for many years. Why not forever?'

Why not, indeed? There were several answers to that question. Leave aside the most important – Original Sin, which means that nations are no better than individuals at behaving themselves – the League was crippled from the start by structural weakness. Conference negotiation and diplomacy is a clumsy beast. The League's ideal of universal and equal membership was all very well, but it made the practical task of reaching agreement on important international issues well-nigh impossible when all nations, big and small, had a vote of the same weight. The Congress of Vienna had got round the problem by remitting the big issues to the Great Powers and using the Congress in plenary to ratify what had been agreed. But, to return to the Old Diplomacy's way of working was anathema to the League's membership.

In 1945, the founding fathers of the United Nations, who naturally sought to learn from the League's collapse, devised a Security Council of permanent and rotating members with the authority to pass resolutions binding on the broader membership. This was not a million miles from the *modus operandi* of Castlereagh and Metternich. It is not perfect, since there is no way to abolish the irreconcilable clash of national interests; agreement, when it can be reached, tends to drift down to the lowest common denominator; and unanimity is bought too often at the price of ambiguity. The United States has repeatedly blocked resolutions uncongenial to Israel, its Middle East ally. Russia and China, with an eye to Iran's energy resources, have regularly diluted action against the Iranians to deter them from developing a nuclear weapon. The famous Resolution 1441 of November 2002, which demanded from Saddam Hussein a comprehensive declaration of his weapons holdings, was agreed unanimously. But, the consensus, built on a masterpiece of ingeniously ambiguous drafting, rapidly fractured on the question of war or peace.

There was an even more serious flaw. In laying claim to universality – which was seen as essential to its moral force and ability to mobilise the membership against transgressor nations – the League was compromised from the start. The big powers were never properly represented. Whereas defeated France in 1814 had been integrated early on into the Vienna negotiations, defeated Germany was punished by the Treaty of Versailles with an enormous bill for reparations and excluded from the League until 1926. It remained a member for seven years only; Hitler withdrew in 1933. Mussolini followed suit in 1937. Communist Russia, adding ideological hostility to the traditional xenophobia and territorial expansionism of its Tsarist predecessor, refused to join the League until 1934. Most damagingly, despite President Woodrow Wilson's role as midwife to the League (for which he was awarded the Nobel Peace Prize), the US Senate refused to ratify its Covenant. The United States, then as now, was not prepared to subordinate its sovereignty to the demands of collective action, unless it could be certain that it was in the driving seat (a close contemporary parallel is the American refusal to submit to the jurisdiction of the International Criminal Court). The absence of America, with its military and economic muscle, was fatal to the whole enterprise.

The inevitable result was that the League of Nations did not have its own standing force. Nor, it will be argued, does the United Nations today, though peace-keeping is one of the UN's major occupations, with thousands of Blue Helmets on duty around the world. But these troops are drawn from battalions voluntarily contributed by member-states; and it has always been the devil's own job to find good-quality troops that can enforce UN mandates. Though the UN has done much better than the League, its reputation for peace-keeping has been sullied over the years by feeble rules of engagement, weak command and control, and the resulting failure to stop mass slaughter in places like Central Africa and Bosnia, despite the presence of UN contingents.

If, because of opposition from its members, it has proved impossible for the UN to acquire a standing army, imagine how much harder it was for the League in the early aftermath of the Great War. European nations were exhausted and impoverished by the cost of war. Gales of pacifism swept through their societies. There was intense pressure for disarmament. The League found itself caught in a dilemma. It needed force as the ultimate deterrent for aggression, yet at the same time it was energetically pressing the moral and practical case for collective disarmament. If arms races had led to war, then the reverse must surely lead to peace. This helped stoke an environment in which, when the authority of the League came under threat, the default reaction of the membership would be to favour economic over military measures. The League's theoretical military options were to remain just that.

It wasn't long before the League was displaying the characteristics of the worst kind of international organisation: a bureaucratic talk-shop, short on action and long on hot air and paper. Though modestly effective in mediating a number of small-scale disputes in the early years – as the historian, Norman Davies, has put it, the

League had a major role in minor issues – by the 1930s, the League found itself overwhelmed by challenges of a higher order, which it had neither the muscle nor the will to meet. The first serious blow against the Spirit of Locarno came in 1931. It happened, not in Europe, but in the East. Japan invaded and seized the Chinese region of Manchuria and declared it the new state of Manchukuo. The League, with thinly disguised impotence, announced an 'urgent' period of consultation. Late the following year, a League commission reported, condemning Japan's actions and denying recognition to the puppet-state of Manchukuo. Economic sanctions, still less military action, were nowhere to be seen. The Japanese reacted to this slap on the wrist by staying in Manchuria and walking out of the League. Collective security had faced its first challenge and had been found wanting.

There was worse, much worse, to come. In December 1934, fighting broke out on the disputed border between Abyssinia, as Ethiopia was then known, and Italian Somaliland. At the oasis of Walwal, shots were exchanged between Abyssinian and Somali troops. It would never be clear who fired first. To Benito Mussolini, Italy's fascist dictator, Walwal was not so much a problem as an opportunity; the Italians had a humiliation to avenge after their crushing defeat by Abyssinian forces at the battle of Adowa in 1896. Though Italy and Abyssinia had not long signed a bilateral treaty of friendship and were also signatories to the Kellogg-Briand Pact,[3] this did not prevent Mussolini from reacting angrily to what he painted as Abyssinian aggression. He demanded an immediate official apology, an indemnity of 200,000 dollars, honour paid to the Italian flag, and the arrest and punishment of the 'guilty' parties. It became clear over the ensuing months that what the dictator really wanted was to turn a skirmish into a *casus belli*. This was Bowring and the *Arrow* Incident (see Chapter 3) all over again.

Fascism's glorification of violence and the purifying properties of war need no repeating here. In Mussolini's case, it was complemented by a strutting vainglory that was at once laughable and dangerous. He was bent on resurrecting the power and the glory of the Roman Empire, but to have an empire, you had to have colonies. Britain, France, Germany and even little Belgium had all done much better out of the 'scramble for Africa' in the late nineteenth and early twentieth centuries. For Mussolini, bent on martial exploits and empire, here was a second chance in the shape of the only remaining independent territory in Africa, flanked already by two small Italian colonies. Abyssinia looked like low-hanging fruit, ripe for the plucking.

Mussolini's ambition challenged the League and its ideals at their very core. European powers were supposed to have put the age of empire behind them and to have embraced self-determination for smaller nations. Worse, both Italy and Abyssinia itself were members of the League. As Mussolini amassed a vast army of Italian regulars on the border, Abyssinia's Emperor, Haile Selassie, appealed for international help. This was surely a clear-cut case: precisely the kind of aggression that the League of Nations had been set up to prevent.

In London, the hosts to the grand signing ceremony of the Locarno treaties a decade previously had to decide their reaction to Haile Selassie's appeal. In principle, the British government was fully committed to the League of Nations. Inside the heart of government, however, there had always been doubts. During the Great War, when the idea of a League of Nations was under discussion, the Cabinet Secretary, Maurice Hankey, had written with striking prescience that:

It will only result in failure, and the longer that failure is postponed, the more certain it is that this country will have been lulled to sleep. It will put a very strong lever into the hands of the well-meaning idealists ... who deprecate expenditure on armaments ... it will almost certainly result in this country being caught at a disadvantage.

In the Foreign Office, the bastion of 'realism', there was a similar scepticism. Sir Eyre Crowe, who was later to become Permanent Under-Secretary, wrote in 1916 that a solemn league and covenant would be a treaty like other treaties. 'What', he asked, 'is there to ensure that it will not, like other treaties, be broken?' Ten years later, with the League a fact of life and the Spirit of Locarno still in the ascendant, a senior Foreign Office official, J.D. Gregory,[4] signed a minute,[5] putting a more traditional gloss on Britain's commitment to the New Diplomacy:

The maintenance of the balance of power and preservation of the status quo have been our guiding lights for many decades and will so continue … At first sight it would seem that British foreign policy is altruistic but in truth His Majesty's Government cannot lay this unction to their souls. The fact is that war and rumour of war, quarrels and friction, in any corner of the world spell loss and harm to British commercial and financial interests. It is for the sake of these interests that we pour oil on troubled waters. So manifold and ubiquitous are British trade and British finance that, whatever else may be the outcome of a disturbance of the peace, we shall be the losers … This is the explanation and the reason for our intervention in almost every dispute that arises, and the justification for the maintenance of the armed forces which enable us to intervene prominently and with authority. Without our trade and our finance we sink to the level of a third class Power. Locarno and the unemployed have an intimate connexion.

Gregory's minute, with a notable absence of 'unction' to the soul, was a worthy, but rather desperate, attempt to ground the New Diplomacy in the national interest. He could see that, without that link, British foreign policy would be little more than a pious whirring noise, with gears unengaged. Britain would back the League, because peace and stability served its global interests. But Britain should have no illusions about the behaviour and motives of other powers, who, even if they talked the talk of collective security, walked the walk of good old *realpolitik*. Now, in 1935, a major European power was threatening the very foundations of the League. Where did Britain's interests lie? Would it be necessary to go to war to uphold the peace?

Much of the responsibility for answering these questions lay with the Permanent Under-Secretary (PUS) at the Foreign Office, Sir Robert Vansittart, known as 'Van' to friends and colleagues. Van was among the best and the brightest, and had risen rapidly in his diplomatic career. He was a powerful and colourful character, who expressed strongly held opinions loudly and often. He had a racy, flamboyant, almost journalistic style of writing, the very opposite of the dry civil service tradition. He even pursued a second career as novelist and playwright. He invested in Alexander Korda's film-making company; and wrote the screenplay and lyrics for some of his films, including *The Thief of Bagdad*. His successor, Sir Alexander Cadogan, an altogether more conventional diplomat, disapprovingly described Van's writing as 'dancing literary hornpipes'.[6]

The PUS is the senior civil servant in the Foreign Office. He (there has yet to be a female PUS) is responsible for managing not only headquarters in London but the entire Diplomatic Service abroad. He is senior to even the most illustrious ambassadors. He also enjoys the role of senior policy adviser to the Foreign Secretary. In modern times the managerial role has tended to overshadow that of adviser. In principle, it is for ministers – the elected politicians – to make policy; and for officials – the civil servants – to execute it. But the line becomes blurred, because ministers rarely act without advice from officials. A really strong-willed, talented official, like Vansittart, can become highly influential in the formulation of policy. In his memoirs, Anthony Eden, who became Foreign Secretary in 1935, called Vansittart a 'sincere, almost fanatical crusader', the sort of man who might have been more suited as Foreign Secretary than PUS.[7]

Vansittart brought strong views to the Abyssinian crisis. Despite having once written, in true Palmerstonian fashion, that 'no capable or trustworthy public servant can be pro or anti any foreign country', he had developed in his youth a strong antipathy for the Germans, whom he thought dangerous, and a corresponding sympathy for the French. After Hitler came to power in 1933, Vansittart wrote that:

The present regime in Germany will, on past and present form, loose off another European war just so soon as it feels strong enough ... we are considering very crude people, who have very few ideas in their noddles but brute force and militarism.

Vansittart's anti-Germanism would harden still further with the passing of the years.

He had also developed an early scepticism about the effectiveness of the League. In a famous minute, entitled 'An Aspect of International Relations in 1930', Vansittart cast doubt on the reality of the transformation which the New Diplomacy was supposed to have wrought on the behaviour of European powers. The minute became known as 'The Old Adam', the term Vansittart used to characterise the old, supposedly discarded, pre-war diplomacy. He wrote:

the continent is still riddled with pre-war thought. Alongside the ideals of the League, the pacts, arbitration and disarmament, material and moral, still runs the old diplomacy with its alliances, insurance and reinsurance treaties, balance of power, military values, and the economic theories represented by tariff walls and tariff combination . . .

After the war the Old Adam – if Professor Elliot Smith still allows the term – fell sick and lived somewhere in the country; many hoped, some even said, that he was dead. The report was greatly exaggerated. He is out and about again, medically reprieved, introducing the young to the overdraft, still capable of sowing a bumper crop of tares among the wheat, and it is an act of intellectual good faith to recognise him. He is something like the average man on an average day in Europe. He is sceptical of League and Pact, and has influence among those who have not got beyond a credo quia absurdum. Those suspect, moreover, that we, too, are full of him, and the evidence alleged is a prudery almost American about entanglements, evidence that we strengthen as we permit ourselves to be anti-this or anti-that, or even pro-this or pro-that, which in practice comes to much the same thing. The 'virtue' of Anglo-Saxons seems a proof of old Adam's virility; and he himself whispers that it is the old game, that nobody knows exactly where we are, that nobody ever did know, that there would have been no war if they had known. This is his story and he sticks to it . . .

Nations, like individuals, do not 'live happily ever after' 1918. . . . It is useless, meanwhile, to be disappointed, more than useless to be irritated, worst of all to shut our eyes. Our task is to take things as they are and make the best of them; any other course would make the League unworkable.

'To take things as they are and make the best of them': the eternal mission of British diplomacy, the permanent national interest. To seek instead to operate on a higher moral plane, in a world infested by fascist dictators, aggressive Bolsheviks, and American isolationists, was, as with Gladstone's foreign policy, a delusion. Vansittart was clear that, without a strong dose of the Old Diplomacy, the British national interest would be at risk. If others were wolves in the sheep's clothing of the League, or just plain wolves, then Britain had to be their match.

Vansittart's 'Old Adam' minute rightly identified Germany as the principal threat to Europe's peace and stability. To counter the threat, Britain would need not only to rearm but to isolate Germany by maintaining good relations with other European powers. This became the *leitmotiv* of Vansittart's European policy. By the time Hitler came to power in 1933, Vansittart judged, again correctly, that Mussolini, for all his military posturing, would be less dangerous than the new Nazi German *Reichskanzler*. As he put it (in a manner, which, in today's Foreign Office, would earn a stiff reprimand and time spent in a race-sensitivity class): 'the Latin says much that he does not mean, and has a sense of humour, in which the Teuton is conspicuously lacking.' Vansittart may have been prejudiced against Germany, but in the context of the times, it was not a bad prejudice to have. Hitler had quit both the Geneva disarmament talks and the League of Nations on coming to power. Vansittart read the Nazi threat exactly right.

The Abyssinia crisis placed the New and the Old Diplomacy on collision course. To deter and contain German ambitions, it seemed plain common sense not to make an enemy of Italy. Britain had to try to keep the two dictators apart. It had been easy enough in the early 1930s, when Mussolini had taken strong objection to Hitler's plans for incorporating Austria into a greater Germany. But by making his lunge for Abyssinia, Mussolini had thrown British diplomatic calculations into disarray. Would it be possible to be true to the League, to protect Abyssinia, and to keep the Italians on side? For Vansittart, the plight of the Abyssinians was a second-order matter, compared with his anxieties over Germany. Colonialism in Africa was preferable to war in Europe, for which Britain was simply not ready.

In a minute of February 1935, Vansittart outlined his approach to the handling of Mussolini:

We should endeavour to dissuade Italy from going the full length firstly, because it can hardly suit her, when she ought to have her hands free for graver matters in Europe; secondly because of the further, and perhaps deadly, blow that this must deal the League; and, therefore, thirdly on account of the consequent reaction of a large section of public opinion here, just at a period when we want and need, all of us, the most complete confidence and collaboration. ... But all this must be done in the quietest, most friendly way ... We cannot afford to quarrel with Italy and drive her back into German embraces.

Not a word about economic sanctions, still less the threat of force. Vansittart would rely instead on quiet diplomacy and an appeal to Italy's own national interest. France, Italy and Britain met at Stresa on the Italian Lake Maggiore in April 1935. Mussolini cut a typical dash by arriving in a speedboat. For a while there was talk of a 'Stresa Front' against Germany, a formation with a distinct Old Diplomacy ring to it. But it all went bad. Mussolini thought that he had received at Stresa a green light from Britain (as he had already from France) to invade Abyssinia; and was aggrieved to discover that he had not. Then, he was infuriated not to have been consulted on the Anglo-German Naval Agreement of June that year, which fixed the size of the German *Kriegsmarine* in relation to the Royal Navy. The game was starting to slip away from Vansittart.

Meanwhile, in Abyssinia, Mussolini was not to be restrained. The dream of imperial glory was too alluring. He had promised the Italian people 'a place in the sun'. He was shrewd enough to have calculated that the League, and its nucleus of European powers, would not risk war to stop him. The build-up of Italian troops continued apace. In June, Vansittart again minuted Eden:

It is as plain as a pikestaff. Italy will have to be bought out – let us use and face ugly words – in some form or other, or Abyssinia will eventually perish. That might in itself matter less, if it did not mean that the League would also perish, (and that Italy would simultaneously perform another volte face into the arms of Germany, a continuation of haute politique and haute cocotterie that we can ill afford just now).

This was as Old Diplomacy as it gets. Pieces of Abyssinia would have to be sacrificed to keep Mussolini out of Hitler's arms. Vansittart began confidential talks with his French and Italian opposite numbers. The goal, wrote Vansittart to Eden later in the month, would be to procure for Mussolini 'something substantive for the shop window without fighting or fever'. It is around this time that hindsight begins to attach the label of appeasement to the Foreign Office, something from which, to this day, it is not entirely free. It did not, of course, look like it at the time to King Charles Street. The last thing on anyone's minds was to appease Hitler. To the contrary, it was for them, and for Vansittart in particular, a matter of distinguishing between a greater German and a lesser Italian evil; and prioritising accordingly. An official report of that month could not have made things clearer:

no such vital British interest is concerned in and around Ethiopia as would make it essential for His Majesty's Government to resist an Italian conquest of Ethiopia.

Unfortunately for Vansittart, a very large chunk of British public opinion took a different view.

At the time of the Bulgarian Atrocities some sixty years previously, a recognisably modern public opinion had burst upon the scene and had had for the first time a material impact on foreign policy. By the 1930s, public opinion had developed still further as an independent force, thanks to universal adult suffrage, radio and newsreel film, as well as mass circulation newspapers. The Foreign Office now had its own News Department in recognition of the need to brief journalists and respond to their questions. But the regular testing of public opinion by the government was primitive, if it existed at all. The focus groups of today would have revealed a public mood that was heavily pro-League, pro-disarmament, and anti-war. What else was it likely to be after the Great War, which had left scarcely a family in the land untouched?

The 1930s became the decade of anxiety. There was an economic depression at home and, yet again, fear of war abroad. Public feeling broke surface in dramatic ways. The Oxford Union debated the motion that it would 'under no circumstances fight for its King and Country', and passed it by a large majority.[8] Then the government candidate suffered an unexpected defeat in the East Fulham by-election, as voters registered their opposition to the policy of rearmament.

As the New Diplomacy came under threat, the pro-peace lobby organised itself as never before to pressurise the government not to yield to the temptations of the Old Adam. In June 1935, the results of a 'Peace Ballot' were announced at a grand ceremony in the Albert Hall. Polling, organised by the League of Nations Union, had started in 1934. There had been a huge response. Over 11.5 million people had taken part. The turnout, at nearly 40 per cent of people over the age of eighteen, was higher than that in most European Parliament elections held in Britain today. No lobbying campaign has ever been bigger, more complex, or attracted more publicity.

There were five questions on the Ballot:

1. Should Great Britain remain in the League of Nations? *[95 per cent in favour]*
2. Are you in favour of the all-round reduction of armaments by international agreement? *[90 per cent-plus in favour]*
3. Are you in favour of the all-round abolition of national military and naval aircraft by international agreement? *[80 per cent-plus in favour]*
4. Should the manufacture and sale of armaments for private profit be prohibited by international agreement? *[90 per cent-plus in favour]*
5. Do you consider that, if a nation insists on attacking another, the other nations should combine to compel it to stop by:
   a) economic and non-military measures? *[86 per cent-plus in favour]*
   b) if necessary, military measures? *[58 per cent-plus in favour]*

Modern pollsters would criticise the unscientific nature of the questions and their in-built propensity to deliver inconsistent answers. Vansittart called the Peace Ballot 'a free excursion into the inane'. But, sheer weight of turnout gave it a moral and political force, which the government could not ignore. Despite its imperfections, the Ballot's overall message to the government could not have been plainer. Britain should stay true to the League of Nations. It should continue to work for disarmament and collective security. It should not abandon the New Diplomacy. Or, as the *Daily Herald* put it,

... from the results of the Peace Ballot one fact stands out with inescapable clearness. The solid mass of British public opinion demands a policy based not on isolation, not on particular alliances or particular antagonisms, but on the collective system which is embodied in the League.

One statistic that leaps from the Ballot is the strong preference for economic sanctions over force in tackling an aggressor. Today, economic sanctions remain a significant weapon in the armoury of the United Nations. But their record is one of persistent failure. In my time as a diplomat, I saw UN sanctions imposed on Rhodesia, South Africa, Iraq, Iran and North Korea, to name but five. Goodness knows how many other regimes were punished in this way. In some cases, they were supplemented by EU and bilateral sanctions. I cannot think of one instance where sanctions on their own were decisive in changing a government's behaviour. Often they had perverse consequences by stimulating domestic production of the very products that were banned. Every sanctions regime has been enormously vulnerable to smuggling. Élites become adept at insulating themselves from the worst effects of sanctions. In Saddam Hussein's Iraq, it was ordinary people who were hardest hit by sanctions as he rationed medical supplies and then used this – pretty effectively, it has to be said – as a propaganda weapon against the UN. Too often, economic sanctions have been simply gesture politics, especially when the imports that are really vital to a state in breach of international law are omitted from the list of banned goods. It is astonishing that, as late as 2009, there was still scope to tighten sanctions further against a regime as mad and bad as that of North Korea.

In the 1930s, this was all to come. Most people thought that collective security based on economic measures alone would do the trick. History has since taught us that this is false. There are times when diplomacy, old or new, must be backed by the credible threat of force. It was necessary after the occupation of the Falkland Islands by Argentina in 1982; after Saddam Hussein's seizure of Kuwait in 1990; and to bring Slobodan Milošević to heel in 1999. Yet, of these three actions, only two benefited from the blessing of a UN Security Council resolution (the Falklands and Kuwait); one was undertaken by one nation alone (the Falklands); and one by NATO without a

UN resolution (Milošević). The invasion of Iraq in 2003 was, of course, also without an enabling UN resolution. In the 1930s it proved impossible to mobilise the membership of the League to take military action against anyone, despite major threats to peace. Things have improved under the UN, but not a lot. The plain truth is that the decision to go to war remains the ultimate bastion of national sovereignty; and it will not be pre-empted by any notion of collective security, unless it happens to coincide with the national interest.

The Ballot threw up several ironies and contradictions. A large section of British public opinion was telling the government that it did not want the League of Nations to have even the theoretical option of going to war to uphold collective security. This hardly reinforced the League's authority, even if the option never came near to being exercised. Despite the disdain of many in the government – and the Foreign Office – for the Ballot, they were, for all practical purposes, at one with the pacifist lobby. Britain was in no position to undertake a serious war; and this would remain the case until late in the decade, by which time the nation had rearmed. Hindsight tells us that Mussolini and Hitler should have been stopped in their tracks early on, by force if necessary, and that this should have been done by the League. But, the temper of the times, the need to rearm, and the fallacies of the New Diplomacy were all against it.

The politicians had to pay attention to the results of the Peace Ballot. The outpouring of public feeling was too large to ignore. The Prime Minister, Stanley Baldwin, met a deputation from the National Declaration Committee in July 1935, and reassured them 'that the League of Nations remains, as I said in a speech in Yorkshire recently, "the sheet anchor of British policy"'. For the rest of the year, the Peace Ballot, and its political consequences, weighed on the minds of the Cabinet.

British foreign policy now had a new public face. Sir Samuel Hoare had replaced Sir John Simon as Foreign Secretary in June 1935, just in time to be hit with the full force of the Abyssinia crisis. Having spent the last four years steering the controversial India Bill through Parliament, Hoare was experienced in the art of the possible. As an elected politician, Hoare had, far more than

Vansittart (though you are unlikely to become PUS without the keenest political antennae), to take account of the public's mood. He was under a double pressure: from the strong views expressed through the Peace Ballot, and the public's wish for Britain to do something about Abyssinia. They were in potential contradiction. In July, Hoare wrote to the British Ambassador in Rome that 'the feeling here is becoming more and more anti-Italian and there is every sign of the country being swept with the kind of movement that Gladstone started over the Bulgarian atrocities'.[9] Doing nothing was not an option. He would have to find a 'third way' between intervention that could lead to war, and amoral isolationism.

Hoare, like Vansittart, was under no illusion that Mussolini could be stopped by economic sanctions. But he had at least to be seen to try the League route. He set out the dilemma in a letter to the British Ambassador in Paris in late August:

Most people are still convinced that if we stick to the Covenant [of the League] and apply collective sanctions, Italy must give in and there will be no war. You and I know that the position is not as simple as this and that the presumptions that, firstly, there will be collective action including full collective action by the French, and secondly that economic sanctions will be effective are, to say the least, very bold and sanguine. None the less, whatever may develop it is essential that we should play out the League hand in September. If it is then found that there is no collective basis for sanctions ... ... the world will have to face the fact that sanctions are impracticable. We must, however, on no account assume the impracticability of sanctions until the League has made this investigation. It must be the League and not the British Government that declares that sanctions are impracticable and the British Government must on no account lay itself open to the charge that we have not done our utmost to make them practicable.

Going through the motions may not look an especially inspired or principled approach to foreign policy. But, this is the reality of democratic politics and an answer to those who protest that diplomats are too divorced from the concerns of so-called ordinary people. What the voter wants, the voter usually gets. In 1935, ordinary people – the voters – demanded the League; and that is what the Foreign Office gave them. The fact that professional diplomats thought that this would get nowhere was neither here nor there. There is a loose parallel with Iraq and the United Nations in 2002. It was important to the British government, less so to the American, that, if it came to war, it should be the UN itself that declared Iraq to be in breach of its international obligations on weapons of mass destruction. This, of course, never happened, to the eternal embarrassment of Tony Blair and his Cabinet.

The government's calculation was that, if Hoare's approach could hold until after the general election in November, it would be on safer ground to try Vansittart's preferred tactic of brokering a deal with Italy. It was no surprise then that the government's election manifesto should play to the voters' love of the League:

the League of Nations will remain, as heretofore, the keystone of British foreign policy ... In the dispute between Italy and Abyssinia there will be no wavering in the policy hitherto pursued. We shall take no action in isolation, but we shall be prepared faithfully to take our part in any collective action decided upon by the League and its members.

As they say in the Foreign Office, true as far as it goes. Where this pronouncement did not go was to the no-man's land of what would happen if the League failed to agree collective action. The Foreign Office would, to use another favourite phrase, have to cross that bridge when it came to it.

Hoare himself gave every appearance of being an apostle of the New Diplomacy. In a speech to the Assembly of the League of Nations in September, he gave the League an extravagant endorsement:

in conformity with its precise and explicit obligations the League stands, and my country stands with it, for the collective maintenance of the Covenant in its entirety, and particularly for steady and collective resistance to all acts of unprovoked aggression.

The audience reacted with jubilation. They took it as a commitment to action against Italy. But Hoare was, of course, committing only to *collective* action. He knew from recent discussions with the French Prime Minister, Pierre Laval (who would be shot in 1945 for collaborating with the Germans), that the French were unlikely to commit to anything which might threaten war. Without France, there was no practical prospect of collective military action against Italy, given their common frontier and France's status as a Mediterranean power.

Then, Hoare's cunning plan was overtaken by events. On 3 October 1935, Italian troops crossed the frontier into Abyssinia. The invasion had finally begun. Mussolini, bathing in the glow of adoring crowds, shared none of the British and French aversion to war, though Italy had suffered terrible casualties during the Great War, fighting Austria in the mountains. Haile Selassie repeatedly appealed for help from the League. In September, his calls having gone unheeded, he mobilised his own troops. On paper, they and their antiquated weapons stood little chance against the well-equipped Italian invaders. To make matters worse, Britain and others had for the last few months maintained an arms embargo against the belligerents. This had a disproportionate impact on the Abyssinians, who desperately needed weapons for self-defence. The situation was akin to that in the early 1990s when an arms embargo against Serbia and Bosnia made it more difficult for the Bosnians to defend themselves against well-armed Serbian attack. The British government was reluctant to relax the embargo on Abyssinia for fear of provoking Italy. In the event, the war brought no glory to the Italians' regimental standards, though it took Mussolini's domestic popularity to its apogee. The Italian armies were repeatedly held up by fierce Abyssinian resistance, which was only broken when, against the very Geneva Protocol that Italy had recently signed, Mussolini allowed his commanders to drop mustard gas on the Abyssinians from the air.

The League condemned Italy for resorting 'to war in disregard of its covenants under Article XII of the Covenant of the League of Nations'. The next step was economic sanctions. These were feeble. Vital raw materials, such as coal, oil, iron and steel were excluded. Even if oil had been included, neutral countries outside the League like the US and Venezuela could have compensated. Vansittart had strongly argued against an embargo on oil. The Italian Ambassador had threatened the possibility of an attack on the British fleet in the Mediterranean, if Britain were to support an oil embargo. For Britain, at this point, war was unthinkable save in the context of collective action by the League. This apparently very New Diplomacy stance was, in reality, dependent on a very Old Diplomacy calculation: namely, where were the French in all this? The League, like the UN, was no more than the sum of its parts, that is the member-states. Any collective military action was wholly dependent, as today, on the contributions of the member-states; and in 1936, with Italy in the League's somewhat palsied sights, the only contribution that mattered for Britain was the French.

This posed a big problem. Vansittart succinctly explained it in a minute to Hoare in advance of a meeting on a possible oil embargo:

The situation, and my anxiety, would be very different, but for our glaring deficiencies, and the impossibility of counting on France – which will make it impossible to count on anyone else. I beg you and Mr Eden to take this into consideration ... To run the risk alone and unprepared would surely be unthinkable.

In January 1935, in a meeting with Mussolini, Laval had almost certainly agreed already to sit on his hands if Italy invaded Abyssinia. The French had good reasons for avoiding conflict. In the Great War they had suffered over five million men killed and wounded, mostly on French soil. In the Franco-Prussian War of 1870–71, also fought on French soil, over one million men had been killed, wounded or captured in only ten months' fighting. This puts American and British casualties in Iraq and Afghanistan in some perspective. Casualties on the French scale do something to a country, physically and morally. France had regularly trounced the Prussian army during the Napoleonic Wars, until one afternoon in the summer of 1815, when Marshal Blücher had come to Wellington's rescue on the field of Waterloo. Now it regarded Germany with fear and loathing. France was in the unenviable position of having Hitler on one frontier, Mussolini on another. If Britain could make the calculation that Germany was a greater threat than Italy, ergo Mussolini should not be driven into Hitler's arms, so could France – with knobs on. Laval had also a domestic political problem: his government was dependent on the support of the resolutely anti-war Radical Party.

Vansittart was, therefore, right to say that the French could not be relied on to support an oil embargo. After Hoare's famous speech to the League on collective security in September, the French sought reassurances that the British would not support any sanctions against Italy which might lead to war. Vansittart, whose onerous task it was to try to strike a deal over Abyssinia with French support, had the Englishman's love-hate relationship with France. For centuries, relations between the two countries had been shot through with a complex concoction of enmity and intimacy. Britain's only comparable relationships are with Germany and the United States, with whom, as with France, we have both fought wars and worked together in the closest harmony. In the Hundred Years' War with France, fought in the fourteenth and fifteenth centuries, it had been difficult sometimes to work out who was English, who French, given the common Norman and Gascon pedigrees. The medieval English royal family was coursing with the blood of French princesses. The persecuted seventeenth-century French Protestants, the Huguenots, found refuge in Britain, as did French aristocrats after 1789, fleeing for their lives from the French Revolution. Yet Britain and France had fought what was virtually another hundred years' war between the early eighteenth and nineteenth centuries, ending only with Bonaparte's final defeat at Waterloo. We had, of course, been allies in the Great War, though this had left a residue of mixed feelings on both sides (one of my grandfathers returned from the trenches with an indelible loathing of the French); and we had not entered into formal alliance until 1904 and the *Entente Cordiale*. The two countries, in a curious mirror-image, attributed to each other an almost bottomless capacity for treachery and cunning. The French called Britain *perfide Albion* (and they still do). When I worked in the 1980s at Britain's mission to the EU, any French initiative was regarded with intense suspicion; and was rigorously picked apart for evidence of diplomatic trickery. Vansittart was frequently exasperated by the French, bemoaning in one October minute 'the danger of an Anglo-Italian war brought about not only by French lack of co-operation but disloyalty and treachery in its dirtiest and blackest form'.

The fundamental weakness of the New Diplomacy was that it would only work if adopted by all. Already in 1930, in his 'Old Adam' minute, Vansittart had noted that France appeared not entirely committed to New Diplomacy's ideals of 'moral disarmament and cooperation'. Old-style balance of power diplomacy, said Vansittart, underlay its public commitment to the League. When Abyssinia was invaded in October 1935, the French government announced that it would agree to action against Italy, only after consultation and 'accord' with Britain. Here was that mirror-image again. Neither would entertain war against Italy unless the other moved first. But, for their own good reasons, neither wanted war. So each was afraid that, if it moved against Mussolini, it would be left dangling on the end of a branch, with the other refusing to move. If that happened, the rest of the League membership would also hang back. Because Britain had taken the contingency step of sending troopships to the Mediterranean, the French already felt themselves absolved from war; the British move had, after all, been made without the 'accord' of France.

These machinations opened a fatal gulf between what the politicians were telling the public and what was going on behind the scenes. The government's formal position was to work with France and others to bring about a solution to the Abyssinia crisis, fully consonant with the League's principles and the norms of the New Diplomacy. But, behind the scenes, Vansittart was busy in talks with the French to find a compromise acceptable to Mussolini. It would be resolutely Old Diplomacy. It could not be anything else. The New Diplomacy was already dead, but nobody had the courage to tell the public so soon after the Peace Ballot. Hoare and Vansittart would pay the price with their careers.

In December 1935, Vansittart and Hoare travelled to Paris to sort out the final elements of an agreement which had been carefully put together by the diplomats. The King had to give a special dispensation to allow the Foreign Secretary and the Permanent Under-Secretary out of the country at the same time, but the importance of the Paris meeting warranted it. Vansittart later revealed that, in the car on the way to the French Foreign Ministry at the Quai d'Orsay, he had seized the moment to nail down once and for all the key point. Would the government fight Italy over Abyssinia? No, said Hoare. 'Then you will have to compromise,' Vansittart replied. 'That will be unpopular but there is no third way.'

Hoare was in no state to resist Vansittart's powerful character and convictions, even had he wished to. He had been unwell for some weeks, suffering fainting fits while at work. Later, he wrote in his memoirs that 'it may be that I was so pulled down by overwork that my judgement was out of gear'. Before leaving London, Hoare had promised Eden (then Minister for the League of Nations Affairs, with Cabinet rank) that he would not commit Britain to anything while in Paris. Once there, however, he signed the agreement which became known as the Hoare–Laval Pact. To this day, it is not entirely clear what happened in Paris. In his memoirs, Hoare blames himself for not getting clearer instructions from the Cabinet, but protests that what was agreed with Laval was subject to government approval anyway. Eden, in a memoir years later, blamed Hoare for not having more political *nous*. But, on the eve of the Paris meeting he had warned Hoare that 'Van can be more French than the French . . .'

The Pact was a classic deal of the old school. Peace was to be purchased at the expense of Abyssinian territory. Italy would be given land in the northern province of Tigray and in the east and south-east of Abyssinia. There would be an economic development zone in the south and south-west, where the League would oversee an Italian monopoly. To compensate the Abyssinians, they would be granted a land corridor to the sea through British Somaliland. Just as the Shah of Persia had not been told about the division of his country into Russian and British spheres of influence until it was a *fait accompli* in the 1907 Anglo-Russian agreement, so Haile Selassie was not consulted about the Pact. The idea was that once it had secured Mussolini's agreement, it would then be presented to Abyssinia and the League of Nations; and made public.

Mission accomplished, Hoare took leave in Geneva. He and Vansittart were well aware of the Pact's imperfections. But, they considered that it was the best that could be done in the circumstances. It would stop the war; and strengthen ties between Britain, France and Italy against Germany. They were reasonably confident that it would be acceptable to the League, which had itself appointed a Committee of Five earlier in the year to investigate the possibility of a deal between Italy and Abyssinia. The Committee's report, published in September 1935, had suggested a plan similar to the Pact's. Hoare went on holiday, confident that 'there was general approval of the double policy that I was pursuing', i.e. negotiating a deal, while imposing economic sanctions. He would soon be disabused.

Before Mussolini could respond formally to the Hoare–Laval Pact (to which he had reacted well in private), it was leaked to the press in Paris. There was an eruption of moral outrage. A *Times* leader was typical:

the Paris Proposals ... were dead for all practical purposes from the moment that their general tenor was known. There has never been the slightest prospect that British public opinion would recommend them for approval by the League as a fair and reasonable basis of negotiation ... Let Ministers make up their mind, then, in the light of this clear manifestation of British opinion, that their representatives cannot possibly press for the acceptance of the Paris proposals by the Council ... No Englishman in his senses has ever contemplated hostilities with Italy or with any other nation. There has never been any question of Great Britain taking sides in the Abyssinian War. Her role is precisely that of fifty other nations. Neither more nor less.

The Times was, of course, one of the leading apostles of appeasement. Its moral fervour, and absolutist interpretation of Britain's role in the League could lead to one practical consequence only: that absolutely nothing would be done to help Abyssinia in its agony. The Hoare–Laval Pact, had it been accepted by Mussolini, would have rescued something from the Abyssinian wreckage. What sticks in the craw, of course, is that the Pact still rewarded *Il Duce* for his aggression. But, as A.J.P. Taylor concluded in his *Origins of the Second World War*, the Pact 'was a perfectly sensible plan, in line with the League's previous acts of conciliation from Corfu to Manchuria'. It would have 'ended the war; satisfied Italy; and left Abyssinia with a more workable, national territory'; but the 'common sense of the plan was, in the circumstances of the time, its vital defect'.

The public, meanwhile, saw the Pact as a gross act of betrayal.

The government went into headlong retreat; and, as governments do, prepared to sacrifice the scapegoats. At first, the Prime Minister, Stanley Baldwin, had assured Hoare that 'we all stand together'. But public pressure was such that the government's very survival was in question unless someone took the fall. Hoare handed in his resignation, after some unsubtle nudging from the Cabinet. So did Laval. The story goes that when King George V gave an audience to Anthony Eden, Hoare's successor as Foreign Secretary, the monarch wryly commented, 'No more coals to Newcastle, no more Hoares to Paris.'

As for Vansittart, he stayed in his post, but his reputation was in tatters. He remembered later how the *News Chronicle* 'cut off my head and pilloried me as the man behind it all'. It seems likely that his resignation from the Diplomatic Service was discussed by the Prime Minister. In the end, Vansittart was kicked upstairs into the vacuous role of Chief Diplomatic Adviser to the government. The Hoare–Laval Pact was buried. Baldwin told the Commons on 19 December that it was 'absolutely and completely dead'.

Mussolini pressed on. Thanks more to the deadly effect of mustard gas than to the ardour and skill of his troops, the Italian army entered the capital, Addis Ababa, on 5 May 1936. Mussolini proclaimed that Abyssinia was henceforth annexed to Italy. A month later, Haile Selassie appeared in person before the League of Nations. Though shamefully heckled by Italian journalists, he delivered a speech that was at once dignified, eloquent and prescient. It should have shamed his audience:

I, Haile Selassie I, Emperor of Ethiopia, am here today to claim that justice which is due to my people, and the assistance promised to it eight months ago, when fifty nations asserted that aggression had been committed in violation of international treaties.

There is no precedent for a Head of State himself speaking in this assembly. But there is also no precedent for a people being victim of such injustice and being at present threatened by abandonment to its aggressor. Also, there has never before been an example of any Government proceeding to the systematic extermination of a nation by barbarous means, in violation of the most solemn promises made by the nations of the earth that there should not be used against innocent human beings the terrible poison of harmful gases. It is to defend a people struggling for its age-old independence that the head of the Ethiopian Empire has come to Geneva to fulfil this supreme duty, after having himself fought at the head of his armies.

The Emperor went on to describe the atrocities perpetrated by the Italian army, in particular the effects of mustard gas:

The deadly rain that fell from the aircraft made all those whom it touched fly shrieking with pain. All those who drank the poisoned water or ate the infected food also succumbed in dreadful suffering. In tens of thousands, the victims of the Italian mustard gas fell.

He also reminded the League how ill-equipped his country had been to defend itself, and of the commitments the League had made to defend the weak. 'God and history will remember your judgement,' he warned the Assembly.

If the audience were not shame-faced and conscience-stricken, they should have been. Either way, it made no difference. The League of Nations was broken-backed. Such authority as it may have enjoyed had gone forever. Collective security had proved a sham, the New Diplomacy impotent. An independent state had been swallowed up; a fascist dictator had gone undeterred. Mussolini would in due course ally with Hitler. The outcome could not have been worse.

In Berlin, they drew the obvious conclusions. The League of Nations would be no impediment to Hitler's ambitions. In March 1936, his troops occupied the demilitarised Rhineland, Mussolini having already told him that he would raise no objection. When Hitler seized the Czech Sudetenland in 1938 and invaded Poland in 1939, no one bothered to consult the League of Nations.

The reputation of Neville Chamberlain, Britain's Prime Minister at the outbreak of the Second World War, has never recovered from his failed attempt to appease Hitler during the Czechoslovakia crisis. But, in the summer of 1936, he made some shrewd observations in a speech as to why a system of collective security based on sanctions had failed. It is as apposite today:

Is it not apparent that the policy of sanctions involves, I do not say war, but a risk of war? ... Is it not also apparent from what has happened that, in the presence of such a risk nations cannot be relied upon to proceed to the last extremity of war unless their vital interests are threatened? That being so, does it not suggest that it might be wise to explore the possibilities of localising the danger spots of the world ... by means of regional arrangements which could be approved by the League, but which should be guaranteed only by those nations whose interests were vitally connected with those danger zones?[10]

In 1936, the idealists of the New Diplomacy had to learn painful truths: that no Western democracy would go to war for the sake of an internationalist idea; that the nation-state, precisely because of the blood-letting of the Great War, would continue jealously to reserve to itself the decision to wage war; and that this decision would be based on a hard-headed calculation of where the national interest lay. In short, if there were any mileage in the concept of collective security, it would be driven by the diplomats of the old school. By devolving some peace-keeping duties to organisations such as NATO, the EU and the African Union, the UN seems, albeit unconsciously, to have taken up Chamberlain's proposal.

The stench of appeasement still sticks to the Hoare–Laval Pact. Vansittart's tragedy is that he sought to appease the minor dictator so as to be better positioned to fight the major dictator, at a time when public opinion was not ready to abandon the delusions of the Peace Ballot. As for the New Diplomacy, it turned out a dangerous diversion from the realities of a dog-eat-dog, Hobbesian world. If there is a charge to be laid at Vansittart's door, it is not that he sacrificed the New Diplomacy on the altar of the Old; but that he was not sufficiently clear-eyed, not 'realist' enough. It was surely his delusion to believe that Mussolini could ever be tempted to throw in his lot with the Western democracies, and not Germany.

The League of Nations, mortally wounded in Abyssinia, died a lingering death, finally put out of its impotent and irrelevant misery in 1946. As a former Foreign Secretary, Lord Hurd, concluded: 'It was an attempt to create a system of rules without power, and it failed.'

But let the last word go to Van – the concluding line of his autobiography, *The Mist Procession*, published posthumously in 1958:

Mine is a story of failure, but it throws light on my time which failed too.

9

THE RETURN OF HISTORY:
Bosnia and the Hour of Europe

I was on a posting to the British Embassy in Washington, revelling in the magnificently Edwardian title of Minister (Commercial), when the Berlin Wall came down in 1989. As number three in the Embassy's hierarchy after the Ambassador and the Deputy Head of Mission, my job was to deal with trade, science and transport policy. It was an interesting job, because it covered subjects where, unusually for the British-American relationship, there were a significant number of disputes: chicken wars, beef wars, rows about transatlantic air services and so on. Most of these were supposed to be handled by the European Commission, which was responsible for the trade policy of the member-states of what was then the European Community, but embassies retained plenty of scope to deal on their own account with the Americans, in the best school of negotiation on earth.

For all its interest, trade was not my natural habitat; and I looked with envy at my Embassy colleagues, who were dealing with all the issues arising from the collapse of Communism. Then in 1992, out of the blue, my prayers were answered. The Ambassador, Sir Robin, now Lord, Renwick, decided to promote me to be his deputy, rather than getting someone from London. Suddenly, the post-Soviet world was my oyster.

Washington DC at this time was awash with an optimism that bordered on euphoria. The demise of the old Cold War enemy; the crushing of Saddam Hussein in a lightning war the year previously; and the emergence of what the Americans called a Europe 'whole and free', had left the United States of America indisputably the world's top dog, the only superpower. The administration of President George H. W. Bush talked of a New World Order, and few were prepared to swim against this flash-flood of optimism. Some anxieties lingered about Japan and the perceived superiority of its economic model. As the Japanese bought the Rockefeller Center and Hollywood studios, alarm spread in some quarters that they would achieve economically what they had failed to secure by force of arms in the Second World War. There were twitches of concern about the impending creation of Europe's Single Market, from the benefits of which the Americans worried that they would be unfairly excluded. As usual, the US was trying to have its cake and eat it. It regularly exhorted the Europeans to get their act together and unify; but, at the first signs of this happening, warnings would fly across the Atlantic that decisions should not be taken that would discriminate against America.

Here and there, more perceptive warnings sounded. After Gorbachev had come to power in Moscow, the French Foreign Minister, Jean-Bernard Raimond, commended to his European colleagues what he called 'double vigilance' in approaching the changes that were taking place in Russia. By this he meant that the West should be vigilant for genuine change that would mark a hopeful break with Soviet Communism and Cold War thinking; and vigilant for what was just window-dressing, concealing the Old Russian Adam. In the new age of Putin's authoritarianism, this now reads as prophetic common sense.

In 1989, the US Deputy Secretary of State, Larry Eagleburger, made a speech of equal prescience. Eagleburger, a chain-smoker, who named all three of his sons Lawrence after himself, prayed for visitors who also liked to smoke. He found one such in Nicholas Ridley, Margaret Thatcher's Trade Secretary (he was later fired for saying that handing over sovereignty to Europe 'was as bad as giving it up to Adolf Hitler'). I went once with Ridley to see Eagleburger. Ridley asked if he might smoke. With a whoop of joy, Eagleburger, who was under doctor's orders to give up tobacco, whipped out his own cigarettes, saying that it would be impolite not to accompany a distinguished foreign statesman in his enjoyment of the weed. The topic of discussion, wreathed in a smokescreen worthy of the Battle of Jutland, was the banning of American chewing tobacco in Britain, to which both objected, though, in Ridley's case, it was official British policy.

In his speech at Georgetown University, Eagleburger implied, to some subsequent criticism, that we might come to regret the passing of the Cold War. In his view, the world was not

necessarily going to be a safer place than the Cold War era ... for all its risks and uncertainties, the Cold War was characterised by a remarkably stable and predictable set of relations among the great powers.[1]

He went on to refer to the instability of the new nation-states after the First World War.

Raimond and Eagleburger had been right to counsel caution. As I started my new job in early 1992, the hubris and hyperbole of the post-Soviet moment were about to dissolve in a violent Balkan mess. The immediate reason was the collapse of Yugoslavia after the death of its long-time dictator, Marshal Tito. But behind Tito hovered the ghosts of the Habsburg and Ottoman Empires, and the old Eastern Question itself. This was not the end of history, but its resumption. Europe and the US found themselves sweeping up the wreckage not only of Yugoslavia, but of those two old empires that, with Russia, had once dominated the Balkans. Even today, well into the twenty-first century, the task is incomplete.

On 18 December 1992, Lord Owen, a former British Foreign Secretary, now the EU's Balkans troubleshooter, stepped on to the tarmac at Sarajevo Airport and delivered a bleakly candid message to the beleaguered Bosnian people: 'Don't live under this dream that the West is going to come and sort this out. Don't dream dreams.'

Owen was walking into an almighty mess, and he knew it. The disintegration of Yugoslavia had resulted in the kind of brutal and organised violence that Europe hoped it would never see again: ethnic cleansing, mass rape, and concentration camps. Later, for the first time since Second World War, the violence would be formally characterised as genocidal. Despite Owen's brutal realism, the powers of Europe could not just stand by as genocide happened on their doorstep. But what exactly could, and should, they do? There was no easy answer; and by the time they found one, over 110,000

Bosnians had been killed, more than two million displaced, and the territory of a multi-ethnic European republic sliced into ethnically pure regions. There were other major casualties too: European pretensions; the reputation of UN peace-keeping; and, for a while, British and European relations with the US.

The New World Order came and went like a shooting star. Peace – kind of – was brought to Bosnia, and Slobodan Milošević hoist by his own Kosovar petard, thanks to the time-honoured combination of diplomacy backed by force. To the immense chagrin of many Europeans, the United States proved once again the only Western power capable of delivering that combination in a manner remotely intimidating to an adversary as tough as Milošević. It was the hour of the Americans; and, as usual with the Americans, that was because they saw their national interest imperilled by Balkan chaos and European impotence. Bosnia buried the New World Order, as effectively as Abyssinia had buried the New Diplomacy.

The first Yugoslav state, the Kingdom of Serbs, Croats and Slovenes, was formed after the First World War and the demise of the Habsburg and Ottoman Empires. It was the fulfilment of the nineteenth-century dream, a state for the southern Slav people, free from the shackles of foreign rule. But, the young state was a jigsaw of different ethnic and religious groups. Between the world wars, it was frequently shaken by their rivalry and, sometimes, mutual hatred. This applied, in particular, to the Serbs and Croats. During the Second World War, after Italian and German invasion, Yugoslavia was riven by pro- and anti-fascist forces, a divide which rendered still more toxic the already poisonous ethnic rivalries. A 'second Yugoslavia' – a socialist federation of six republics – emerged from the war. It was ruled with an iron fist by the hero of partisan resistance to the German occupation, Josip Broz Tito. For thirty-five years, under the doctrine of 'Brotherhood and Unity', Tito ruthlessly suppressed expressions of ethnic separatism going beyond what was permitted under Yugoslavia's federal structure. After his death in 1980, and the fall of Communism a few years later, the ties that had held Yugoslavia together began to unravel.

The vacuum left by the death of Tito and his brand of socialism was filled by fierce nationalisms, stoked ironically by the first genuinely democratic elections to be held in Yugoslavia since the Second World War. These returned nationalist party majorities in many of the constituent republics, notably in the two old rivals, Croatia and Serbia. Slobodan Milošević, President of Serbia, would have liked to step into Tito's shoes. But, if Yugoslavia was going to break up – in part because of the very pressure of centralising Serb nationalism – he argued that internal boundaries would have to be redrawn so that the Serb diaspora in the other republics could be brought into an enlarged Serbian state. This was something for which the original drawing of Yugoslavia's internal boundaries in 1945 had never provided. Croatia, Bosnia-Herzegovina, and Montenegro – three other republics of the Yugoslav federation – each had significant Serb populations. The implication was clear. If Milošević were to achieve his ambition, it could mean only war; and that was what happened.

In the summer of 1991, Slovenia and Croatia walked out of the Yugoslav Federation. They knew that Milošević was unlikely to let them go without a fight. He had gained control of the JNA, the Yugoslav People's Army, a fighting force that was supposed to be for the protection of the whole Federation. Most of it, with equipment and munitions, soon became the military arm of the Serbian regime. Slovenia and Croatia pleaded with the international community for recognition as independent nations. At the same time, units of the JNA moved to crush their aspirations.

At that moment, Europe's leaders were at a European Community Summit in Luxembourg. They too were touched by the optimism of the hour; on the verge of taking another big step for European unity as the European Community converted itself into the European Union (EU). The Single Market, agreed by Margaret Thatcher at a European Council in Luxembourg in 1985 – apparently to her eternal regret – was about to come into effect. There was much talk of further integration, with a common foreign and security policy. And then the Balkans immediately threw up the new Europe's first challenge. With sublimely fatuous hubris, Jacques Poos, the combined Deputy Prime Minister and Foreign Minister of Luxembourg – the EU's smallest state, with an army of 800 men – declared: 'The hour of Europe has dawned.' It certainly had; but not as Poos intended. It was an hour of shame and humiliation, one of those moments when history exacts a harrowing retribution from the foolish.

The outbreak of war in the crumbling Yugoslavia was not supposed to happen under the New World Order. Perhaps Poos and others had got carried away by reading Francis Fukuyama's treatise *The End of History*, which, on its publication, enjoyed an immediate *succès d'estime* in academic and think-tank circles. Fukuyama wrote:

What we may be witnessing is not just the end of the Cold War, or the passing of a particular period of post-war history, but the end of history as such: that is, the end point of mankind's ideological evolution and the universalisation of Western liberal democracy as the final form of human government.[2]

Here was somebody else setting himself up for history's retribution. Europe, far from bringing the curtain down on its history, was about to resume it after the long hibernation of the Cold War. The first awakening would be in the land of the southern Slavs.

The Europeans were determined to deal with the Yugoslav crisis without American help. This suited the Republican administration of President George H.W. Bush fine. They had just won the first Gulf War in February 1991. There was little American appetite for engaging in further foreign conflict. As James Baker, Bush's Secretary of State, put it in good old Texan fashion: 'We don't have a dog in that fight.' But I remember, from talking at the time to contacts in the White House, that there was already a fear that, sooner or later, the Europeans would be calling for rescue by the US cavalry.

David Owen, with characteristic bluntness, dismisses any notion of neo-Gladstonian, humanitarian motives in the EU's approach:

Yugoslavia was the virility symbol of the Euro-federalists. This was going to be the time when Europe emerged with a single foreign policy and therefore it unwisely shut out an America only too happy to be shut out.

In short, it was a European power-play that would end in tears – mainly Bosnian Muslim tears.

The task of bringing peace was daunting. Between the outbreak of fighting and the Dayton Agreement at the end of 1995, at least seven identifiable Balkan belligerents were involved. This was the period of Yugoslav disintegration, in which the two largest republics, Serbia and Croatia, sought to grab the lion's share of the spoils, mainly at the expense of Bosnia[3] and, sometimes, each other. There were three Serb belligerents: Serbia itself and mini-Serb republics carved from Serb communities in Croatia and Bosnia; two Croatian, Croatia itself and a Croat mini-republic, amputated from Bosnia; Bosnia, which, after the secession of its Serb and Croat communities, was largely, but not exclusively, Muslim Slav in character and whose inhabitants were known as Bosniaks; and Slovenia, which after a ten-day war in 1991, broke free for good from Serb clutches.

In a second phase, which reached its climax in 1999, and provided Tony Blair with his finest hour on the world stage, Milošević tried, and failed, to purge the province of Kosovo of its native Albanians. This dragged in the former Yugoslav republic of Macedonia, which had a significant Albanian population.

The multiple wars of 1991–95 were fought by a combination of regular army formations from the old JNA and irregular units comprising former soldiers, policemen, intelligence officers, criminals and mercenaries, domestic and foreign. As the plight of the Bosniaks deepened, Muslim fighters from around the world came to help them. Civilians were a strategic target and atrocity became a strategic weapon. Since the objective of the Serbs and Croats was to take and hold territory, they visited an extreme and deliberate violence on civilians of other ethnic groups. In a warning to the Bosniaks not to follow Slovenia and Croatia in declaring independence, the Bosnian Serb leader, Radovan Karadžić, could not have been clearer about the consequences of breaking away from the Yugoslav Federation:

You want to take Bosnia-Herzegovina down the same highway of hell and suffering that Slovenia and Croatia are travelling. Do not think that you will not lead Bosnia-Herzegovina into hell, and do not think that you will not perhaps make the Muslim people disappear, because the Muslims cannot defend themselves if there is a war. How will you prevent everyone from being killed in Bosnia-Herzegovina?

The purpose was either to intimidate civilian populations to flee their homes or simply to exterminate them. It was called 'ethnic cleansing', a euphemism of vile proportions. Much of the violence was carried out by paramilitary groups, such as Arkan's Tigers, who were little more than a Serbian criminal enterprise. But General Ratko Mladić, who was in command of the Bosnian Serb army – and is at the time of writing on the run from an international arrest warrant for genocide – was a former high-ranking officer in the JNA. It was he who laid siege to Sarajevo and carried out the Srebrenica massacre, twin emblems of this latest chapter in the interminable history of Balkan disasters.

The result: mass slaughter, mass rape, torture, concentration camps, and long trails of civilian refugees, much of which was to be seen daily on television. In the village of Voćin dozens of Croats were shot in the face or burned alive by Serb paramilitaries, and then left in the streets as a warning to other Croats. In Croatian Vukovar, after a long siege by Serb forces, some 300 Croat men, who had sought refuge in the town's hospital, were taken to a nearby farm and executed. In the Serbo-Croat war alone, casualties on both sides are reckoned to have reached 15,000, with 500,000 Croats and 230,000 Serbs displaced. A third of Croatia fell under Serbian control. Bad as this was, it would be the fate of the Bosniaks that seized the public imagination in the West, and finally moved the US and its allies to intervene effectively.

The extreme violence – the like of which had not been seen on European soil since the Second World War – was matched only by the extreme duplicity of the ex-Yugoslav leaders. This deadly combination proved too much for the EU, the UN, and European governments, softened by decades of peace and easy living. Mediators came and went with their plans. In early 1992, Lord Carrington and Jorge Cutileiro, respectively a former British Foreign Secretary and a Portuguese diplomat, and now mediators for the EU and the UN, came up with a devolution plan for Bosnia, based on ethnic cantons. It was signed by Bosniak, Serb and Croat alike on 18 March; and then repudiated by the Bosniaks on 28 March. In early 1993 a new team of mediators took over: Lord Owen for the EU, Cyrus Vance for the UN, former Foreign Ministers of the UK and the US. In August they presented a partition plan for Bosnia, which the

Serbs rejected. Later in the year, with a new partner, Thorvald Stoltenberg, a former Norwegian Foreign Minister, Owen came up with another plan, which this time the Bosniaks rejected. Then in 1994, the Contact Group of nations (US, Russia, Britain, France and Germany) put forward a plan, which the Serbs rejected. It would take full American engagement, and a NATO bombing campaign, to concentrate Balkan minds and finally achieve in 1995 a settlement that held.

The negotiators had to watch their backs as well as their fronts. The problem for the various mediators was not only devious and ruthless Balkan leaders, but also disagreement among those who had appointed them as to how to proceed. From the start, the hesitations and anxieties of the governments behind them left the mediators firing blanks. In the early days of 1991, there was still a hope that Yugoslavia could be held together. The Carrington–Cutileiro mediation proceeded on that basis. But when Slovenia and Croatia broke away and pleaded for recognition as independent states, the international community had to decide what to do. Lord Carrington felt strongly:

If they recognised Croatia and Slovenia then they would have to ask all of the others whether they wanted their independence. And if they asked the Bosnians whether they wanted their independence, they inevitably would have to say yes, and that this would mean civil war [in Bosnia]. And I put this as strongly as I could.

The British government agreed with him. But, Germany did not. Douglas Hurd, then Foreign Secretary, recalls Hans-Dietrich Genscher, Germany's Foreign Minister, advising him that 'as a general principle, Germany, in view of its awful past, could not afford to find itself on the wrong side of any moral issue'. The moral purity of this position was not quite as undiluted as it seemed. Germany had something of a special relationship with Croatia. In the Second World War, the Croats had sided with Hitler and had been governed by their own brand of Nazism through the *Ustaše* party. The Germans had controlled the Croatian economy, which was rich in the raw materials that Germany needed to prosecute the war. German influences remained in post-war Croatia. Germany pressed its case hard. If its EU colleagues refused to recognise Croatia, it would go ahead anyway. The Germans won the day: the EU agreed to recognise Croatia and Slovenia.

So much for EU solidarity and a common foreign policy. There are many who believe recognition to have been a cardinal strategic error, though it is possible that Yugoslav disintegration had already gone beyond the point of no return. Either way, it cleared the path for the Bosnian war. As Carrington had predicted, Bosnia-Herzegovina declared independence in March 1992. For the next three years it would be Serb and Croat open season on the Bosniaks. The Germans, for their part, did little to help tackle the situation that they themselves had created. Having salved their conscience on the matter of independence, they then refused to contribute a single soldier to the UN's peace-keeping operations that followed. Of course, there were historical reasons for that too. German troops did not fire a shot in anger outside their own frontiers until a 1997 incident in Albania, where they were part of a peace-keeping force. As Britain's Ambassador to Germany, I happened to be meeting the German Foreign Minister, Joschka Fischer, on the day that he had to take part in an historic parliamentary debate to give retrospective approval to the German shot.

Of all the governments that were dragged into the Balkan *imbroglio*, none created more turbulence for the mediators than the United States. In January 1993, Bill Clinton became President. Clinton had during the presidential campaign the previous year criticised George Bush for abdicating American responsibilities in the Balkans. But on taking office, the new President found little appetite either in Congress or among the American people to get involved in Europe's backyard. There appeared to be no national interest at stake that warranted putting American servicemen in harm's way. Something, nonetheless, began to shift in US attitudes.

As the plight of the Bosniaks deepened in 1992, and the siege of Sarajevo tightened, the idea of 'lift and strike' inserted itself into American political debate. It had been part of the Clinton campaign platform. Since September 1991, the United Nations had imposed an arms embargo on the warring parties. This hit the Bosniaks disproportionately, since the Serbs had seized most of the JNA's equipment. 'Lift and strike' would raise the embargo for Bosnia and allow air-strikes on the Serbs in the hills around Sarajevo. The Bush administration was against the proposal, as were Britain, France and Germany. Douglas Hurd took the strongest objection to a policy that, as he put it, said: '*Here are the arms: fight it out.* That is the policy of the level killing field.' The Europeans were afraid also that it would put their soldiers and aid workers in peril. Pro-Serb Russia was against the idea as well. The UN mandate was exceptionally soft, confining the lightly armed troops to the role of protecting the delivery of humanitarian aid. The UN rules of engagement had virtually disarmed them, turning them into little more than boy scouts with armoured cars. It had even been possible for the Serbs to murder Hakija Turajlić, the Bosnian Deputy Prime Minister, under the noses of an armed UN escort.

In early 1993, the Clinton administration decided to push 'lift and strike'. It was supported by two well-placed and eloquent members of the administration, who were appalled by Serb aggression and the suffering of the Bosnian people. One was an old friend of mine from Moscow days, the late Warren Zimmerman, who was US Ambassador to the Yugoslav Federation. Some believe that Warren was responsible for persuading the Bosnian President, Alija Izetbegović, to repudiate the Carrington–Cutileiro proposal on the grounds that it gave too much to the Serbs. He was later to resign from the US Foreign Service in protest at US policy in the Balkans. The other was Jennone Walker, Director for European Affairs in the White House. I used to see the formidable Jennone regularly. They were not always comfortable meetings. She was unashamedly pro-Bosnian, a sentiment stoked by apparently frequent conversations with the Bosnian Ambassador to the UN, Muhamed 'Mo' Sacirbey. He was straining every nerve to get the international community behind 'lift and strike'. Every time I called on her, she seemed to have just finished a conversation with 'Mo', as if to check on what she ought to tell me. Like the Israeli Prime Minister, Binyamin Netanyahu, he sounded like an American (he was a naturalised US citizen), and this made his diplomacy all the more effective in Washington. As I offered the usual reasons against 'lift and strike', Jennone would flash a cold blue eye at me, tinged with contempt. She took pleasure in telling me that the French contingent in the UN force was much more aggressive than the British in interpreting their rules of engagement (which seems to have been true).

In May of that year, the US Secretary of State, Warren Christopher, embarked on an ill-advised tour of European capitals to take soundings on 'lift and strike'. He got a flea in his ear wherever he went. Nor were the Europeans impressed by his downbeat style. There was much negative briefing in the European press, including in London. It was my misfortune to walk into Jennone's office the day after Christopher's return. She was enraged at his humiliation. One lesson that the Clinton people learnt from this episode was that you don't ask the Europeans, you tell them.

All in all, 1993 was a bad year for transatlantic relations. Things were not helped by some disobliging remarks about US policy that appeared in the *New York Times* attributed to David Owen by their star reporter, the late Johnny Apple, Owen then went on American television to tell the viewers that 'lift and strike' was a 'delusion' – 'you will not solve the problem at 10,000 feet'. The intense irritation was mutual. On the European side, the Americans were seen to be indulging in dangerous back-seat driving. Unwilling to put in troops of their own, they were espousing a policy that would endanger the European contingents without bringing a conclusion to the war any closer. This looked less like Madeleine Albright's 'indispensable nation', more like an interfering, moralistic busybody.

While all this was going on, there was agony in Bosnia. The Serb siege of Sarajevo had begun in April 1992. Before then, the city had had a reputation for two things: as the place where the assassination of Archduke Franz Ferdinand and his wife had triggered the First World War; and as a place where different ethnic groups appeared to live in harmony and mixed marriages were fairly common. Sarajevo now found itself at the sharp end of a vicious Serb campaign. The siege would last for four years. The Serbs not only shelled from the surrounding hills, but took up positions in some parts of the city centre and suburbs. Artillery, mortar and sniper fire accounted for around 10,000 civilian deaths. There were particular atrocities that seized the attention: an attack on a football game, where 15 people died and 80 were injured; the Markale marketplace massacre in 1994, where 68 civilians were killed and 200 injured. After the Markale massacre, the UN threatened air-strikes if Serb artillery were not withdrawn beyond a certain line. The Serbs complied, for a while.

In 1994, during a lull in the fighting, I visited Sarajevo with Britain's Prime Minister, John Major, when I was his press secretary. Sarajevo was the headquarters of the UN Protection Force (UNPROFOR), whose commander in 1994–95 was a British General, Sir Michael Rose. The city was enjoying a period of pre-carious renaissance, now that the Serb artillery had gone quiet. The airport had been in the hands of the UN since early in the siege. To diminish the risk of being shot down by Serb forces, landing and take-off from the airfield entailed hair-raising manoeuvres by the pilots of the C-130s, which were the UNPROFOR work-horses. I can remember clinging on like grim death as, inside a shaking, unsoundproofed cabin, we took off almost vertically from Sarajevo.

Rose showed us around the city. I was in some kind of armoured vehicle, with an SAS escort, which included an American from US Special Forces. I asked him what he was doing with the Brits. 'Just looking, just looking,' he said with a grin. Here and there in the streets were signs saying, '*Pazite, Snajper!*' (Beware, Snipers!) We went to the famous Latin Bridge, not far from the spot where Gavrilo Princip had assassinated Archduke Franz Ferdinand. The bridge marked a demarcation line between the Bosnian and Serb parts of the city. On the Serbian side was a block of flats with all the windows shot out, like blinded eyes. It had been a favourite hiding place for snipers. With a mixture of swagger and insouciance, Rose took the Prime Minister and me over the bridge. I did not like those blinded eyes right above me. At one end of the bridge was a smart French armoured car with some smart French soldiers. At the other end was a clapped-out, rusty thing, which belonged to the Russians. There was no sign of Russian soldiers. Rose banged on the door of the armoured car. It eventually opened and out clambered three or four dishevelled soldiers, who had clearly been asleep. So much for the Russian national interest.

Prosecuting counsel at one of the war-crimes trials in The Hague had this to say about the siege of Sarajevo:

The siege of Sarajevo, as it came to be popularly known, was an episode of such notoriety in the conflict in the former Yugoslavia that one must go back to World War II to find a parallel in European history. Not since then had a professional army conducted a campaign of unrelenting violence against the inhabitants of a European city so as to reduce them to a state of medieval deprivation in which they were in constant fear of death. In the period covered in this Indictment, there was nowhere safe for a Sarajevan, not at home, at school, in a hospital, from deliberate attack.

Elsewhere in Bosnia, Serbian forces made rapid gains, within months occupying 70 per cent of the country. The mainly Muslim inhabitants of eastern Bosnia were driven out or killed. Refugees poured into Croatia, bringing with them tales of mass killings, the burning of villages and mass rape. The UN estimated that just a month into the conflict 520,000 people, a twelfth of the population, had been displaced from their homes. Aid convoys destined to help these people were blocked by ground troops. It was a vast humanitarian disaster that would only get worse. Something had to be done.

But what? In Britain, agonised debate ensued. There were two main questions: Should Britain get involved? If so, how? In the Cabinet and House of Commons, opinion split broadly between those who did not believe that the national interest was engaged – and that therefore Britain should keep out of what would undoubtedly be a Balkan quagmire; and those who thought that, as a great European democracy and permanent member of the UN Security Council, there was a moral duty for Britain to intervene to stop the worst violence on European soil since 1945.

As with the Bulgarian atrocities a century previously, the media and public opinion rallied behind the underdog, Bosnia (but this time, a Muslim, not Christian, underdog). Once again, a former Prime Minister emerged from retirement to issue a thundering pronouncement. In 1992 Margaret Thatcher told the world:

Serbia will not listen unless forced to listen ... waiting until the conflict burns itself out will not only be dishonourable but also very costly: refugees, terrorism, Balkan wars drawing in other countries, and worse.

For good measure, she added that the inaction of the West made it 'a little like an accomplice to slaughter'. In the end, Thatcher was proved right. Her argument was implicitly accepted in 1995 by the

US and others. Her crucial insight was that, for strategic and other reasons, a humanitarian intervention that stopped Milošević and Mladić by force would also be good *realpolitik*. It is not invariably the case that values and power politics have to diverge in diplomacy.

None of this was obvious in 1991–92. The default position of the international community was to work through the United Nations. After all, that was what the UN was for. But the UN has shown a habit over the years of sending peace-keepers into action where there is no peace to keep. As in Bosnia, this can turn them into hostages, even victims, of a violent situation, which neither their numbers, weapons, nor mandate allow them to subdue. It happened to the Pakistanis in Somalia in 1993 and the Belgians in Rwanda in 1994. Too often, the Blue Helmets become part of the problem, not the solution.

Britain, if it were going to do anything to help the Bosniaks, could not send a fleet to the Adriatic Sea, as Disraeli had done to the Dardanelles during the Bulgaria crisis. Britain had to move at the same pace as the international convoy. This had automatic consequences for Britain's margin of manoeuvre. But, there was also the question of how the British government judged the British interest. Britain's Foreign Secretary at the time, Douglas Hurd, put it this way in a recent interview for the companion BBC television series to this book:

Britain had no interest specifically in the former Yugoslavia. It was not important for trade. Not important strategically. Our interest was simply to make it a more decent place. To stop people killing each other and we were trying to do that the whole time with diplomacy. By sanctions. By applying pressures. We weren't trying to do it by bombing them into submission as it were.

As public outrage mounted, Hurd, like Disraeli before him, argued in the House of Commons in April 1993 that:

Anger and horror are not enough as a basis for decisions. It is a British interest to make a reasoned contribution towards a more orderly and decent world. But it is not a British interest, and it would only be a pretence, to suppose that we can intervene and sort out every tragedy which captures people's attention and sympathy. I have never found the phrase 'something must be done' to be a phrase which carries any conviction in places such as the House or the Government where people have to take decisions. Governments and Parliaments have to weigh and judge. Bosnia is not the same as Kuwait or the Falklands, in history or terrain or calculation of risk.

Decisions cannot be based either on false analogies or on a desire to achieve better headlines tomorrow than today. That is particularly true when those decisions affect human life, and more especially still when the lives are those of British service men or civilians.

A few months later, Hurd took aim at the editors and leader-writers in a speech at the Travellers' Club:

Most of those who report for the BBC, *The Times*, the *Independent*, the *Guardian*, have all been in different ways enthusiasts pushing for military intervention in Bosnia [...] They are founder members of the something-must-be-done club.

An American journalist once said that a picture was worth a thousand words. That was the British government's problem throughout the Bosnia crisis, one that neither Disraeli nor Vansittart had had to face. It was forced to deal with the impact of television. Hurd argued that the medium of moving pictures and sound distorted the situation:

like it or not, television images are what forces foreign policy makers to give one of the current 25 crises in the world greater priority.

One critic turned this around and dubbed it 'Hurd's law': that governments can get away with inaction over conflicts that do not receive media coverage. Hurd was not alone in his view of the power of television. General Wesley Clark, the senior military member of the US negotiating team at Dayton, and later Supreme Allied Commander, Europe at the time of the Kosovo crisis in 1999, commented that

... the information age technologies ... impacted powerfully at the political levels. The instantaneous flow of news and especially imagery could overwhelm the ability of governments to explain, investigate, coordinate and confirm. We called it the 'CNN factor' ... CNN correspondent Christiane Amanpour, whose stunning on-the-scene visuals and reporting could make a distant crisis an instant domestic political concern ... the new technologies could put unrelenting ... pressure ... on policymakers ... from the very beginning of any operation.[4]

In June 1992, the UN peace-keeping force, UNPROFOR, deployed to Bosnia. It had been created the previous September during the Serb-Croat war. It had no peace-making authority. Besides the protection of humanitarian convoys and refugees, its main task was to hold and protect Sarajevo's airport. A couple of months later the British government decided to contribute a battalion of 1,800 men. After France, Britain became UNPRO-FOR's largest contributor.

The story of Britain's intervention in Bosnia was not a happy one. The unhappiness, however, was not uniquely British. It illustrated what happens when the UN agrees a course of action which falls far short of what is needed. In some ways, a UN intervention at half-cock is worse than no intervention at all. The presence of the Blue Helmets can convey a sense of false security, especially when, as at Srebrenica, the troops are equipped with light arms and feeble rules of engagement, making them no match for seasoned forces bent on serious violence. Time and again, words were not matched by action. The greater the pressure from the media and the public, the more the outraged rhetoric of the politicians soared, while on the ground handguns faced tanks. Bismarck had once said that the Balkans were not worth the life of a single 'Pomeranian Grenadier'. For several years, major members of the Security Council – France, Britain, Germany, and, above all, the United States – behaved as if they agreed with him. John Major, in his autobiography, protested that UNPROFOR did good work on the humanitarian side, which was often overlooked by those who wanted a much tougher approach to Serb and Croat ethnic cleansing. But, emphasised Major, the very humanitarian mission – the protection of aid convoys and of normal civilian life – demanded neutrality of UN forces. This could not be reconciled with armed defence of

Bosnia against Serb and Croat attack. Margaret Thatcher's riposte was that Britain and the UN could not go on with this policy, 'namely feeding people but leaving them to be massacred'. The dreaded word 'appeasement' began to hang over the British government.

Nor was it an incentive to decisive action against Milošević and Mladić that Russia, an unsentimental and unabashed exponent of the spheres-of-influence school of foreign policy, saw itself as the Serbs' protector in a region that Moscow considered its own backyard. It would not be until 1995 that the twentieth-century version of the Great Powers broke free of these contradictions and special interests and put an end to the fighting.

A week after the decision to send in British troops, a joint EC–UN conference was convened in London, hosted by the British Prime Minister, John Major, and the UN Secretary General, Boutros Boutros-Ghali. The conference brought together thirty nations, including representatives of the Yugoslav republics. The aim was to halt the violence, alleviate a mounting humanitarian crisis, and put in place a framework within which a final peace could be negotiated. There was particular concern that, as winter approached, over a million refugees could die of exposure and starvation.

Major opened the conference with words appropriate to the seriousness of the crisis:

In this room are the people who can stop this war, end the bloodshed, reach a lasting settlement. I do not believe that world opinion will easily forgive anyone who impedes that work over the next couple of days and beyond. The people who we represent have been appalled by the destruction, the killing, the maiming, the sheer cruelty which has disfigured Yugoslavia. We all seek a just peace.

The London conference reached tough conclusions. The warring parties were ordered to halt ethnic cleansing and agree to peace talks in Geneva – or face harsh consequences:

If they do not comply the Security Council will be invited to apply stringent sanctions leading to their total isolation.

For a while the conference looked like a triumph for diplomacy. The warring parties had been brought to the table. There appeared to be a framework in place to deal with the crisis. Then the parties reneged on it. The promised UN retribution was nowhere to be seen: no stringent sanctions, no total isolation. Above all, there was no use of force to stop the fighting and the atrocities; the threat had not even been made in the London communiqué.

This set a disastrous precedent. It led Milošević and Tudjman, the Croat leader, to believe for over three years that they could face down the international community. The aftermath of the London conference as good as gave the Serbs and Croats *carte blanche* in their ethnic cleansing. It was hardly surprising that four successive peace plans subsequently foundered. Neither the Serbs nor the Croats had any incentive to submit to the mediators' plans, when they thought that, without fear of retribution, they could acquire more territory by force of arms.

The cycle of violence was reversed only when the gap between tough talking and weak action became intolerable. This happened with the sorry tale of the safe havens. Six of these had been created by Security Council resolution in 1993. They included Srebrenica. The idea was that there should be areas where Bosnian refugees could find sanctuary from the violence. Their integrity would be guaranteed by UNPROFOR. The initiative was flawed from the start. The commander of UN forces requested some 30,000 troops for the task of protecting the safe havens; he got around 7,500 instead. The Security Council had provided for air-strikes, should the havens come under attack. But the strikes had to be authorised by a UN/NATO 'dual key' – a clumsy arrangement, which guaranteed impossibly slow responses, if any at all. The havens became places where Bosniak forces rested before combat. This prejudiced their integrity in Serb eyes and invited attack. UNPROFOR found itself stranded once again in an ill-defined no-man's land between peace-keeping and peace-making. The result was predictable. The safe haven of Srebrenica came under Serb attack in July 1995. The few hundred lightly armed Dutch troops of UNPROFOR could do nothing to protect the thousands of refugees. In one of the most notorious incidents of the whole conflict almost 8,000 men and boys were massacred by General Mladić and his Bosnian Serb army.

It required an atrocity of this scale finally to lead to decisive action. It was taken by an informal club of Great Powers, called the Contact Group, led by the United States. The Group comprised the US, UK, France, Germany and Russia. All five were on the UN Security Council. Four were members of NATO. The Group, which was almost automatically self-selecting, took formal shape in 1994. It seized the reins of Bosnian policy from inside the UN and NATO. It showed how far the US had come since 1992. The Clinton administration had reached the reluctant conclusion that violent Balkan disorder had become a direct threat to the American national interest. The credibility of NATO and the UN; the stability of Southern Europe; and the gains from the end of the Cold War were all at risk. The lead American negotiator, Richard Holbrooke, Assistant Under-Secretary for Europe at the State Department, later described July 1995 as a 'dreadful month', when the situation in Bosnia was at 'its low ebb'. But, it was cathartic. John Major convened a crisis meeting in London. Agreement was taken to send a well-armed Anglo-French Rapid Reaction Force to protect Sarajevo. Immediately after, NATO convened to draw 'a line in the sand' around Gorazde, the next safe haven to come under threat; and to agree that the decision to use air power to defend the town would be NATO's alone.

The tide began to run against the Serbs. After a further atrocity in August, when dozens of civilians were killed by a mortar shell in the second massacre to occur at Sarajevo's Markale market, Bosnian Serbs came under heavy NATO bombing attacks, while the Croats comprehensively defeated the Croatian Serbs in a lightning campaign the same month. Holbrooke observed that

the success of the Croatian ... offensive was a classic illustration of the fact that the shape of the diplomatic landscape will usually reflect the balance of forces on the ground ... as diplomats we could not expect the Serbs to be conciliatory at the negotiating table as long as they had experienced nothing but success on the battlefield.

For Holbrooke and his team, the Croat victory over the Serbs was the turning point. Milošević, the eternally cunning tactician, distanced himself from the puppet Serb mini-states in Bosnia and Croatia.

Ivor Roberts, the British Chargé d'Affaires[5] in Belgrade, put it like this:

His vision of becoming a strong man of the whole of Yugoslavia had collapsed, his vision of pulling together a greater Serbia was also in the throws of collapsing, he was then negotiating his own retreat to a situation, which he could control, controlling the whole of Serbia and as much as other parts of the Serbian territories as he could. He was coming seriously unstuck at that time because his Frankenstein's monster in the shape of Radovan Karadžić [the 'President' of the Bosnian Serb 'Republic'] was refusing to take orders from his creator.

Now, Milošević needed diplomacy to consolidate to the maximum possible what he had achieved by force.

Roberts – a highly talented diplomat, with whom I had worked twice in the Foreign Office – had been observing Milošević from close up since his arrival in the Yugoslav capital the previous year. Beneath Roberts' unflappable exterior, there beat a passionate heart, as might be imagined of someone with the incendiary combination of Welsh and Italian parentage. We were squash partners for much of the seventies and were once officially warned at the Oxford and Cambridge Club for our swearing and shouting on court (I, too, have Italian blood on my father's side). He nearly always had the beating of me. Ivor Roberts had the courage to speak his mind. When Ambassador in Italy, he got into trouble with the Foreign Office a couple of times for stating the obvious: for example, that our participation in the Iraq invasion would prove a recruiting sergeant for terrorists, something said at a private event that was subsequently leaked to the press.[6]

Roberts made it his business, as an ambassador should, to get alongside Milošević to try to find out what made him tick. I would have done the same. You don't do diplomacy just with your friends. Needless to say, he was accused of going native. He was nicknamed Ratko Roberts, or Roberts the Red, and Dick Holbrooke judged him 'excessively pro-Serb'. But, in diplomacy, as in warfare, it is no bad idea to know your enemy. He secured a level of access to Milošević that few others enjoyed. In my interview with him, Roberts recounted that the message from both the Foreign Secretary Douglas Hurd and the European Union negotiator David Owen was quite clear. I think they decided that Slobodan Milošević was not only the problem but he was probably also the solution to the problem and they therefore said to me, in a nutshell, get inside his head. What is it he wants? What is it that motivates him? How can we put pressure on him to bring an end to the war?

Sometimes, you have to talk to bad men. But, you must have a clear purpose. Talking for the sake of it is pointless. In 1995, Roberts was given a clear purpose when, as the British government had always feared, a NATO air-strike in response to an attack on the Gorazde safe haven provoked the Bosnian Serbs into taking hostage some 350 UN peace-keepers, including 33 Royal Welch Fusiliers. The hostages were used as human shields against further NATO air-strikes. In Britain, Parliament was recalled for an emergency sitting. There were calls for British troops to be withdrawn. As Chargé, Roberts' job was to secure the release of the hostages. He succeeded: no mean feat, illustrating yet again the importance of having a diplomat on the ground who has the access, the contacts and the local knowledge to safeguard British lives and interests. He related that

[it] was quite tricky because of course it did occur to me that one of their plans might be to take me hostage while I was there. There was no protection or anything to stop them doing so. And I went to see Milošević and impressed on him how much we needed the British soldiers out in one piece and, when I went to Bosnia to see the Bosnian Serbs, I said to them, 'It's a matter of prime national interest and the consequences of any harm coming to them would be visited on the Bosnian Serbs if you do not release them.' They got the message.

It was a classic exercise in diplomacy backed by the credible threat of force.

Holbrooke, meantime, was using much the same weapon on a far broader negotiating canvas. General Wes Clark later observed that 'Holbrooke had a clear sense for using military force to back diplomacy'. By now, the US was fully engaged and in charge. Holbrooke led the diplomatic offensive. His robust, sometimes abrasive, style is not to everyone's taste, though I always found his ability to cut to the core of issues refreshing and admirable. Nor was his astute use of the media to influence both Balkan opinion and those back home. If television put enormous pressure on governments, it could also be used to buttress diplomacy. Holbrooke, the 'Balkans Bull-dozer', was exactly what the tough, duplicitous, and devious Balkan leaders needed and deserved. He and Roberts, who met from time to time in Belgrade, were not soul-brothers, perhaps because they had more in common than either would wish to admit. Roberts has observed that

Holbrooke behaved like a latter-day Metternich, endlessly wheeling and dealing and not entirely trusted by anyone, including and indeed especially perhaps by his so-called Allies. Certainly he was a very tricky customer, with whom I enjoyed perfectly reasonable personal relations but I wouldn't have trusted him. And indeed subsequent events demonstrated that I was right not to trust him. He was telling us one thing and doing something quite different.

But, Holbrooke delivered where the Europeans had failed. Apart from slippery Slavs, he had to deal with fractious European allies who did not take kindly to being taken off the pitch and relegated to the stands. In his shoes, where improvisation was often a negotiating necessity, I too might have been guilty of saying one thing and doing another. In the isolation of Wright-Patterson airbase, outside Dayton, Ohio, Holbrooke banged Balkan heads together. On 21 November 1995, after twenty days of negotiations – of late-night, alcohol-fuelled sessions, of near breakdowns, of last-minute renego-tiations of borders – Izetbegović of Bosnia, Tudjman of Croatia and Milošević of Serbia were finally brought to initial a deal. It was solemnly signed a month later in Paris. The deal has stuck so far. It was, perhaps, the most significant American diplomatic achieve-ment since the withdrawal of Soviet forces from the old East Germany five years previously.

The Dayton Agreement has its critics. To his credit, Holbrooke is frank about some of its weaknesses in his memoir, *To End a War*. The old, multi-ethnic Bosnia-Herzegovina had gone. The country was now divided into two entities – the Bosniak-Croat

Federation of Bosnia and Herzegovina and the Bosnian Serb Republic, the Republica Srpska. The issue of Kosovo, already identified as a potentially dangerous flash-point, went unaddressed. Some see Dayton as a reward for Serb and Croat violence, though many of those responsible for war crimes have been brought to justice and imprisoned (Milošević himself died during his trial in The Hague; and, of the big names, only Ratko Mladić remains, at the time of writing, on the run). But what was the alternative?

Others thought that Holbrooke took too much of the credit for a deal that was built on the previous efforts of European mediators. But the American team was never going to come up with a wholly novel approach, because there was none to be had. The outcome was always going to be some form of cantonisation; and it would have been perverse to have ignored the work of previous mediators. The problem with the previous plans was not that they were fundamentally unworkable, but that neither the Europeans nor the UN had the power or the will to enforce them. As David Owen, the co-author of two of the plans, put it in an interview for our television series with unvarnished candour,

Well, if the politicians are refusing to use force, and if there isn't the structures available to use force, then diplomats are sent in to play for time. And I was part of that diplomatic thing.

By the time the Balkan Bulldozer went into action, the Americans were ready to use force. That was the watershed. Lurking behind Holbrooke's shoulder was the prospect not only of further air-strikes, but of 25,000 US troops on the ground to enforce a deal. As Wes Clark put it,

... we had stood the weakness of UNPROFOR exactly on its head. Under UNPROFOR, the obligations of the force had been unlimited – protect civilians, assist aid deliveries, secure safe zones, and so on – but its authority was very limited. We were seeking to limit the obligations of the military – you can't do everything with military forces – but to give the commander unlimited authority to accomplish these limited obligations.

This was the philosophy that lay behind the American-led NATO force that imposed the Dayton Agreement – a force, in Clark's words, 'capable of serious combat'. To illustrate what he called the Balkans' 'acute sensitivity to military power', Clark described an encounter with a self-pitying Milošević (Holbrooke's team found it as necessary to deal with the Serb leader as had Ivor Roberts), in which he lamented that 'it was your NATO, your bombs and missiles, your high technology that defeated us. We Serbs never had a chance against you.' It was a lesson that Milošević had to learn all over again in the Kosovo crisis of 1999.

The hour of Europe, when it finally came to Bosnia in 2007, was a modest thing, a sapling in a forest of acronyms. Until then, NATO forces – IFOR (Implementation Force), followed by SFOR (Stabilisation Force) – had policed the Dayton Agreement under American leadership. Twelve years later, things were considered stable enough to risk handing over the policing role to a European command, EUFOR (European Force) Althea. But NATO, with American officers, has still a presence in Sarajevo; and if things get too difficult for EUFOR, its website helpfully tells us that 'EUFOR can be easily reinforced by KFOR [Kosovo Force] and Over the Horizon Forces'.[7] As of 22 July 2009, EUFOR comprised 2,012 troops, of which the third largest contingent was that of Turkey (not an EU member), and the smallest that of 'hour of Europe' Luxembourg, with one soldier. For some strange reason, there is a South American contingent, in the shape of Chile.

The Bosnia crisis differed fundamentally from those provoked by the Bulgarian Atrocities and Mussolini's invasion of Abyssinia. It did not present a stark choice between 'realist' and 'idealist' diplomacy. Nor was the Dayton Agreement a triumph, after four long years, of values over *realpolitik*. It was something much more complicated; and Bosniaks, Serbs and Croats paid with their lives for the complexity, as the international community, by timid trial and error, worked out what it should do.

Throughout the crisis, there was always an undercurrent of opinion in Western capitals that nobody had a dog in the Balkan fight. This was not an argument for appeasement, nor one drained of all humanitarian feeling. It was one that argued that, when societies fall out, however violently, only they can bring the crisis to a permanent resolution. Even today, we cannot be certain that the Dayton and Kosovo settlements are not just truces in a longer conflict; and that, by intervening, we have simply postponed the inevitable day of reckoning. We just do not know whether the republics and communities of the old Yugoslavia are capable of peaceful coexistence, once foreign forces leave their soil. Much the same set of considerations applies to Iraq and its three-way split between Sunni, Shi'a and Kurd.

Hindsight is a wonderful thing in foreign policy, as anywhere else. If Milošević and Mladić had been confronted by the full force of the United States and NATO in 1991, instead of 1995, over 100,000 lives would have been saved. But in the beginning, nobody thought the situation worth the bones of anyone's grenadiers. It required violence, atrocity and instability to seize the world's attention. The interaction of public opinion and the press had demonstrated its power to influence government in the Bulgarian and Abyssinian affairs. By 1995, television – the live audio-visual communication of emotive images – had taken this power to a higher plane (a phenomenon which the internet has developed still further). The 'CNN effect' – for example, the symbiosis between the viewer and CNN's superb reporter, the intrepid Christiane Amanpour – became an objective factor in the making of Bosnian policy. It helped push the US and the rest of the international community into using lethal force against the Serbs.

If this were enough, we would have intervened similarly in other areas of gross violence and human suffering: Rwanda, the Congo, Darfur or Zimbabwe. The pictures that we see on television or our laptops are no less harrowing than those transmitted from the Balkans. But, nations pick and choose. They always will. The decisive factor is the national interest. Do we have a dog in the fight? By and large, the Great Powers will not go to Africa. Britain's (successful) intervention in Sierra Leone in 2000 and the US' (unhappy) intervention in Somalia in 1993 were the exception that proved the rule. The result is UNPROFOR-syndrome all over again, but worse. African conflicts are cursed by weak UN peace-keeping operations: poorly equipped, second-rate troops, with inadequate mandates.

Lord Owen once told me that the price of a human rights policy is inconsistency. Lord Hurd put it to us this way in our interview with him:

It's very easy to do what Tony Blair did and President Clinton did to go and say oh these things will never happen again. They will happen again and we won't always be able to intervene. It won't always be sensible to intervene. Sometimes by intervening we will kill more people and post-pone peace instead of solving it. You have to judge that case by case. It's extraordinarily difficult.

It is extraordinarily difficult also because of the structural weakness in multilateral diplomacy and international organisations. We are light years away from what is called the post-modern state, so frequently trumpeted nowadays, where national frontiers are sup-posed no longer to matter. Time and time again, multilateral dip-lomacy, and concepts of global values, break down on the Old Adam of national interest. To argue that transnational problems demand multilateral solutions misses the point. Even inside reasonably homogeneous groups like the EU and NATO, the most important dynamic is the interaction of national interests, which defines what is collectively possible. If Germany, out of step with its European partners, had not been so selfishly determined to recognise Croatia's independence, it might have been possible to preserve Yugoslavia and to have avoided war.

In the end, Bosnia was Gladstone and Disraeli combined. The Grand Old Man's shade stalked Blackheath, fulminating against the slaughter of the Balkan innocents. Meantime, the ghost of the Old Jew, as Bismarck called him, was whispering into the ear of any diplomat who would listen: 'remember the national interest.' It took a while for the penny to drop in the chancelleries of the West – that hard interests were in the Balkan pot, along with everything else. Left to their violence, the southern Slavs could have destabilised the whole of southern Europe, wrecking NATO, humiliating the UN, dragging in Greece and Turkey, and creating a serious antagonism with Russia, just as we were all celebrating the end of the Cold War. No one on either side of the Atlantic wanted that (though the Russians would have been happy to see NATO disappear). The Dayton Agreement reflected a fusion of all the elements that make up modern foreign policy: interests, values, the media and public opinion.

This was why we had to 'do' Kosovo as well in 1999. That year, Tony Blair, the Messiah's Messiah, told a Chicago audience that NATO's campaign against the Serbs to protect the Kosovar Albanians was 'a just war, based ... on values'. It was a just war. But, it was not exclusively about values. The justice of the war was enriched by a heavy dose of *realpolitik*, without which Milošević would never have been brought to book. Perhaps Blair came to believe his own propaganda. When values become detached from reality, and tip over into ideology and messianism (usually when they are wrapped inside a doctrine of supposed universal application), the first casualty is the national interest. Who paused to think in March 2003, as Britain and America invaded Iraq, that the strategic beneficiary would be Iran?

Politicians and diplomats ignore history at their peril. Sitting on his cloud, Winston Churchill shouts down in frustration to our commanders in Afghanistan and diplomats in Pakistan: 'Read my 1898 *Malakand Field Force: An Episode of Frontier War* – it's all in there!' Then, there's General Sir Aylmer Haldane shouting likewise from his cloud: 'Read my *Insurrection in Mesopotamia 1920–22* – it's all in there!' Robert Castlereagh, by contrast, is quite content on his cloud. The Contact Group, led by America, is just like his Great Power directorate that ran the Congress of Vienna and kept multilateral diplomacy on a disciplined leash. Finally, there is the great British statesman from the 1820s, George Canning. After Bosnia, Iraq and Afghanistan, he is shaking his head in despair. He has decided to hang a large sign from his cloud. It repeats one of his most famous precepts that

... our true policy has always been not to interfere except in great emergencies, and then with a commanding force.

Exactly.

CONCLUSION

The qualities that make a good diplomat have not changed in five hundred years. Sir Henry Killigrew would have survived and prospered in the murderous labyrinth of Bosnian politics; Viscount Castlereagh would have handled the Hong Kong negotiations with the necessary finesse and firmness; Sir David Ormsby-Gore would have been in his element at the Congress of Vienna; and so on.

The ability to negotiate; to win the confidence of the powerful and to influence them; to drill down deeply into a foreign society and understand what makes it tick; to acquire and analyse high-grade information and to report it accurately, succinctly and fast; to have the courage to tell your government what it may not want to hear without losing its confidence in you; to have the courage also to act on your own initiative without instruction from London: to do all this, guided always by the lodestar of your nation's interests, has been the mark of effective diplomacy since the beginning of time. It requires a quick mind, a hard head, a strong stomach, a warm smile and a cold eye.

These talents should be as in demand in the early twenty-first century as at any time in our history. This is the age of transnational issues, managed and negotiated within permanent, multilateral conference systems under the umbrella of institutions like the UN, the EU and the World Trade Organisation. They are by definition hotbeds of intergovernmental bargaining. Some will argue that the rise of multilateralism has ushered in – again – an age of New Diplomacy. In the 1930s, the idea was suffocated by its delusions and naïvety. The danger today is that history may repeat itself. There is barely a speech made on foreign affairs that does not contain the clichés of 'globalisation' or 'interdependence'. These terms are used interchangeably without any serious effort to define what actually they mean. They are frequently deployed to uphold two dubious propositions: that the age of the traditional nation-state is over; and that in international relations there is necessarily a new harmony of interests created by the mutual dependence of nations. The second argument is made explicitly by Britain's Department for International Development (DFID) to justify its enormous budget and to lay claim to a role in the safeguarding of national security.[1]

It is perfectly true that, in the EU, member states are willing to limit sovereignty in specific areas of domestic and foreign policy. But, the EU is unique in this respect; and, even here, it is because the member-states judge that their national interest is better served through common action agreed by majority vote. What else is the EU if not the arena for the resolution of the rivalries and ambitions of twenty-seven European states? I remember hearing Chancellor Helmut Kohl say in 1997 to a Rhineland audience that a united Europe best served German interests, because it would allow Germany to dominate the continent without reawakening fears of German hegemony.

Nor is it to be denied that there is such a thing as globalisation – that national frontiers have become increasingly porous, as electronic information, money, business, culture and people move back and forth across them in ever growing volume. But, the phenomenon does not have the automatic consequence of finally making feasible an international system based on 'global values', as some like Tony Blair have argued.

To the contrary: globalisation has, if anything, strengthened around the world the sense of nationhood and nationalism. Five minutes in Beijing, Washington, Moscow, New Delhi will tell you that. Far from stimulating convergence around common political, social and economic models, underpinned by common values, globalisation has, in apparent paradox, promoted an extraordinary diversity of national forms. What does the governance of big global players like India, China, Russia and the United States have in common? Not a lot.

Henry Kissinger said to me a few years ago, when I interviewed him for a radio programme,[2] that, in the age of globalisation, we were seeing the rise of Great Power rivalries redolent of the late Victorian age. The struggle for control of natural resources was today's 'Great Game'. Witness China's drive to gain pole position in the competition for the natural wealth of Africa, Central Asia and Latin America. Or, take Russia's determination, driven by an equally single-minded nationalism, to regain control of its natural resources. Or, observe the growing tensions between powers, including Russia, caused by their competing claims on the mineral wealth lying beneath the Arctic ice cap.

The lesson from this is not that we are at the dawn of a new era in international relations; but that the Old Adam, to use Vansittart's phrase, is back in town and has taken up residence in the very citadel of multilateral diplomacy. On the great global issues, such as the environment, energy, food production and the like, the key to cooperation and agreement does not lie in great conferences and international bodies. It is to be found in capitals. This is where the policies are made and the instructions to conference negotiators formulated. You can be quite sure that in the capitals of the G20 group of nations – those that will shape the world in which our children live – policy-makers will not have as a first, second or even third priority the elevation of wispy ideas about global values. They will start and end, as should we in Britain, with a hard-headed calculation based on a view of their national interest – an unsentimental cost/benefit analysis of competing policy options. It is the job of diplomats in capitals to understand and, where possible, to influence the decision-makers. That is why abandoning the notion of national interest is a form of unilateral disarmament.

In its actions overseas, the state has a number of instruments and assets at its disposal: aid workers, spies, entrepreneurs, members of the armed forces, diplomats, BBC correspondents. In the last decade, diplomacy has been the under-utilised poor relation. We have pursued grinding military expeditions and spent a fortune on international development aid, for all practical purposes inside a foreign policy and diplomatic vacuum. If I have heard it once, I have heard it a dozen times from army reservists returning from Iraq and Afghanistan: there has been scant joined-up government between the soldier, the aid worker and the diplomat. How many times does Clausewitz have to be invoked so as to remind our leaders that war is the extension of politics by other means? I recall putting down this marker in a report to London in late 2001 about US policy in Afghanistan. War has no meaning unless directed by a political goal. As of August 2009, after nearly eight years in Afghanistan – longer almost than both World Wars put end to end – there is still no clarity about why we are there. Is it to stop al-Qaeda returning on the shirt-tails of the Taleban? Or, are we trying to create the conditions to transform Afghan governance and society? Depending on who you speak to – British or American – it is either, both, or something in the middle. A punitive expedition against al-Qaeda is one thing; but to seek, against the grain of history, to rebuild Afghanistan from the ground up, in the name of a Western concept of democracy and human rights, is futile. If this madcap venture is to take forty years, as General Sir David Richards, Chief of the General Staff, averred in 2009, no conceivable national interest can be served by such an eccentric concentration of resources on a country of marginal importance. To the contrary, while the US, Britain and others waste lives and treasure in this benighted land (in our case for the fourth time in little more than 150 years), al-Qaeda has moved its training camps elsewhere. Worse, we continue to pursue an illusory stability in Afghanistan at the cost of destabilising Pakistan, where the risk of nuclear weapons falling into the hands of *jihadists* threatens the core of our security, the supreme national interest.

Recent history has taught hard lessons. The more grandiose our proclamation of values, the more we lay ourselves open to the charges of incoherence and hypocrisy. We are self-appointed apostles of Democracy and Moderation around the world. But these two fixed points of our foreign policy are in permanent contradiction. Our 'moderate' Arab friends are despotic regimes like those of Saudi Arabia and Egypt. We judge Hezbollah and Hamas to be extremist, though each has been legitimately elected to legislatures in Lebanon and Palestine. By bringing elections to Iraq, we have entrenched ethnic, religious and tribal divisions by giving them democratic legitimacy.

In his interview with us, Henry Kissinger reckoned that 'prophets' had done more harm in history than 'statesmen'. British foreign policy needs a little more statesmanship, a little less prophecy; a little more Disraeli, a little less Gladstone. It needs to regain a clear understanding of the articulation between war and politics and between force and diplomacy. It needs to relearn some of the old arts of negotiation: that no agreement is better than a bad agreement (make sure the other side knows that you will, if need be, walk away from the negotiating table); that reciprocity is the heart of a good agreement; that it is sometimes more necessary to play hardball with your friends than your enemies; that a negotiator without a bottom line is like a helmsman without a compass.

Because of the strain on our armed forces, Britain may well need a defence review. But, before that, the paramount requirement is for a foreign policy review – or, if the American terminology has to be used, a review of national security. Its purpose would be to define Britain's national interest: to decide what advances it; what damages it; what our priorities should be; and what we can afford. Then, it becomes possible to construct a coherent foreign policy, backed by a correspondingly resourced diplomacy.

Such a review will be so much wasted effort unless one matter is clearly understood from the outset. There has to be a single, guiding hand on the tiller of British foreign policy in all its dimensions, the guardian of a strategic vision, to which all else is subordinate, including, especially, defence and development policies. The alternative, as in the past decade, is strategic incoherence, poor coordination between departments, military expeditions without clear political goals, and even rival foreign policies pursued respectively by the Foreign Office and the Department of International Development. This cannot go on. Nor is the right answer to look across the Atlantic for inspiration. There is talk of creating a British equivalent of the White House National Security Council; or even a Whitehall version of the American Defense Policy Review Board, a kind of council of foreign policy wise men. But, the last thing Britain needs is American bureaucratic gigantism, with its turf wars and agonisingly complex decision-taking, just to ensure that the Prime Minister has all the options laid before him.

The answer is less, not more bureaucracy. If in Margaret Thatcher's time, a notably successful period for British diplomacy, policy could be made by a combination of two senior advisers Percy

Cradock and Charles Powell;[3] a properly functioning Cabinet committee system to ensure coordination across Whitehall; the occasional seminar for the Prime Minister's benefit with outside experts; and a Foreign Office, with a Secretary of State who, to quote the 1978 government White Paper,[4] was responsible 'for the overall conduct of overseas relations in the broadest sense of the term' – there is no reason why the next Prime Minister could not do the same. Government is energised when bureaucracy is cut back.

In the preceding pages, we have had the Hour of Europe and the Hour of America; the New Diplomacy and the Old Diplomacy; the End of History and the Return of History; Collective Security and the Balance of Power. Heaven knows what historians will call the first half or so of the twenty-first century. But of one thing we can be sure. It will be the Hour of Diplomacy, because it is always the Hour of Diplomacy – not New, not Old, just good, effective diplomacy that, in a world of menacing uncertainty and turbulence, does what it has always been designed to do: safeguard our security and prosperity. We have never needed it more.

NOTES

INTRODUCTION

1. Summary from 'A Cultural Audit of the Foreign and Commonwealth Office' by Couraud, human resources consultants, Crown copyright © August 2008
2. Foreign Secretary three times between 1830 and 1851; and Prime Minister twice between 1855 and 1865.
3. cf. Tony Blair's foreign policy speech of 21 March 2006, in which he calls for a 'common global policy based on common values' and an 'international community, based on core, shared values'. He sets this utopian vision against what he calls 'narrow' national interests.
4. Secretary of State for Foreign and Commonwealth Affairs, 1983–89
5. Sir Ewen Fergusson, Ambassador to France 1987–92.
6. Lord Renwick of Clifton, Ambassador to the United States 1991–95
7. Now Burkina Faso
8. General Anthony Zinni, Commander-in-Chief, US Central Command, 1997–2000. Zinni was reported to have used this colourful phrase when telling the Obama White House where it could stick its offer of an ambassadorship to Saudi Arabia.
9. Acheson, the son of an English clergyman who had emigrated to the US, took a notably unsentimental (and historically accurate) view of Britain, saying that 'a unique relation existed between Britain and America . . . but unique did not mean affectionate.

We had fought England as our enemy as often as we had fought by her side as an ally.' [Quoted in the magnificent *Old World, New World* by Kathleen Burk]
10. We finally got in in 1973.
11. *The United Kingdom's Overseas Representation*, Her Majesty's Stationery Office, August 1978
12. Private conversation in London, February 2008
13. Department for International Development

CHAPTER 1

1. Knox is famed for his attacks on the 'monstrous regiment of women'. Less delicately, he once described a woman 'as a dressed-up turd'. These Renaissance Scots had a thing about fecal matter. When James VI became James I of England, he told a bishop, 'I care not a turd for thy preaching.'

CHAPTER 2

1. The same Robert Armstrong who later told a court in Australia that, on the matter of the ex-MI5 officer Peter Wright's book, *Spycatcher*, which he was seeking to have banned, he had been 'economical with the truth'.
2. See a speech by the then Foreign Secretary, David Miliband, on 27 August 2008, which attacks the Congress of Vienna and the notion of balance of power. http://www.davidmiliband.info/speeches/speeches_08_012.htm
3. Although French rehabilitation was to be rudely interrupted for the one hundred days between Napoleon's escape from Elba and his last hurrah on the battlefield of Waterloo.
4. The Viennese remain addicted to balls. There is a full season of them in the early months of each year, which reaches its climax with the Opera Ball. For the making of the companion television series to this book, my wife and I attended the Officers' Ball, a magnificent affair where the sound of clicking heels was almost as loud as the orchestra's rendition of polkas, quadrilles, mazurkas and the like.

CHAPTER 3

1. Excerpts of diary in the author's possession
2. That was the thinking behind the crudely crisp instruction that I received from No. 10, just before leaving for Washington in 1997, 'to get up the arse of the White House and stay there'.
3. House of Commons debate, Hansard, 7 November 1945, series 5, Vol. 415 cc1290–390
4. So named after the Victor, Vulcan and Valiant bombers.
5. I was in the Moscow Embassy at the time. We were well aware of a fearful mood enveloping the Soviet capital, but it was the Soviet defector, Oleg Gordievsky, head of the KGB station in London, who provided direct evidence for Soviet fears of nuclear war in 1983.
6. Tony Blair to House of Commons, 4 December 2006

CHAPTER 4

1. The wars of Spanish and Austrian Succession, for example.
2. The Seven Years War, the War of Jenkins' Ear, and various campaigns in India.
3. Contrast and compare with the 'great clunking fist' of another famous son of Kirkcaldy, Gordon Brown.
4. The passage of time has not changed much. China today sits on vast mountains of foreign currency, especially dollars, with an imbalance of trade that works roughly 4:1 in its favour.
5. The controversy today about extradition arrangements between UK and the US springs from the fact that it appears easier to extradite to America than to Britain. If so, it shows that the British negotiators neglected to stand firm on the principle of full reciprocity, an elementary mistake.

CHAPTER 5

1. Palmerston to Sir Charles Elliot, 1841, cited in Wollaston, N., *The Travellers Dictionary of Quotation*, 1962, p.448

2. Cited in Webster, C.K., *The Foreign Policy of Palmerston*, 1951, pp.750–51
3. A lorcha was a curious Chinese-European hybrid vessel, generally comprising a Portuguese hull fitted with Chinese junk rigging.

CHAPTER 6

1. Extensive interviews with Cradock and Patten are to be found in the second programme of the companion television series of *Getting Our Way*. Some interview material cited here is also taken from the 1997 BBC series *The Last Governor.*
2. The Non-Aligned Movement (NAM) had been established in 1955 as a grouping of largely Third World nations that would be independent of power blocs, i.e. they would steer a course in the Cold War between the US and the Soviet Union. Since the genesis of the NAM owed a great deal to the end of the colonial era and the emergence of new, independent states, its natural political posture was to lean more to the Russians than to the Americans.

CHAPTER 7

1. Colin Thubron in the *New York Review of Books*, Vol. LVI, number 10. He also points out that: '... Victorian women travellers – with an access denied to men ... identified the Turkish harem as ... a domestic sanctuary, often rather boring.'
2. The Sublime Porte was the seat of the Ottoman government and the literal name of the gateway leading to the State departments in Constantinople.
3. For example, the 1907 Anglo-Russian agreement which divided Persia into Russian and British spheres of influence without consulting or even informing the Persians beforehand.
4. Conversation with Dr Steven Richmond, Istanbul Technical University
5. *Flashman at the Charge* and *Flashman in the Great Game.*

6. *The Times*, Friday, 26 May 1876, p.8
7. FO 78/2463/966
8. Blair, Tony, 'The Kosovo Conflict: A Turning Point for South Eastern Europe', Speech by the Prime Minister, Tony Blair, to the Atlantic Club of Bulgaria, Sofia University, Bulgaria, Monday, 17 May 1999

CHAPTER 8

1. *The Times*, 1 December 1925, p.15
2. *Time Magazine*, 27 September 1926
3. Another piece of New Diplomacy architecture by which states solemnly pledged '... the renunciation of war as an instrument of national policy'.
4. Gregory was an Assistant Under-Secretary. Titles like his have recently been abolished and replaced by terminology borrowed from a mixture of Continental European and business practice.
5. Foreign Office terminology for a memorandum.
6. http://www.fco.gov.uk/en/about-the-fco/publications/ historians1/history-notes/history-pus/the-new-diplomacy- 1920–46
7. Lord Avon, *The Memoirs of Anthony Eden: Facing the Dictators*, p.242
8. This was shocking even to those who yearned for peace. Both my grandfathers had fought in Flanders, one of them had been gassed, and neither ever wanted to talk about the experience. They became strong supporters of the League of Nations. Both, however, thought the Oxford Union vote a disgraceful dereliction of duty by the younger generation (some thirty years later, one of the grandfathers was to express relief that I was going to Cambridge, not Oxford).
9. 27 July, Cambridge Univ. Library, Templewood MSS. VIII–I. FO 800/295, fo
10. *The Times*, 11 June 1936

CHAPTER 9

1. Speech at Georgetown University, 13 September 1989
2. Fukuyama, Francis, *The End of History and the Last Man*, 1992
3. Formally the Republic of Bosnia and Herzegovina
4. General Wesley K. Clark, *Waging Modern War*, Public Affairs, 2001, pp.8–9. Clark received an honorary knighthood, for his role in commanding NATO during the Kosovo affair. I was honoured to give him the decoration in a ceremony at the Embassy.
5. Ambassador in all but name.
6. That was not the only time Roberts was the victim of a leak. In the Introduction to this book, I have related the leaking of his Valedictory Despatch, in which he strongly criticised the Foreign Office for its obsession with process and navel-gazing.
7. KFOR is the NATO force keeping the lid on things in Kosovo, to which American troops still contribute.

CONCLUSION

1. See the 2009 White Paper *Building a Common Future* and its website introduction by the Secretary of State, Douglas Alexander.
2. *Lying Abroad*, BBC Radio 4, 2007
3. Now Lord Powell of Bayswater
4. See page 13

BIBLIOGRAPHY

1. All Secrecy and Circumspection: Killigrew in Edinburgh
   Amos, C., Sir Henry Killigrew: *Elizabethan Soldier and Diplomat* (1963)
   Anderson, M.S., *The Rise of Modern Diplomacy, 1450–1919* (1993)
   Calendar of State Papers (Scotland, Holland, Domestic)
   Darvill, Giles, *Little Sir Hal Killigrew* (1994)
   Guy, John, *Tudor England* (1988)
   Machiavelli, Niccolo, *The Prince*
   MacMahon, Luke, 'Killigrew, Sir Henry (1525x8–1603)', Oxford Dictionary of National Biography, Oxford University Press, Sept 2004; online edn, Jan 2008 [http://www.oxforddnb.com/view/article/15533, accessed 11 April 2009]
   Mattingly, Garret, *Renaissance Diplomacy* (1955)
   Potter, Harry, *Edinburgh Under Siege 1571–73* (2003)
   Raab, Felix, *The English Face of Machiavelli* (1964)

2. A Just Equilibrium: Castlereagh at the Congress of Vienna
   Anderson, M. S., *The Rise of Modern Diplomacy, 1450–1919* (London, 1993)
   Bartlett, C. J., *Castlereagh* (London, 1966)
   Brown, Michael Edward, *Offense, Defense and War* (2004)
   Chamberlain, Muriel E., *Pax Britannica? British Foreign Policy 1789–1914* (London, 1988)

Crawley, C. W. (ed.), *The New Cambridge Modern History, Vol. IX: War and Peace in an Age of Upheaval 1793–1830* (Cambridge, 1965)

Derry, John W., *Castlereagh* (London, 1976)

Gronow, Captain Rhys Henry, *Reminiscences and Recollections* (London, 1900)

Hayes, Paul, *Modern British Foreign Policy: The Nineteenth Century 1814–80* (London, 1975)

Kissinger, Henry, *A World Restored* (1957)

Kissinger, Henry, *Diplomacy* (1994)

Morgan, Kenneth O., *The Oxford History of Britain* (Oxford, 1984)

Otte, T. G. (ed.), *The Makers of British Foreign Policy: From Pitt to Thatcher* (London, 2002)

Thorne, Roland, 'Stewart, Robert, Viscount Castlereagh and Second Marquess of Londonderry (1769–1822)', *Oxford Dictionary of National Biography*, Oxford University Press, September 2004; online edn, January 2008 [http://www.oxforddnb.com/view/article/26507, accessed 28 April 2009]

Webster, C.K., *The Foreign Policy of Castlereagh 1815–22* (London, 1925)

Wright, Jonathan, *The Ambassadors* (2006)

Zamoyski, Adam, *Rites of Peace: The Fall of Napoleon and the Congress of Vienna* (London, 2007)

3. Keeping Up with the Joneses: Our Man in Washington and the Nassau Deal

Ashton, Nigel, *Kennedy, Macmillan and the Cold War: The Irony of Interdependence* (2002)

Ball, George, *The Discipline of Power* (1968)

Brandon, Henry, *Sunday Times*, 9 December 1962

Harlech, Lord, 'Suez SNAFU, Skybolt SABU', in *Foreign Policy*, 2 (1971)

Horne, Alistair, 'The Macmillan Years and Afterwards', in Louis & Bull (eds), *The Special Relationship* (1986)

Horne, Alistair, *Macmillan* (1991)

Jenkins, Roy, 'Gore, (William) David Ormsby, fifth Baron Harlech (1918–1985)', rev., *Oxford Dictionary of National Biography*, Oxford University Press, 2004 [http://www.oxforddnb.com/view/article/31518, accessed 17 May 2009]

Macmillan, Harold, *At the End of the Day 1961–1963*

Matthew, H.C.G., 'Macmillan, (Maurice) Harold, first earl of Stockton (1894–1986)', *Oxford Dictionary of National Biography*, Oxford University Press, September 2004; online edn, January 2008 [http://www.oxforddnb.com/view/article/40185, accessed 12 May 2009]

Neustadt, Richard, 'Report to JFK: The Skybolt Crisis in Perspective' (1999)

Owen, David, *The Politics of Defence* (1972)

Schlesinger, Arthur, *One Thousand Days: John F. Kennedy in the White House* (1965)

Trachtenberg, Marc, *A Constructed Peace: the Making of the European Settlement, 1945–1963* (1999)

'BRITAIN GETS FACTS OF LIFE ON SKYBOLT', *Chicago Daily Tribune (1872–1963);* 16 December 1962, p.10

The Times, Saturday, 8 December 1962; p.8; Issue 55569; col. C http://www.nato.int/docu/speech/1946/S460305a_e.htm

The Times, Wednesday, 12 December 1962; p.10

Documents consulted in the National Archives
FCO 73/171
PREM 11/4229
CAB 21/5967

4. Heaven is High, the Emperor Distant: Macartney's Mission to China

Barrow, John, *Travels in China* (1805)

Cradock, Percy, *Experiences of China* (1994)

Cranmer-Byng, J.L. (ed.), *An embassy to China: being the journal kept by Lord Macartney during his embassy to the Emperor Ch'ien-lung, 1793–1794* (1962)

Gelber, Harry G., *The Dragon and the Foreign Devils* (2007)

Marshall, P.J., *The Oxford History of the British Empire*

Morse, H.B., *Chronicles of the East India Company Trading to China*, Volume II (Oxford, 1926)

Murphey, R., *The Outsiders* (London Library)

Peyrefitte, Alain, *The Immobile Empire*, Alfred A. Knopf (New York, 1992)

Robbins, Helen H., *Our First Ambassador to China* (1908)

Roebuck, Peter (ed.) *Macartney of Lisanoure 1737–1806 – Essays in Biography* (1983)

Smith, Adam, *The Wealth of Nations* (1776)

Thorne, Roland, *Oxford Dictionary of National Biography –* Biographical Entry for Macartney

Walvin, James, *Fruits of Empire: Exotic Produce and British Taste, 1660–1800* (New York: New York University Press, 1997)

Web Resources

Morgan, Kenneth, *Symbiosis: Trade and the British Empire*

http://www.bbc.co.uk/history/british/empire_seapower/trade_empire_01.shtml

Watt, John R., *Qianlong meets Macartney – Collision of Two World Views*

Wang, Y., *A study on the size of the Chinese population in the middle and late eighteenth century.* Chin J Popul Sci. 1997; 9(4):317–36. The adjusted total population is 388,150,057 in 1799.

5. The Hour of the Gunboat: Bowring in China

Bartle, G.F., 'Sir John Bowring and the Arrow War in China', Bulletin of the John Rylands Library, 43.2 (1961)

Bartle, G.F., *An Old Radical and His Brood* (1994)

Bowring, Sir John, *Autobiographical Recollections of Sir John Bowring* (1877)

Fairbank, John K., *Trade and Diplomacy on the China Coast* (1953)

Hurd, Douglas, *The Arrow War, An Anglo-Chinese Confusion 1856–60* (1967)

Kissinger, Henry, *Diplomacy* (1994)

Lowe, Peter, *Britain in the Far East* (1981)

Pelissier, Roger, *The Awakening of China 1793–1949* (1967)

Rose, Sarah, *For All the Tea in China* (2009)

Wong, J.Y., *Deadly dreams: Opium, Imperialism and the Arrow War (1856–60) in China* (1998)

Web Sources

http://www25.uua.org/uuhs/duub/articles/sirjohnbowring.html

Unitarian Universalist Historical Society (UUHS) 1999–2009

6. Hong Kong: A Tale of Two Systems

Cradock, Percy, *Experiences of China* (1994)

Howe, Geoffrey, *Conflict of Loyalty* (1994)

Hurd, Douglas, *Memoirs* (1993)

Major, John, *The Autobiography* (1999)

Patten, Chris, *East and West* (1998)

Tsang, Steve Yui-Sang, *Government and Politics, A Documentary History of Hong Kong* (1995)

EU Warns China on UK Trade, *New York Times*, 1 March 1994

'Signing of HK Treaty Heralds New Era', *Financial Times*, 20 December 1984

Web sources

The Economist, 'Bad Day for Business', 11 September 2008

http://www.economist.com/world/asia/displaystory.cfm?story_id=12209864

7. The Grand Turk and the Russian Bear: Disraeli, Gladstone and the Eastern Question

Adams, R.J.Q. 'Hoare, Samuel John Gurney, Viscount Templewood (1880–1959)', *Oxford Dictionary of National Biography*, Oxford University Press, September 2004; online edn, January 2008 [http://www.oxforddnb.com/view/article/33898, accessed 25 June 2009]

Blake, Robert, *Disraeli* (1966)

Elliot, H.G., *Some Revolutions and other Diplomatic Experiences* (1922)

Freely, John, *The Companion Guide to Istanbul* (2000)

Gladstone, W.E., 'Bulgarian Horrors and the Question of the East' (1876)

Hayes, Paul, *The Nineteenth Century, 1814–80* (1975)

Kennedy, Paul, *The Realities Behind Diplomacy* (1981)

Kissinger, Henry, *Diplomacy* (1994)

Jones, Raymond A., *The British Diplomatic Service 1815–1914* (1983)

Seton-Watson, R.W., *Disraeli, Gladstone and the Eastern Question* (1972)

Shannon, Richard T., *Gladstone and the Bulgarian Agitation 1876* (1963)

St John, Ian, *Disraeli and the Art of Victorian Politics* (2005)

Stojanovic, Mihailo D., *The Great Powers and the Balkans 1875–1878* (1939)

Twain, Mark, *The Innocents Abroad* (1869)

Washburn, George, *Fifty Years in Constantinople and Recollections of Robert College* (1909)

8. Hobbes Rules, OK: Vansittart and the Fall of the New Diplomacy

Barnett, Corelli, *The Collapse of British Power* (2002)

Birn, Donald S., *The League of Nations Union, 1918–1945* (1981)

Ceadel, Martin, 'The first British referendum: the Peace Ballot, 1934–5', *English Historical Review* (1980)

Cross, J.A., *Sir Samuel Hoare, a Political Biography* (1977)

Eden, Anthony, *Facing the Dictators* (1962)

Goldman, Aaron L., 'Sir Robert Vansittart's Search for Italian Cooperation against Hitler, 1933–36', *Contemporary History* IX, no. 3 (1974)

Hamilton, K. and Langhorne, R., *The Practice of Diplomacy: its evolution, theory and administration* (1995)

Medlicott, W.N., Dakin, D., et al, *Documents on British Foreign Policy, 1919–1939* (1981)

Mowat, C.L., *The New Cambridge Modern History, Vol. 12: The Shifting Balance of World Forces 1898–1945* (1968)

Northedge, F.S., *The Troubled Giant: Britain Among the Great Powers 1916–1939* (1966)

Parker, R.A.C., 'Great Britain, France and the Ethiopian Crisis 1935–1936', *English Historical Review* 89 (1974)

Rose, Norman, 'Vansittart, Robert Gilbert, Baron Vansittart (1881–1957)', *Oxford Dictionary of National Biography*, Oxford University Press, September 2004; online edn, January 2008 [http://www.oxforddnb.com/view/article/36630, accessed 25 June 2009]

Vansittart, Sir Robert, 'An Aspect of International Relations in 1930'

9. The Return of History: Bosnia and the Hour of Europe

Ashdown, Paddy, *The Ashdown Diaries*, Vol. 1 (2001)

Burg, Stephen L. and Shoup, Paul, *The War in Bosnia-Herzegovina* (1999)

Clark, General Wesley K., *Waging Modern War* (2001)

Holbrooke, Richard, *To End a War* (1998)

Hurd, Douglas, *Memoirs* (2003)

Major, John, *The Autobiography* (1999)

Power, Samantha, *A Problem from Hell* (2003)

Ramcharan, B.G. (ed.), *The International Conference on the Former Yugoslavia* (1997)

Seldon, Anthony, *Major: A Political Life* (1998)

Silber, Laura and Little, Allan, *The Death of Yugoslavia* (1996)

Stuart, Mark, *Douglas Hurd, The Public Servant* (1998)

Taylor, Philip M., *Global Communications, International Affairs and the Media since 1945* (1997)

Web sources:

British Diplomatic Oral History Programme – Ivor Roberts Interview: http://www.chu.cam.ac.uk/archives/collections/BDOHP/Roberts Ivor.pdf

INDEX